Living
with
Herbs

Living with *Herbs*

*A Treasury of
Useful Plants for
the Home &
Garden*

Jo Ann Gardner

Illustrations by
Elayne Sears

The Countryman Press
Woodstock, Vermont

Library of Congress Cataloging-in-Publication Data
Gardner, Jo Ann, 1935–
     Living with herbs : a treasury of useful plants for the home and garden /
  Jo Ann Gardner.
            p.   cm.
     Includes bibliographical references and index.
     ISBN 0-88150-359-2 (alk. paper)
     1. Herb gardening. 2. Herbs. 3. Herbs—Utilization. I. Title.
  SB351.H5G355   1997
  635'.7—dc20   96-2828
                                                          CIP

Cover design by Trina Stahl
Text design by Sally Sherman
Illustrations © 1996 by Elayne Sears
Cover and interior photographs by Alan Dorey
"Jo Ann's Favorite Pita Bread," originally published in *The Herb Companion*, Oct/Nov 1992, is reprinted with permission from Interweave Press. Excerpts from *Herb Gardening in Five Seasons*, © 1964 by Adelma Grenier Simmons, are reprinted with permission from the author and Dutton Signet, a division of Penguin Books USA, Inc.

First Edition.

Printed in the United States
10 9 8 7 6 5 4 3 2 1

Published by
The Countryman Press
PO Box 748
Woodstock, Vermont 05091

Distributed by
W.W. Norton & Company, Inc.
500 Fifth Avenue
New York, New York 10110

To Jigs,
my love and partner-in-all-things,
who grew herbs first.

*I am very grateful to my
editor, Helen Whybrow,
for her unfailing support,
good cheer, and seeming ease
in creating the book I envisioned
from the original manuscript.*

Contents

Introduction 11

PART I

Chapter One
BASIC GROWING METHODS   19
    Starting Herbs From Seed 20
    Starting Herbs Indoors 24
    Starting Herbs Outdoors.. 27
    Soil, Site, and Planting... 29
    A Sample Harvest Bed 34
    Growing in Containers 35
    Care and Propagation... 39
    Growing Herbs Indoors.. 44

Chapter Two
HANDLING THE HARVEST   49
    Traditional Method of Harvesting and Drying Herbs.................. 50
    Alternative Method of Harvesting and Drying Herbs.................. 53
    Other Alternatives: Microwave and Freezer 59

Chapter Three
USING HERBS IN THE HOME   61

Aromatherapy 61
Bath Herbs.. 62
Butters.. 63
Candied Flowers... 64
Cheese Herbs.. 64
Cooking with Herbs 65
Decoctions 65
Dried Flowers 65
Edible Flowers.. 66
Essential Oils 67
Fines Herbes 67
Fixatives 67
Infusions 68
Jellies 68
Medicinal Herbs 69
Oils 70
Potpourri.. 70
Sachets 72
Swags 74
Teas 74
Tussie-Mussies.. 74
Vinegars 77
Wreaths 78

Chapter Four
THE INTEGRATED LANDSCAPE   81

The Starting Point.. 82
An Island Bed... 83
The Art of Naturalizing 86
A Harvest Bed 87
A Rose Bed 89
Gardening at the Edges.. 90
Herbs for Landscaping 91

PART II

Chapter Five
THE HERBS IN MY LIFE: 74 HERB PORTRAITS 95

Bibliography 277
Source Appendix 279
Index 281

Introduction

I cannot say that I have always been interested in herbs. For many years, I was wholly absorbed in caring for our four children and learning the basic culinary and household arts, in which I was very deficient. It's no exaggeration to say that when I married at 19 I couldn't boil an egg.

These days I live at the end of a dirt road on a lonely peninsula, miles from the nearest neighbor, with neither a phone nor a vehicle, and my life revolves around herbs. The useful plants I grow, and those that nature has kindly grown for me, fill a variety of needs for food, flavoring, teas, and so on, and they provide the raw material for my little business, Jo Ann's Kitchen & Garden. The name aptly sums up where I have spent most of my time over the past two decades and more, ever since we moved to an old farm on Cape Breton Island in northeastern Nova Scotia.

When we first lived in northern Vermont, it had been my husband, Jigs, who experimented with growing herbs, selected solely on the basis of their interesting names. At a time when few other gardeners were growing them, he raised such plants as horehound, pennyroyal, angelica, and calendula from seed. There was very little information available on how to use these herbs, and since I was busy with other matters—such as learning how to feed our family of six with no income and a limited food supply—I left their care to Jigs.

In the years before we moved to Cape Breton, Jigs continued to grow unusual herbs, though we never harvested or used them, and we grew culinary herbs—parsley, basil, marjoram, and thyme—as row crops in the family vegetable garden. Although the growing season in Vermont is short, our harvests were always huge. I recall evenings spent stripping the dried herb bunches that hung from wooden beams in our kitchen, bunches so numerous they darkened the large room. My only problem then (incredible as it now seems to me) was what to do with the bounty.

Our lives were radically reorganized when we moved to Cape Breton in 1971. Once farming became our sole occupation (before we had also run a tutoring school in Vermont), Jigs no longer had the time or the inclination to seek out unusual herbs, so he bequeathed them to me. It was a fateful step, for these plants became the seeds, as it were, of a lifelong interest.

With the children growing up, I found that, even with the addition of farm work—making butter and cheese, cutting wood with a crosscut saw in winter, loading hay with a pitchfork in summer—I had time to lay out my first garden, my very own, in which I could plant whatever appealed to me. As it happened, my husband's Old World herbs—elecampane and hyssop, among others—were sturdy and attractive plants that proved winter hardy over many seasons. Once planted, they meant to stick around. These and similar, vigorous plants formed the backbone of my first flower garden, having proved themselves well suited to my rough-and-ready landscaping needs.

Gradually, all the herbs, even those formerly grown in the family vegetable plot, came under my domain, as I expanded plantings around the farmhouse—never too far away for quick gathering. I learned to incorporate herbs into beds of annuals, into shade gardens, into perennial beds, and into container plantings. I never made much of a distinction between the useful and the ornamental, since virtually everything I grew was pressed into service in one way or another. Even plants more often considered cutting flowers than herbs—glads and dahlias, for instance—were dried and preserved for use in potpourris.

All this growing did not come about at once. It has involved a long process of learning (a process that is still going on, I hasten to add) to beat the odds of a short season, combined with heavy, poorly drained soil leached of nutrients, generally cold summers, and wind—always wind. In Vermont, where we had always had a large garden, we considered ourselves master gardeners. And why not? Everything we planted grew well. But this was more the result of gardening in rich, deep, loamy soil than of our superior knowledge. In fact, as we soon found out after moving to Cape Breton, we really knew very little about gardening.

Over the years, I have devoted a lot of care and attention to the techniques of gardening, learning the secrets of seed germination, how to raise healthy seedlings, and how to create microhabitats outdoors to reduce plant stress, selecting those types and varieties best suited to our conditions. In a way, learning to garden in the face of adversity has been salutary, since I have become a more conscious gardener. Once the general principles of sound gardening have been mastered, moreover, they can be applied to any situation. So no matter where you live, I think you can benefit from what I've learned through hard experience.

Aside from practical needs, herbs assumed an economic importance in our lives with the establishment of my business. At first, the thought of including herbs among the goods we marketed locally—butter and cheese and smoked bacon—never crossed my mind. I rarely have a surplus of the traditional cooking herbs that prefer a warmer climate and that we once grew so easily: basil, marjoram, and thyme. And those herbs that *do* thrive in our cool, damp environment—chives, lovage, and the mints—somehow failed to suggest themselves as candidates for a cottage industry.

But necessity is a powerful stimulant. Almost 10 years ago, when I was invited to sell my jams and jellies at a Christmas craft show in the city (58 miles away), I jumped at the chance to increase our sluggish winter cash flow, which at times was confined to $25 a week from the sale of eggs. Having overcome the logistics of traveling to the sale (we hired a friend and his truck), I decided to make the trip truly worthwhile by packing something new to peddle: two 6-pound sacks of "Mrs. Gardner's Herb Salt."

Working with herbs that thrive here in my gardens, I had concocted this all-purpose seasoning, the base of which is table salt with varying quantities of dried herbs and spices mixed in. The dominant flavoring comes from either lovage *(Levisticum officinale)*, an herb that tastes sharply of celery and parsley with spicy overtones, or the dark green leaves of celery itself. To these I add chopped chives (leaves and flowers); parsley (both curled and Italian flat-leaved types); deep orange calendula petals; small amounts of paprika, garlic powder, onion powder, and ground black pepper; plus a top note of pulverized dill. Flecked with bright colors, the salt is attractive, the aroma mouthwatering. But would the island's conservative cooks buy a strange homegrown condiment?

My jams and jellies sold like hotcakes that December weekend, but no one lingered to ask about the modest sign advertising HERB SALT. A DOLLAR A SCOOP. At least not until I started literally pushing samples under people's noses.

(I discovered then that I'm a very persuasive salesperson.) The reaction was invariably the same—a cautious sniff or two, then a sudden smile of anticipated gustatory pleasure. Almost everyone purchased a few fragrant scoops; in the end I sold out my stock, and thus was born, a few years later, Jo Ann's Kitchen & Garden, featuring a variety of flavorings, teas, potpourris, and vinegars, products I had been making for years to satisfy our own family's needs.

On a deeper level, herbs have been the source of a spiritual awakening to my Jewishness, long dormant. As a garden writer and as a Jew, I was drawn to the subject of the bitter herbs eaten at the Passover Seder, the banquetlike meal at which the Exodus story is retold. As a child, I, like most Jews of European origin, ate horseradish as a reminder of our ancestors' former status as slaves in Egypt. However, as I discovered over two years of research, the *true* bitter herbs are common weeds, among them chicory, whose stems become hard stalks, whose leaves assume their most bitter taste precisely at the season of Passover in Israel. Thus, when these plants are at their most unpalatable, Jews are commanded to eat them, in bulk equal to the size of an olive, to remember how they had been welcomed in Egypt and later enslaved, just as the plant undergoes a transformation from its soft, tasty winter leaves to extreme bitterness at the Passover season in the Middle East. These were difficult lessons to absorb on a backcountry farm on a cold, remote peninsula in Cape Breton, where snow still covers the semifrozen ground at Passover time (March or April), and the only available true bitter herb is chicory in its softest, most palatable form. But like the Children of Israel who sojourned in the desert and found their way to the Promised Land, after years of wandering I found my spritual home in Judaism by discovering my roots in its moral and ethical teachings, often through plants like the five common weeds of Passover.

My interest in biblical flora compelled me to travel to Israel to see the plants growing in their native habitat. My first trip was wholly financed through the sale of herbs at a local craft sale. Herbs, it seems, have carried me through the latter part of my life onto strange and interesting byways.

In Israel, I was bowled over by the beauty and vigor of many Mediterranean herbs, seeing for the first time how they grow in optimum conditions. "So that's rosemary," I remember saying when I saw the streets of Jerusalem lined with its blue flowers, growing elsewhere as a weed, as did the striking Spanish lavender (*Lavandula stoechas*), various salvias, and a larger-than-life rue

(Ruta chalapensis), much showier than the European type, crowned by flocks of swallowtail butterflies feeding on the flowers' nectar.

When I returned home, I began to grow some of these as potted plants, with varying success. I learned that they are connoisseur herbs, grown by enthusiasts from coast to coast in North America. Cyrus and Louise Hyde of Well-Sweep Herb Farm in Port Murray, New Jersey, for instance, have long specialized in selling them to an increasing number of gardeners. In Canada, Richters, herb specialists based in Goodwood, Ontario, have been enlarging the herb grower's palette with some of the very herbs I had studied for years as biblical plants, such as the true Bible hyssop, *Majorana syriaca*. I feel blessed to have experienced such plants in their native habitat, and I still enjoy the challenge of growing them as potted plants, wintered over indoors. Herb growers in warmer, Mediterranean climates like California, of course, can grow these herbs outdoors year-round.

I don't know where herbs will take me next, but I'm ready for the journey. In the meantime, my days are busy with herbs from March to late October: sowing seeds, planting, harvesting, drying, storing, creating new products, and then enjoying the bounty over the winter. I am thankful to my husband, Jigs, for introducing me to his herbal oddities. They have suited me just fine.

Living with Herbs is a book that springs directly from my life on a remote, self-reliant farm, where every growing thing is regarded as potentially useful. As we moved farther and farther into the country and had to rely more and more on our own efforts to meet our daily needs, I had to push each of my limited number of plants to its utmost, finding many uses for the table, for the household, or to enhance our outdoor living space. All of the herb descriptions in this book are based on direct experience: I have grown and used every plant.

Although certain plants are by custom viewed as herbs, this was once the generic term for all seed-bearing plants, as the Bible tells us. Most of the plants I describe in *Living with Herbs* are generally regarded as herbs, but a few are also known as wildflowers (chicory, pearly everlasting, sweet white clover) or as shrubs (elderberry, roses). The point is, though, that these are the useful plants in my life, and they are, moreover, common ones, whose uses may give you a fresh way to look at them in your own life.

The greatest challenge to me as a gardener has been to discover and make use of plants that will grow, even thrive, in a hostile climate. Although not all gardeners have to contend with the special conditions that prevail in Cape Breton, few have ideal growing conditions. It is my hope that wherever you garden, *Living with Herbs* will suggest some simple strategies for dealing with common problems: poor soil, wind, early frost, limited water.

As the 19th-century horticulturalist Samuel Fuller noted about growing small fruits, there is nowhere in North America, unless it be underwater, where a few herbs may not be grown for "use and delight." And there are even some herbs, as you will learn, that prefer wet feet.

Living with Herbs is guided by three principles—economy, simplicity, and conservation—which are reflected in the way I handle herbs from seedling stage to the table, to attain maximum benefit by the simplest means. These principles are natural components of our life; we do not consciously strive to fulfill them. They are just there, underlying all our activities.

I believe *Living with Herbs* is unique among the plethora of contemporary books on herbs. It is intimate rather than encyclopedic; deeply personal rather than coldly distant. In our thirst for plants and gardens, we sometimes forget that what makes them interesting is the human dimension, our interaction with the natural world. A book about herbs, as I hope my readers will agree, can be much more than a compilation of vital statistics (although I have included these, too, of course). It can be about life itself.

This is one gardener's testament.

Part I

CHAPTER ONE

Basic Growing Methods

The very act of planting a seed in the earth has in it . . . something beautiful
. . . I watch my garden beds after they are sown, and think of how one of
God's exquisite miracles is going on beneath the dark earth out of sight.
—Celia Thaxter, *An Island Garden*

My knowledge of growing herbs, and plants in general, developed after we moved to Cape Breton and I had to face the challenge of struggling with poor land and a harsh climate. Once, when I was describing the growing problems on our remote, backlands farm—cold, wet, late-warming soil; vigorous weeds; wind, insects, and diseases—I was asked if I was ever tempted to give up. The thought has never occurred to me. Gardeners everywhere will know just what I mean: The urge to sow seeds and guide plants to maturity is not easily discouraged.

Gardening in difficult circumstances has had beneficial consequences, for it forced me to examine and question accepted gardening practices and to revise them according to my needs. This is a healthy, even exciting exercise, very rewarding for those who enjoy challenges and solving problems. Some of the most widely held notions do not, I have discovered, work under all circumstances. For instance, clay soil should not always be dug out and replaced by "better" soil; in fact, digging in general can often be avoided altogether. And mulching can sometimes lead to more problems (such as slugs) than it solves.

You don't have to live as I do, or garden in such difficult circumstances, to benefit from my experiences. From the moment a seed is sown or a root is planted in the earth, we all need to know, master, and have the ability to question the basic principles of growing. Such knowledge gives us the confidence to discover new gardening worlds, to try different types of plants, and to create enjoyable landscapes in which to live and work.

In this chapter you will learn my strategies for successful growing, based on simple methods that work and are within the reach of every gardener, such as making a greenhouse from old storm windows or creating a microhabitat inside a recycled truck tire (it's an appropriate and elegant use of found materi-al). However, let's begin at the beginning.

STARTING HERBS FROM SEED

Growing herbs from seed is an economical way to have a variety of plants for general use or for landscaping. If you plan to make herb vinegars and jellies with basil, for instance, or use parsley as an attractive edging plant in the bed or border, it makes sense to grow your own plants from seed. For a fraction of what it would cost you to buy them, you can raise a virtual army of seedlings.

You should know, however, that not all herbs are easy to start from seed, and others can't be grown from seed at all. Seeds of some plants, like parsley, germinate very slowly. Certain seedlings, like those of rosemary, thyme, and lavender, are slow growing, a disadvantage in regions where summers are short. And some cultivars or strains (named plant variations), like *Achillea ptarmica* 'The Pearl', as well as all the mints, do not come true to type from seed (in other words, plants grown from seed do not look exactly like the parent plant).

If you're just beginning with herbs, it's wise to start with the easy ones first; your success will give you confidence to try the more demanding ones later on. Consult the Growing section in each herb portrait to find out more about the herbs you'd like to grow from seed.

The following herbs are easy to grow from seed:

* Arugula
* Basil
* Borage
* Calendula
* Chamomile
* Chervil
* Coriander
* Cress
* Dill
* Lemon Balm
* Mallows
* Marigold, Signet
* Nasturtium
* Sages

Make Your Own Sowing Guide

Some time in the winter I draw up a plan for sowing herbs, making a list of those I want to raise indoors—some need a head start before being planted out-doors—and those that can be sown directly in the soil *(see fig. 1)*. Since sowing times vary considerably, this list can get rather complicated. To simplify my job, I make a chart on 8½-by-11-inch paper, using the long end as the top of the page to write the following column headings: NAME, WHEN TO START, TREATMENT, SOWING TEMPERATURE, GERMINATION TIMES.

Figure 1. Sample Sowing Guide

NAME OF PLANT	WHEN TO START	TREATMENT	SOWING TEMP. (IN DEGREES F)	GERMINATION TIMES EXPECTED (ACTUAL)
Arugula	outside; BF	just cover	59–68	7–10
Basil	inside; 6–8	⅛–¼" deep	70–85	14 (3)
Borage	outside; AF	D; ½" deep	70	5
Calendula	inside; 4-6 outside; AF	D; ¼" deep	70	4–14 (3–4)
Chamomile	inside; 4–6 outside; BF	L; barely cover	50	10–12 (3)
Chervil	outside; BF	barely cover	55	14
Coriander	outside; AF	D; ½" deep	55–65	10
Cress	outside; BF	just cover	59–68	7–10
Dill	outside; AF	L; on surface	60–70	21–25
Lemon Balm	inside; 10–12	just cover	70	14–21
Mallows	inside; 6–8	⅛" deep	70	5–21 (2)
Marigold, Signet	inside; 8–10	just cover	70–85	5–14 (1)
Nasturtium	inside; 2–4 inside; 6 *(climbing)* outside; AF	D; ¼" deep	65	7–12 (4)
Sages	inside; 6-8 *(cooking)* inside; 10 *(clary)* inside; 12 *(tender)*	D; just cover	70–85	4–12 (5)

Key

WHEN TO START   BF = a week before last frost date
AF = after chance of frost has passed
4–6 = number of weeks before last frost date to start seeds

TREATMENT   D = seeds need darkness to germinate
L = seeds need light to germinate

When to Start

Herbs, among them slow- and fast-growing annuals and perennials, should never be started indoors at the same time or you'll end up with too many over-grown, potbound plants before planting time rolls around (usually just after the last expected frost date). So under this heading I write whether the herbs I decide to raise indoors should be sown 12, 8 to 10, or 4 to 6 weeks before the last frost date, depending on their growth rates. Purple basil, for instance, needs more time to grow than salad burnet, so they are sown at different times. The herbs I sow outdoors are divided into two groups for early and later sowing (BF for before frost; AF for after frost), since some plants, like chamomile, germinate best in cooler temperatures, while others, like feverfew and the mallows, need warmer soil temperatures to trigger germination.

Treatment

This refers to sowing depth, whether seeds require stratification (prechilling) or soaking overnight, and whether they should be exposed to light or kept in total darkness to trigger germination. These considerations are crucial for success, so be sure to look in the Growing section under each plant portrait for the required information.

❋ 1. To determine **sowing depth**, a rule of thumb is to cover seeds with soil equal to twice their thickness; seeds smaller than a pinhead should be just pressed into the soil. If in doubt about planting depth, or if no figures are given, sow shallowly. Remember that seeds are small for the work they have to do, pushing new life upward toward the light. Planting seeds too deep is a major cause of germination failure.

❋ 2. **Prechilling**, also called **stratification** or breaking dormancy, mimics what nature does outdoors in winter: exposing moistened seeds to cold temperatures. This process breaks down inhibitors in the seed that prevent it from germinating at the wrong time of year (in winter, for instance); stratified seed germinates outdoors in spring at the beginning of a new growing season. I prefer to stratify most seeds indoors in late winter or early spring rather than planting them outside in fall. Outdoors, germination is less reliable due to the vagaries and hazards of nature, such as heavy rains or the activities of birds, insects, or animals. Stratification indoors is readily achieved by storing seeds in the refrigerator at approximately 40 degrees F (an average setting) for 3 to 6 weeks. To do this, I use the paper towel method: Fold a sturdy paper towel three times; open up the third fold and sprinkle both sides with water; spread the seeds out in an uncrowded single layer on one side and refold the towel, placing it in a loosely folded plastic sandwich bag (not an airtight Zip-Lock type, where seeds could rot); then slip a label identifying the seed between one of the dry folds of the paper towel. After stratification, most seeds germinate readily if they are sown on or close to the surface of the soil. Keep in mind that seeds must be moist, not wet, at all times; check the bag occasionally.

❋ 3. Seeds with **hard coats** can be encouraged to germinate: Place them in a teacup, pour boiling water over them, and leave the seeds in the teacup for 24 hours. They should be planted right away, before they have time to dry out. You can also encourage hard-coated seeds to germinate by making a hole in them with a pin, chipping the seeds with a sharp knife, or rubbing them lightly with sandpaper (always away from the seed's hilum or "eye," the small dent where the seed was attached to a pod).

❋ 4. Some seeds need **light** to trigger germination; these should be sown on the moistened soil surface and just pressed in. Herbs that need light to germinate include angelica, borage, dill, and wormwood. Other seeds require total darkness to trigger germination; these should be sown at the recommended depth, then covered with newspaper, brown paper, or black plastic to exclude all light. Herbs that need darkness to germinate include calendula, nasturtium, and viola. Fortunately, most seeds will germinate in light or in darkness but their rates of germination will vary.

Sowing Temperature

The seeds of most herbs will germinate readily in the 70-degree range, the approximate indoor room temperature. I put down the desired germination temperatures in this column; they usually range from 55 to 80 degrees. Those herbs that germinate best at lower temperatures, like chamomile, are sown directly in the ground outside; those in the middle range, from 60 to 70 degrees, are sown either indoors or outside, depending on their growth rate. Herbs requiring higher temperatures to germinate, like the basils and sages, are usually started indoors.

Expected and Actual Germination Times

First I fill in the expected days to germination, say 10; after the seeds have germinated, I add in parentheses the actual number of days it took. Having a record of expected and actual germination times will tell you if you're doing a good job, or if you should improve your methods. (Perhaps your seed is old; most germination rates decline with the age of the seeds.)

If you follow my method and prepare a chart along the lines I have described, without even sowing a single seed you will have greatly enhanced your chances to achieve excellent germination rates, simply by acknowledging that not all seeds should be sown at the same time or in the same way.

STARTING HERBS INDOORS

Now it's time to sow the seed. Let's start with sage as an example: The seeds are nice to work with, round, not too small, and easy to handle.

Sowing

Ten to 12 weeks before our last frost date, I gather together my sowing materials, which consist of soil, containers, and seeds.

First, I spread a double layer of newspaper on the kitchen table, so I won't have a mess to clean up. Then I work *warm,* not cold, water into a bag of commercial soilless seed-starting mix (a blend of sphagnum moss, perlite, and vermiculite, which creates a porous growing medium with excellent drainage and sufficient water retention), until it feels *damp,* not wet, to the touch.

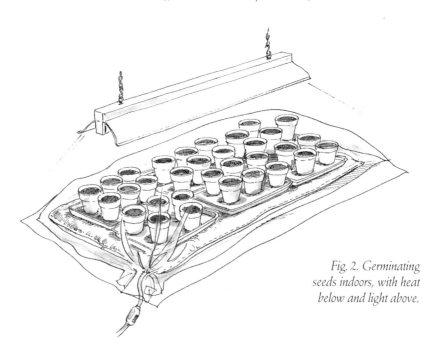

Fig. 2. Germinating seeds indoors, with heat below and light above.

I fill my containers to the top and tamp down the soil with a kitchen spoon handle so there is a quarter of an inch space for watering. My containers are nothing fancier than recycled Styrofoam cups. I like them because they take up so little room and you can easily write plant names on their sides with a permanent marker. Containers of whatever type, store-bought or recycled cartons, should be clean and not much more than 2½ inches deep, with a few drainage holes punched in the bottom.

Sage seeds should be planted on the surface, so I gently press them into the moistened soilless mix, spread them out so they aren't touching one another, then sprinkle a little of the dry growing mix over them, just enough to cover the seeds. The dry growing medium soon absorbs moisture from the dampened mix underneath.

When the cups are planted, I place them in a tray for easy handling and move my operation upstairs. There I place the cups on recycled Styrofoam meat trays, by twos or however they will fit, and arrange them on top of an old heating pad (wrapped in a plastic bag to prevent it from getting wet) set at medium, under a single 20-watt fluorescent light. I wrap a sheet of thin, clear plastic over and around the trays, tucking it in just tight enough to allow moisture to condense on the top of the inside of the bag. This ensures that the seeds will be in contact with moisture at all times and eliminates the need for further watering. The light stays on 24 hours a day until the seeds have germinated. The setup I have described is remarkably efficient for quickly germinating most seeds but is inadequate for growing the plants *(see fig. 2)*.

Care of Seedlings

As soon as the seedlings have sprouted, I remove the plastic and move the trays under two 40-watt fluorescent grow lights, positioned 4 inches above the containers. When the surface of the soilless mix is dry to the touch, the containers are easily watered from the bottom (the preferred method) by pouring lukewarm water into the meat trays. The first watering should be made with a liquid fungicide to prevent the disease known as *damping-off,* which can afflict seedlings grown in moist conditions, even destroying whole plantings.

When the seedlings have their second set of leaves (which are their first *true* leaves), I begin transplanting them to roomier quarters, using 2-inch plastic cups with drainage holes for each plant, or 2- or 3-inch plant cells (depending on plant size) with narrow bases that force seedlings to form a good, strong root system, crucial for their success in the ground.

Removing the seedlings from their Styrofoam cups is easy. I just turn the containers upside down, keeping one hand cupped over the growing plants, then tap the bottom of the container, allowing the whole block of soil and seedlings to ease out onto a Styrofoam tray, where I gently separate each seedling with a kitchen fork. Holding each seedling by its leaves, I then plant it into a hole I have prepared with my finger in its new container, which is filled with friable potting soil. I use a homemade potting mix consisting of 1 part finished and sifted compost and ½ part each of vermiculite and perlite.

Moving to the Greenhouse

I continue to grow the seedlings under lights until our lean-to greenhouse warms up sufficiently, at which time I transfer my operation there. This greenhouse is a rough affair put together in 1975, a few years after we moved to the farm. Built onto a south-facing wall of the house, the greenhouse measures 8

Fig. 3. Our lean-to greenhouse

feet by 25 feet with single-paned, used storm windows all around the front and sides of the structure. These windows reach down on the outside to a base (about 2½ feet tall) of wooden barn boards, and up to a sharply angled, translucent fiberglass roof *(see fig. 3)*. Inside, an old potbellied wood stove at one end provides heat on the coldest days and nights during spring. Even with the additional heat, the greenhouse cools down considerably at night, so there is no need to harden-off my plants (to gradually introduce them to outdoor growing conditions). All my seedlings are tough customers by the time they're ready to go into the garden.

This very unsophisticated greenhouse has produced thousands of healthy plants over the years at virtually no expense, and has served other functions as well. In spring the plants share quarters with day-old chicks, who pass their first weeks of life there under a heat lamp. In summer, I use the intense heat to infuse my herb vinegars. In fall, we use the greenhouse warmth to ripen 70 gallons of tomatoes, and to dry onions and other crops, like soup beans and peas.

STARTING HERBS OUTDOORS

I occasionally sow perennial herbs outdoors in a coldframe in the late summer or fall and plant out the resulting seedlings the following spring. I use this method if I have limited space indoors or if I'm unsure of the plant's germination requirements. The main advantage is that you only need a suitable south-facing site for the coldframe and friable, early-warming, well-drained soil inside. The rest is up to nature, since once the seeds are planted, nature alone will determine when the soil has reached the magic temperature for germination to occur. It's always a thrill to find seedlings in the spring, sprouting on last fall's bare ground. It is important, though, to be patient. If the ground is still bare, don't be alarmed and don't disturb the soil. The seeds may still be viable, just waiting for warmth to germinate.

The Coldframe and the Hotbed

These simple structures are invaluable aids for the gardener, providing places to grow or store hardy plants (the coldframe) and to raise heat-loving types (the hotbed); both are easy to construct and can be made almost entirely from recycled materials *(see fig. 4)*.

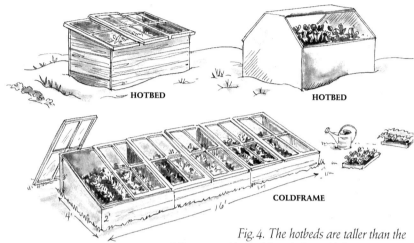

HOTBED

HOTBED

COLDFRAME

Fig. 4. The hotbeds are taller than the coldframes and heated from below with horse manure.

A coldframe is a four-sided wooden structure built into a south-facing slope. Mine measures about 4 feet wide and 16 feet long, with the back 9 to 12 inches higher than the front. The top of the frame is covered with a series of standard-sized windows (all secondhand) that capture solar heat. These are tied down with stout rope to hold them firmly in place. The rope is easily removed when the windows are opened—either partially or all the way—by sliding them to the back of the coldframe, with one end resting on the ground.

The coldframe is filled with friable soil at least 6 inches deep to create a favorable medium for seeding, the rooting of cuttings, plant divisions, or for temporary storage of extra or new plants. It's comforting to know there's a handy, deep bed around when you need it, a veritable treasure chest filled with a variety of plants at all seasons. In the beginning, my plants shared the cold-frame with Jigs's vegetables, but over the years I've taken over the whole thing, using one end to propagate roses and favorite hollyhocks and the other end for seeding, rooting, and temporary plant storage.

The two hotbeds located nearby are heated from below with fresh horse manure (the best comes from horses bedded with straw), and from above by the sun. They are similar in appearance to a coldframe but taller, since they need room at the base to store the heating medium. Jigs makes low, flat piles of manure and bedding outdoors in the early spring near one of the hotbeds, which is actually an old 4- by 8-foot meat cooler salvaged from a local market;

the glass front and the sliding doors at the back are ideally suited for raising plants inside. The other hotbed, made from an actual wooden bed, is covered with storm windows just like the coldframe.

When the manure starts to heat up, after about a week's time, Jigs mixes it all up into a big heap to get it even hotter. He checks it every day and when the pile is heating throughout, or nearly so, he shovels the manure into the bottom section of the hotbed and stamps it down to make a firm bed about 3 feet deep and the length of the cooler (8 feet). It is most important, when shoveling it into the hotbed, to make sure the manure is not dried out; if any white mold is evident, the manure should be watered.

After the manure is in place, Jigs adds a 4-inch layer of seeding medium, similar to what I use indoors. This is where he raises tomatoes, peppers, cabbage, cauliflower, broccoli, zucchini, and melons, and where I grow heat-loving herb seedlings like basil. It's fun to stop by the hotbed on the way to the barn on a particularly cold, blustery day in early spring, slide open the back door of the meat cooler, feel the rush of warm air, and read the temperature on the thermometer inside—80 degrees. A hotbed is a simple and inexpensive gardening aid, especially valuable where the growing season is short. If you know anyone with a horse, it is not difficult to collect the 100 cubic feet of manure needed to heat a 4- by 8-foot structure like our meat cooler.

Later, after Jigs plants out the vegetables, I take over one of the hotbeds (the converted bed) to raise the basil plants to maturity. In this favorable environment—warm, sheltered from the wind—I'm able to get three cuttings in a single season. Best of all, I shovel out all the soil and rotted manure at the end of the season to add to nearby plantings.

SOIL, SITE, AND PLANTING

Herbs, with a few exceptions, thrive in well-drained garden soil, moderately enriched. "Well drained" or "sharply drained," repeated like a mantra throughout this book, means that the soil is loose and friable; in other words, you can scoop up a handful and it will be crumbly and easy to pour from your hand. The soil should allow water to penetrate its surface and reach the plant's roots before draining off; there should never be any standing water around the root crowns of plants. The loose soil particles encourage the production of a strong root system, just as compacted soils discourage good root growth. If you plant herbs in the soil conditions they prefer (consult the Growing sections for each herb) and in the proper site (sun or shade), you will have met their basic growth requirements. Let's first consider the soil.

Soil

Pick up almost any gardening book and you'll find the accepted wisdom on the subject of soils: If it's heavy clay, you can "open it up"—separate the sticky clods—by working in sand and organic matter (sphagnum moss, rotted saw-dust, compost); if your soil is thin and sandy, you can add organic matter to give it body. My only experience is with clay, the kind of soil that sticks togeth-er in a ball when you squeeze it. We tried all the usual methods to improve the soil when we moved to Cape Breton over 25 years ago. Countless wagonloads of rotted manure from the old barn were spread on the area we used for our first vegetable garden, to which we added eelgrass from the shores of the near-by lake and rotted sawdust. As charter members of the organic gardening movement in the 1950s (when it was hardly a movement), we were ideologi-cally committed to improving the existing soil, even though year after year we saw no improvement in its tilth or texture. Indeed, germination rates decreased, and there never seemed to be any soil to cover the tiny carrot seeds. Where had all that rotted manure and the other choice organic amendments gone?

When I decided to establish a planting of flowers on the knoll underneath the old lilac trees, again I followed accepted wisdom: I dug out the offending clay sludge, laid down gravel for drainage, and filled the dug-out area with loamy soil. The result was a depression that has never filled in, no matter how much soil I've added. I had inadvertently created a sunken garden.

Our enlightenment was slow in coming, so committed were we to the methods we were using. We timidly made our first raised beds, merely raking up the soil in mounds to improve drainage. The next year we enclosed the mounds with logs or boards. Weeds were the bane of our gardening lives. Yes, I know, all gardeners complain about weeds. But in an area where they naturally thrive and cultivated plants must fight for existence, weeds will win every time.

Then our Dutch friend, a marvelous, undaunted gardener, told us about his method: raised beds with a difference. Basically, the idea is to use the land as a table on which to build a growing bed. Our friend lays down plastic bags (we use plastic grain bags, of which we have a plentiful supply), encloses them with some sort of barrier so that the plastic extends beyond it, and fills in the area with friable loam.

We have adapted his method and added variations of our own: For vegetables, and for some annual and shallow-rooted perennial herbs and flowers, we use the plastic-bag method; for other types of plants, we line beds with thick layers of newspaper. Whichever method we choose, the idea is to suppress weeds and create a favorable growing medium.

Making Soil

I'm sure I never thought about making soil. It's just there, after all, something you take for granted. It's what you walk on and dig in. Some soils—and ours is an example—are so resistant to improvement that it's a waste of time and energy to try to change their basic structure, especially since there are easier, quicker ways to achieve the same result.

Our problem was to find enough good soil to substitute for the God-given land. Living miles away from any settlement, without a vehicle, and with a small cash income, what could we do? We could never afford to buy enough topsoil for all our plantings. The answer came directly from our life, from the animals that sustain us, from the cows that give us milk and butter and cheese, from the chickens that give us eggs, from the pigs and steers that give us meat, from the horses that plow the land. You guessed it: composted barn manure.

It takes 2 years to make soil from composted manure from the pens we clean out in the summer and fall months. Wheelbarrow loads of manure mixed with bedding litter—either sawdust or straw—are stacked outside in a square pile that is turned once in late fall to encourage decomposition. Over the winter, the manure begins to break down, but because our climate is so cold and damp, the process is very slow (which is why the soil does not immediately benefit from uncomposted manure), so the compost is still rough by the following spring. It takes another season of composting to make friable earth, to which we add hardwood ashes. The ashes sweeten the soil's acidic content to some extent (lime does the same thing, only better). Rough compost goes in the bottom layer of our raised beds, while the finer-textured finished compost goes on the top 6 inches, creating favorable conditions for excellent germination. The loose soil particles encourage good root formation and allow rain to penetrate.

Even if you don't need to use compost as a soil substitute, it's invaluable for adding nutrients and tilth to existing soil. Compost any organic material you can find, especially in quantity: leaves, plant waste, old hay, shredded or crumpled newspaper. There are innumerable recipes for making the perfect heap, but take the directions with a grain of salt; making a compost heap is not all that difficult. Basically, organic matter is piled up within an enclosure 3 to 5 feet square (it can be made of wood, wire, brick, or any rigid material); turned at least once to provide oxygen (this speeds decomposition); and left until all the materials have broken down. The resulting organic matter is then referred to as finished compost and is ready to use in the garden. It should be dark, moist, and crumbly. The original heap, when completely decomposed, will be reduced by about half.

Jigs made our compost bin from wooden timbers. The area, partially shaded to reduce the need to water dried-out compost, is 10 feet long and 5 feet wide. It is divided into two bins, each 5 feet high, which are open at the far end for shoveling out the finished compost. When the first bin is full it is turned into the second, and a new heap started in the now empty first bin, so there are always two heaps on the go: one ready to use and one decomposing. We always make sure that decomposing fruits, vegetables, or manure are well covered with plant waste to discourage flies. Odor is never a problem. A well-regulated compost heap has a pleasant, earthy aroma.

The length of time it takes to turn organic waste into nutrient-rich compost depends on how frequently you turn the pile; whether you keep the pile moist, not wet; the ratio of "brown" material (leaves, straw, sawdust) to "green" material (grass, vegetable and fruit waste, and manure); and whether chunky matter is shredded or reduced before it is composted. With diligence, you can make compost in as little as 2 to 4 weeks. Just turning the pile regularly, however, will help ensure finished compost in 4 to 8 months.

Site

The Growing section under each herb entry will give you the basic exposure requirements (sun, partial shade, or shade). When deciding just where herbs will grow best in your landscape, consider the following:

❋ **1.** Plants preferring *full sun* need a minimum of 6 hours of direct sun each day; partial shade will work, too, as long as the 6-hour sun requirement is met.

❋ **2.** *Partial sun* means that plants receive less than 6 hours of direct sun a day (this should be morning sun for best results).

❋ **3.** *Shady* conditions include the dappled shade of a tree or shrub all day, or just 2 hours of morning sun.

Whatever the chosen site, keep in mind that buildings, walls, fences, rocks, and structures of any kind effectively protect plants from wind. Plant stress is every bit as real as human stress. Herbs growing in unfavorable conditions will not be happy. The remedies are often within every gardener's reach, as in the wise choice of site. I became aware of the importance of site one summer when my impatiens grew to three times their usual size, simply because I had planted them on the east side of the house in a corner between the back door and the cellar entryway, where they were protected from cooling winds.

Planting

Now you are ready to plant out seedlings (if you raised herbs from seed) or purchased plants. The classic advice is that you should do so only in cloudy, windless conditions. It is traumatic enough for the plants to move from their coddled environment (whether indoors or outside) to the actual growing site, without having to contend with scorching sun or drying winds; seedlings are not well enough developed to handle stress.

This is sound advice, but not always easy to practice. Sunny, windy conditions invariably prevail here in Nova Scotia (and in many other regions) just when it's time for the seedlings to be planted; waiting for the right time often proves frustrating and futile. It's a Hobson's choice between putting stress on the plants by letting them outgrow their containers or by planting them outside in less than ideal conditions. A gardener should be flexible, willing to take risks. If you have raised your seedlings in containers on the small size, like plant cells, these encourage the formation of a sturdy block of roots that, in my experience, are seldom disturbed by transplanting.

Here's how I plant out my seedlings to protect them from any unfavorable conditions that may prevail:

* **1.** The soil in the containers should be damp so seedlings just slide out after being turned upside down and lightly tapped (keep one hand over the top to catch the plant).

* **2.** Both annuals and perennials are planted deep and relatively close together (at the low end of recommended spacing) to make use of available ground moisture and to encourage shading (which, in turn, discourages weeds).

* **3.** After planting, seedlings are fertilized with a dilute solution (one-third the regular strength) of a soluble organic plant food high in phosphates and potash. Whatever you use, be sure it is mixed up in water first.

A SAMPLE HARVEST BED

If you're like me, you're torn between admiring the beauty of growing herbs and wanting to harvest them for use. The solution is a harvest bed, where plants can be cut all season long without guilt. One Mother's Day nearly 10 years ago, Jigs and I made a simple raised harvest bed applying our new techniques.

Measuring 50 feet long and 4 feet wide, the bed is positioned adjacent to the house with a southern exposure (suitable for most culinary herbs) and protected from north winds by a 6-foot-high slab fence that encloses a turkey yard. First we laid woven plastic grain bags over the sod ground, then we enclosed them with softwood logs cut for the purpose. In laying down the bags, we avoided any digging, which, as we had discovered, never improves our soil. The bags extended about 6 inches beyond the logs to discourage weeds from creeping into the bed *(see fig. 5)*.

Next, we filled the enclosure with lots of rough compost, stamped the mixture in place, and allowed things to settle for a week or so. (Ideally, we would have done this the fall before so the compost would have been more decomposed by spring.) Finally, we topped the entire bed with several inches of prize aged soil, a rich mixture of composted barn manure, rotted sawdust, and hardwood ashes or agricultural lime.

By then, the soil depth was about 8 inches, sufficient for annual herbs and the few perennial herbs I wanted to include in the bed. Deep-rooted perennials like lovage and invasive herbs like the mints were not included here.

The herbs planted in this bed form 3-foot blocks rather than rows, a strategy that saves space, discourages weeds, and promotes high productivity—about 14 pounds of each leafy-type green herb (chives, lemon balm, parsley, for example) can be harvested two or three times a season. Hand-weeding is minimal, confined mainly to pulling out the witchgrass that inevitably sneaks through the plastic at the bed's edges, but the soil is soft and it's easy to pull out the weeds.

Fig.5. The foundation of our harvest bed consists of grain sacks, which cut down on weeds and provide a base for richer soil.

In a separate patch of sod ground just beyond the long bed, we planted a 3- by 15-foot bed of lovage (since expanded to meet the needs of my Kitchen & Garden herb products) using the no-dig method I often employ: I just made slits with a sharp spade and inserted the lovage roots trimmed to fit. A heavy mulch of organic material—including a thick layer of composted turkey manure from the nearby pen, and either straw or rotted sawdust—killed the surrounding grass and weeds and fed the lovage. It wasn't long before new shoots were poking through the mulch. A new planting was thus established with minimal effort for maximum results.

GROWING IN CONTAINERS

Growing herbs in containers is part of my battle plan to grow heat-loving plants in a cool climate. Rosemary and the basils may spend the early summer in the greenhouse until outdoor temperatures are more conducive to their healthy growth. I use containers for other reasons, too: I can create microhabitats for herbs that need soil conditions I can't easily provide in the garden proper (thin, light soil for nasturtiums, for instance); I can place favorite culinary herbs close at hand for quick picking; new herbs that might get lost in a garden setting stand out and can be admired and studied; a variety of herbs in an assortment of containers provides striking accents in the landscape and complements other plantings; and, finally, container-grown herbs can be easily moved indoors over the winter without being transplanted (see fig. 6).

I use just about any container that comes my way; I refuse nothing Jigs offers me. Despite the fact that he sometimes moans—eyes rolling heavenward—over my expanded plantings, his containers are often the cause of their expansion. Fish tubs, an old wooden wheelbarrow, tires, truck tire rims (they come in various sizes, some with attractive wavy edges), old machine parts, wooden nail kegs, wine barrels, sap buckets, even an old, leaky boat (which I declined) have been filled with a variety of herbs over the years. Keep in mind, though, that the smaller the container, the faster the soil inside will dry out. Tall and wide containers (whole or cut-in-half barrels) look best with trailing plants at their edges; lower containers, such as tires, are most effective with taller plants at their center.

I especially enjoy being able to move the smaller containers around to create combinations I would never otherwise have conceived, such as green and purple basils rising up in front of the tall black hollyhock, prostrate rosemary growing over the rock edging with golden creeping thyme. In late summer, I can freshen up the look of plantings by placing containers I keep in reserve for the purpose. Set among other plants, the container-grown herbs often look as if they, too, were planted in the ground.

I don't put gravel or other drainage material in the bottom of my containers because I've found it unnecessary; all of them are leaky and drain quite well. I usually fill the bottom third of the container with a lightweight organic material such as well-rotted sawdust or wood shavings. Then I add a layer of compost, topped by 4 to 6 inches of porous topsoil, amended with perlite and vermiculite if necessary (the first promotes drainage, the latter retains moisture). I group containers for easier watering and mulch every one with moss to keep the soil cool and moist. Even in a drought, I don't need to water the plants very often; I use recycled lettuce-rinsing water most of the time. My container-grown herbs don't really need fertilizing during the summer, since the compost slowly releases nutrients to them. Herbs are regularly trimmed for use as they are in the garden.

Fig. 6. Heat-loving herbs thrive
in containers placed in the sun near the kitchen door.

A word about tires. Folks down-country are incredulous when I extol their virtues as containers. People who garden where I do, however, set great store by them. Almost anything can be grown in a tire. Jigs has 96 of them planted with strawberries, potatoes, zucchini, and cucumbers. Their advantage is that they absorb and retain heat and discourage weeds. What more could you want? Turned inside out they are urn-shaped, with a cast-iron look (much cheaper, though); the rim makes a convenient stand to keep the tire off the ground *(see fig. 7)*. I put a plastic grain bag in the bottom of the tire to hold the soil, add rough compost, then fine soil. I can plant a whole garden of culinary

Fig. 7. To make a simple but elegant (believe it or not) urn, select the thinnest tire you can find without a steel sidewall. Then follow these steps:

1.

1. With a heavy knife, carefully cut through the tire's sidewall close to the tread. Cut it all the way around, discarding the sidewall when you're through.

2.

2. Turn the tire over to the uncut side and stand on it. Now reach over to grasp the cut edge. Pull it up, turning it inside out, working your way around the tire. Once you're half done, the rest is easy.

3.

4.

3. The result is a container that—if you left the tire on the wheel rim— has a built-in stand.

herbs in one tire, and the brilliant yellow 'Lulu' marigold and mealycup sage (Salvia farinacea) in another.

CARE AND PROPAGATION

Caring for and propagating herbs are not difficult. My methods are simple, by necessity, but they can be universally applied.

Mulching

Mulching—the practice of covering the ground around plants with an organic or inorganic material—protects plants during prolonged dry periods by reducing water evaporation from the soil. It also cools the soil surface, creating a microclimate that is conducive to the continued production of leaves and flowers. Also, organic mulches break down eventually, adding tilth and nutrients to the soil. Plastic mulch is especially effective in preventing weed growth around plants. But be forewarned: Mulching also provides a wonderful home for slugs, which may feast on your delicious, tender herbs at night while you are sleeping.

I mulch as a water-conservation measure when dry conditions set in (it beats lugging buckets of water to the garden site). To do its job, an organic mulch should be 1½ to 2 inches thick: Consider using grass clippings, well-rotted sawdust or wood shavings, straw, bark, leaves, even compost, if you have that much on hand. If you decide to use fresh sawdust or wood shavings, you can prevent possible nitrogen loss—evident in yellowing leaves—by making sure the soil is well fertilized before you add the mulch. Most balanced soils don't suffer adversely from the addition of such mulches, certainly not ours, which is high in nitrogen anyway.

Watering

The ideal condition for maintaining herbs in healthy growth is steady moisture—no problem if you have a drip irrigation system in place. We have no sophisticated water system for the garden, relying solely on the rains from heaven. In a drought we mulch, as I have described, and also lug many buckets of water to the site. Barrels and tubs are placed around the house underneath downspouts that carry rain along gutters. These are used to water all the plantings close to the house.

We also use graywater, a euphemism for dirty water, water that has been used once and has been saved to use again. Irrigating plants with graywater is encouraged these days in line with water conservation. As we have discovered, graywater not only keeps plants moist, it fertilizes them at the same time, but it is too strong to use full strength on seedlings, so we dilute it by half. It can be used full strength on established perennials and shrubs with great results; water plants in a circle around the root area.

In the May 1992 issue of *Flower & Garden* magazine, the former chief floral decorator for the White House, Dottie Temple, confirms the benefits of graywater and gives directions for reusing washing-machine water as follows: Direct the drain hose into 6-gallon plastic jugs stored alongside the washer, and stay close to make sure they don't overflow. She uses liquid laundry detergents to avoid the sodium salts contained in some powdered detergents, which, she says, could damage plant roots.

General Maintenance

How do you encourage your herbs to thrive all summer long, even under adverse conditions? It could be cool and rainy, good for hardy perennials like sweet cicely, but awful for tropical plants like basil. Once in the ground, it's difficult to protect plants from cool, wet conditions; the best defense is a deep, humusy soil that drains well. Good air circulation, as in a sunny, exposed site, will discourage fungus disease. If plants are close together, they should not be touching; keep them trimmed to avoid this situation.

If you are growing herbs primarily to use them, frequent cutting will keep plants healthy, encouraging fresh growth. If your aim is to produce lots of foliage, pinch off buds or cut plants back before they flower and they will grow more leaves. Don't feel guilty if you don't use every one or even *any* of the herbs you grow. You may just want to admire their beauty, their green-hued foliage and enticing scents. But *do* pick them for bouquets. Virtually every herb has value in a vase of flowers: Cool green mint leaves, for instance, look lovely in a bouquet. Once you get in the habit, you will want fresh bouquets all summer so you can enjoy the beauty of herbs indoors at your leisure.

Tall plants, like hollyhocks, will need staking in most situations. The only way to avoid this dreaded job is to cut back plants when they are about one-third of the way through their growth cycle; this works well with plants like white mugwort *(Artemisia lactiflora)*. Although blooms will be sacrificed, plants will be bushier. If cutting back plants is not desirable, it's best to stake plants when they're in their early growth. The type of stake you use will depend on the growth habit of the plant: a stout wooden stake for hollyhocks, for instance, nearly as tall as the expected height of the plant. In tying plant stems to stakes, it's best to use flexible material such as strips of pantyhose tied in a loose figure eight from the stake to the stem, so plants aren't strangled. Sometimes strategically placed brush is sufficient to hold up plants with weak or lax stems. For wide plants like comfrey that threaten to smother their neighbors, I tie two pieces of baling twine together and loosely encircle the plant with a sort of hoop.

To ensure their continued leaf production, I harvest herbs like lovage, lemon balm, and mints in quantity. I spread a layer of compost over the bed in midsummer after the plants have been cut back once, then water them for several days with graywater and they grow back quickly. It's best not to harvest perennial herbs in late summer or fall, since they may become weakened and unable to survive over the winter.

I don't provide any of my perennial herbs with a winter cover, but all the plantings on the farm receive a blanket of aged manure during the winter months, when manure is regularly spread on the fields. Spruce boughs or similar material could be used to cover perennial plantings, but only after the ground has frozen. The best protection for perennials over the winter, however, is snow; for this reason, do not cut back perennial herbs to the ground in the fall, but leave a foot or so of branching "arms" to catch the snow and protect the plant's crown from alternate freezing and thawing.

Insects and Diseases

Most herbs are not much troubled by disease and insect infestations. The problems that do occur are largely based on local conditions (a dry or wet climate, soil type, for example). We never had a major problem with slugs when we lived in Vermont, for instance, but we do here in Nova Scotia, where the climate is very damp. While slugs don't bother herbs much (except for basil and costmary), they can ruin a strawberry crop. In my experience, the best way to keep down the slug population is to keep the grass well trimmed at the edges of the beds and to hand-pick the offenders (I look under containers and around wooden barriers, where whole families can sometimes be found biding their time until dusk, when they begin their nighttime predations).

Your garden will be free of most pests if you follow three simple principles. Always try to match plants to their preferred habitat (sun or shade, dry or moist soil, for instance) to prevent plant stress; plants growing under stress are more likely to succumb to disease or insect damage than are healthy plants. Clean up plant debris in the fall to eliminate insect habitats. And, if all remedies fail, remove and destroy plants by burning.

Diseases have been mainly confined in my garden to powdery mildew on the basils and monardas (bee balm). I avoid moving basil from a warm to a cool temperature, which seems to trigger the disease; with the monardas, I pull out and destroy any affected plants ('Panorama Mix' is a mildew-prone cultivar here) or change the planting site.

The most serious infestations we see are due to whiteflies, which affect lemon balm and other members of the mint family. Whiteflies look like tiny white specks on the undersides of leaves and move in a cloud when you disturb the plant. Leaves infested with whitefly turn yellow, and the whole plant looks very ill. When the plants are small, insects can be destroyed with a strong spray of water, or with a soap spray made from 1 teaspoon of liquid detergent to 1 quart of water, to which a few drops of cooking oil have been added. This will cause the spray to cling to the leaves and kill the offending insects. It's important to spray the insects on the leaf undersides. Continue this treatment as needed, but be sure to thoroughly wash plants before harvesting them for consumption, or wait until they have been washed by a good soaking rain.

In general, it's a good idea to keep track of what's going on in the garden. I am in the habit of examining the undersides of leaves for whitefly, watching out for powdery mildew among susceptible types, and poking among crowded plants for slug nests. It's easier to deal with such problems in their early stages.

Propagating Herbs

The easiest herbs to propagate are those that seed themselves. These include angelica, arugula, calendula, chamomile, coriander, cress, dill, feverfew, hollyhocks, mallows, sweet cicely, sweet rocket, and violas. Dig up the seedlings in the early spring and replant them where you want them.

Most of the hardy perennial herbs are easily propagated by simple root division: In the fall or spring, simply chop off a piece of root and replant it. Early-blooming plants, like lungwort, are usually divided in the fall; later-blooming plants, like feverfew, can be divided in the spring. In my experience, all of the hardy perennials can be divided well into late fall, when they are dormant. That way they will be ready to go the following season, early or late.

Some of the hardy perennials and most of the tender ones are easily propagated by stem cuttings taken during the summer from tender (not woody), healthy shoots 3 to 6 inches long. It doesn't seem to matter if the cut is made above or below a leaf node, depending on the length of the stems. Remove the lower leaves, lightly dip just the cut end in rooting hormone powder, then insert it deep into a favorable rooting medium, such as a commercial seeding mix amended with perlite and vermiculite in equal parts. Loosely cover cuttings with a plastic bag to create moist, not wet, conditions *(see fig. 8)*. If too much moisture starts to collect under the bag, remove it or let in some air. Cuttings kept at 70 degrees should root in about 6 weeks. Repot them in

Fig. 8. Stem cuttings are an effective way of propagating lavender, rosemary, sage, and other herbs.

regular potting soil until they are mature enough to plant out, then bring them into the house over the winter (for tender types), or plant out in a coldframe until needed.

Herbs to grow from stem cuttings include hyssop, lavender, the mints, oregano, rosemary, sage, and thyme. You might consult Tom DeBaggio's excellent guide, *Growing Herbs: From Seed, Cutting & Root* (see Bibliography) for more detailed information.

Mints, basils, rosemary, and lavender will all root in water, but in my experience it's tricky to then grow them in soil.

GROWING HERBS INDOORS

You can grow a number of herbs indoors for the winter, for culinary use (basil, marjoram, parsley), for decoration (flowering sages), or to carry over until the next growing season (tender sages, rosemary). I sow seeds of annual culinary herbs during the summer, grow the seedlings in pots, then bring them indoors in the fall. This is a better practice than digging up mature annual herbs near the end of their growth cycle.

Except for the mints and chervil, most herbs need about 3 or 4 hours of sun a day during the winter when grown indoors. Unless you use artifical light, a cool, sunny window is the best location, and some extra humidity should be provided. We always have a pot of water, uncovered, steaming on the parlor wood stove; I set potted plants on Styrofoam meat trays filled with water and pebbles, keeping the water level near the top of the pebbles. Do not crowd plants and remember to turn them occasionally so growth will be even, not one-sided.

The soil for growing herbs indoors should be porous and friable. Commercial potting soil, amended with extra perlite and vermiculite, to which a handful per pot of sifted compost is added, works well. Whatever type of container you use (terra-cotta or plastic), it should have a drainage hole in the bottom. A layer of small pebbles in the bottom of the pot will ensure that water drains away from the roots: Use a ½-inch layer for a small- to medium-sized pot, a 1-inch layer for a deeper pot.

Overwatering is a major cause of houseplant death. To avoid this problem, scratch beneath the soil surface with your finger and water when it feels dry, alternating the watering from above and from below, and always using tepid, not cold, water. Herbs that are heavily trimmed for use should be fertilized about every 2 weeks with a liquid fertilizer such as Rx–15; otherwise, fertilize once a month.

Inevitably, in my experience, most indoor plants, including herbs, suffer from some sort of insect infestation. Good plant hygiene is one defense: Keep plants trimmed, dispose of debris (dead leaves), and allow plenty of air circulation around them. When a plant is seriously attacked, isolate it and cut it back severely. Don't overwater, and remove the affected plant from direct light. When it shows signs of healthy regrowth, lightly fertilize the plant and return it to its former place. Soap spray often works well: Use 1 teaspoon liquid detergent to 1 quart of water, to which a few drops of cooking oil have been added. Turn plants upside down, holding your hand over the top of the pot, and give the leaf undersides (where the insects usually live) a strong spray. If all of the above measures fail to produce the desired results, I dispose of the plant.

These are some of the herbs you can grow indoors in winter:

* Basils: Keep the soil moist, and pinch back the leaves; the plants will eventually become woody and should then be discarded.
* Burnet: The pot should be deep to accommodate the plant's long tap root.
* Chervil: Grow in indirect light, not full sun.
* Chives: Leave the potted plant outside and expose it to freezing temperatures before bringing it indoors; this stimulates new growth.
* Coriander: Grow it for its leaves (cilantro), for use in sauces and curries.
* Cress: Sprout for salads on moist paper towels set in a tray; harvest when the sprouts are about 2½ inches tall. (See the Cress entry for directions.)
* Dill: Grow the fern-leaf type, which is more manageable in a pot and yields a better supply of leaves than the traditional tall dill.
* Lemon balm: Keep the soil moist, and pinch back the leaves; use the leaves for tea or herb butters.
* Lovage: Keep it cut back to 12 to 15 inches for a striking foliage plant; use leaves sparingly in salads and with tuna fish or oysters.
* Marjoram: This is a fine indoor plant for a hanging basket in a sunny window; keep it trimmed to 8 inches.
* Mints: Indirect light, moist soil, and pinching back will keep plants growing well.

* Oregano: Grow the true Greek oregano with white flowers *(Origanum heracleoticum)* for culinary use; keep trimmed.
* Parsley: Grow it in a deep pot to accommodate the plant's long tap root; keep it pinched back to prevent flowering; eventually, by late winter or early spring, the plant should be discarded.
* Rosemary: This plant needs a cool, sunny window and a little lime in the soil (crushed eggshells work well); it also needs constant moisture, but is most often killed indoors by overwatering.
* Sages: Sages also benefit from a little lime in the soil; tender types like Texas sage will flower indoors all winter and can be cut back in spring and put outside.
* Savory: Summer savory *(Satureja hortensis)* needs more moisture than winter savory *(S. montana);* keep both trimmed.

CHAPTER TWO

Handling the Harvest

*Harvesting is an odd blend of glamour . . . and strain . . . Ultimately,
there is great satisfaction in the large, filled harvest baskets.*—Margaret
Brownlow, *Herbs & The Fragrant Garden*

The importance of harvesting herbs at their peak of flavor cannot be stressed
often enough. The right time varies according to the specific herb but, generally
speaking, foliage should be picked just when the plant is beginning to form
buds, at which time the leaves have the highest concentration of essential oils.
Herbs like chamomile, on the other hand, whose flowers are of interest, should
be harvested when the blooms are freshly opened. There are always exceptions: With lavender, for instance, it is the flower *buds* that contain the most flavor and fragrance. If you want to preserve herbs for dried flower crafts, the
right time for picking also varies, depending on the desired effect. Look up each
herb in the plant portraits section of this book for the details.

Overripe herbs become stalky as plants put their energy into flower and
seed production at the expense of their leaves. The point is that the longer you
wait to harvest most herbs after their time of maximum flavor, the less you will
have to enjoy. Homegrown, processed herbs *should* surpass anything you can
buy, because more care can be taken in gathering small amounts at the right
time, in handling them, and in carefully turning them into a variety of flavorful
products.

For many years I followed the methods established from our Vermont
days. When harvest time came, we cut the plants back and tied them up into
bunches with string. Our large kitchen was darkened with basil and other herbs
hanging from the beams. Later, many hands were enlisted in the evening to
strip the crackling dry leaves while Jigs read to us a Dickens novel. *Nicholas
Nickleby, Martin Chuzzlewit, David Copperfield, Great Expectations* lightened our
task as we filled bowls and packed the dried herbs into jars, labeled and stored
in what came to be known as "the herb closet."

In Cape Breton, without the extra hands to help and with the establishment of my herb business, I gradually had to change and streamline my harvesting and drying techniques to deal with both larger quantities and a wider variety of herbs than I had in the past. The initial success of Jo Ann's Kitchen & Garden—a seat-of-the-pants enterprise that successfully created a market for flavoring and tea herbs where none had existed before—put ever greater pressure on me to refine my methods, which at first were very crude—herbs drying on every available surface, laid down on layers of newspaper under and on top of beds and on floors all over the house.

I should mention at the outset that air-drying is still my preferred method of preserving herbs for future use. I don't have a microwave oven, and I don't like the texture of frozen herbs. If done with care, many air-dried herbs (even chives, not usually recommended for drying) retain both their color and their flavor and are convenient to use in cooking: Use half as much in any recipe as you would use fresh herbs. Those herbs that don't dry well, such as chervil and burnet, are preserved in other forms as in vinegars, or I only use them fresh.

The struggle to achieve better results is an ongoing one. Increasing demand for the herbs, combined with more time taken up in doing farmwork (including berry picking and making jams to sell), has provided the impetus to constantly improve my methods. The rewards for all this labor and experimentation are high-quality dried herbs, still green and packed with flavor. They are superior to anything I have ever seen in a store, and, best of all, these results have been achieved by the simplest means. They have to be simple, for I have no alternatives, and they have to be efficient since I work alone. Jigs is busy harvesting hay at the same time that I'm harvesting the first herbs, lovage and chives. And I'm the one who builds the wagonloads of hay.

TRADITIONAL METHOD OF HARVESTING AND DRYING HERBS

This is the same technique, with a few changes, that we used in Vermont. Now, however, I'm more discerning in its application, using it only for fast-drying herbs like peppermint and savory. On a sunny day, after the dew has dried (no point in having to contend with extra moisture), herbs are cut with a stout pair of kitchen scissors to the lowest set of clean leaves. I grasp a small bunch in one hand and cut the stems with the other, quickly checking each handful for weeds, discolored leaves, debris, and insects—all of which are easy to discard at this stage. Then I lay down the stems in my gathering basket so that they all point in the same direction for easy bunching later on. Once indoors, the herbs are gathered into small bundles and secured with a thick rubber band wrapped tightly about 1½ inches from the end of the stems. I used to use string, but rubber bands are more efficient, contracting as the herbs dry so bunches remain intact. I have never actually counted the number of stems in a bundle, but there are probably between 12 and 15, depending on the type of herb involved, the amount of foliage it has, and the thickness of the stems.

The bunches are hung from rods suspended on hooks in the ceiling around the kitchen and above the wood stove, uncrowded so air can circulate around them, and away from direct light, which destroys an herb's essential oils and color. Some people tie a brown paper bag around each bunch to prevent dust from accumulating on the herbs. I've tried this and find it cumbersome, with dubious benefits. Besides, the herbs add panache to the kitchen decor. The first things one sees on entering the front door are pretty patterned bundles of greenery, some with other colors, suspended from the ceiling. Bunches should be taken down as soon as they are dry (they could take up moisture during a damp period), unless you have hung them solely for their looks, which is fine, too.

If you only use this method for quick-drying herbs (see the list below), the herb bunches should be crispy dry within a week to 10 days, depending on air moisture. In a period of humid weather or if you're in a hurry, you can finish drying the herbs by laying them out on a cookie sheet (don't crowd them, and roughly remove some of the stems to reduce bulk) and placing them in a gas or electric oven on the lowest setting (no higher than 150 degrees F). If you smell the herbs, the oven is too hot. I do most of my initial drying of herb bunches in a cool, airy, dark loft above the kitchen, which benefits from the heat below.

Once the leaves are crispy dry and the stems are brittle, it's time to strip the bunches. On a flat surface, spread a double sheet of newspaper under a large, wide bowl. Hold the bundle of herbs over the bowl, pull off the rubber band, then, taking one stem at a time, remove the leaves with a quick downward motion of your free hand. With some herbs, you can do several stems at a time. An alternative stripping method is to roll the whole bunch back and forth between the palms of your hands. The leaves will fall into the bowl, probably leaving bits of leaves still clinging to the stems. I try to leave the herbs as whole as possible to retain flavor (especially for tea herbs), unless I decide to process them further into flakes for convenience. You can, at this point, discard the stems or retie them in little bundles to use as aromatic kindling for special occasions. A friend of mine decorates these herb stems with ribbon and a few dried flowers, selling them at craft sales, where they are very popular around Christmastime.

Now it's time to store the dried herbs in labeled jars or containers of some sort; I use plastic tubs for large amounts. The easiest way to accomplish this is to pour all the leaves from the bowl onto the newspaper (fold it back to its original crease so it is not spread out), shape it into a funnel, and pour the herbs directly into containers. These must be stored in a cupboard or closet in total darkness, where the herbs should keep for a year in about the same condition in which you originally stored them.

Herbs to Dry by the Traditional Bunching Method

NAME	PREPARATION
Bergamot	Leaves and flowers
Catnip	Make small bunches
Chives	Flowering stalks only
Feverfew	Flowering stalks
Hops	Flowering stalks
Lady's Mantle	Flowering stalks
Lamb's-Ears	Flowering stalks
Lavender	In bud
Lemon Balm	Leafy stalks
Marjoram	Use traditional method if stalks are long enough; otherwise spread on cookie sheets to dry in the oven
Marjoram, Wild	Flowering stalks
Mints	(Except for apple mint) Leafy stalks
Mugwort, Common	In bud or flower for dried crafts
Mugwort, White	Flowering stalks
Pearly Everlasting	In bud
Sages	Leaves and flowers, depending on type
Savory, Summer	Leafy stems
Sorrel	Flowering stalks

Southernwood ....Long or short branches, not too woody

Sweet White Clover ....For small amounts of flowering stalks

Tansy...............................Foliage or flowering stalks

Yarrows...........................Flowering stalks

Wormwood.....................Tender, leafy stems

Wormwood, Sweet........Flower sprays

ALTERNATIVE METHOD OF HARVESTING AND DRYING HERBS

The techniques described here are noncommercial, adapted for home use (my business is still a kitchen-table affair). They can be used for small or large amounts of herbs of every type, even those I have listed under the traditional bunch-drying method. The most important elements involve: 1) how the herbs are cut and chopped to reduce bulk and speed up drying; 2) the construction of simple drying racks; and 3) the use of a homemade riddle, or round screen, which produces uniform herb flakes, most useful in making blends of several different herbs.

Harvesting

I was introduced to the long-handled brush hook quite by accident. One spring Jigs and I were in a well-stocked hardware store and I proclaimed that I needed a trimmer to cut the grass close around the beds where the mower can't reach it. I no longer had the time to use an ancient pair of sheep shears for the job, or, as was more often the case, to get down on my hands and knees and rip out the grass by hand. I envisioned myself, the busy craftswoman, zipping around the various beds with my sleek, gas-powered instrument. I would be just like those lovely ladies in the magazine ads, no sweat, no effort, doing things the modern way. Then reality appeared in the form of Jigs triumphantly handing me something he'd picked up in the hand tool section for under $10. It was a sort of brush hook, but with a long wooden handle affixed to a wicked-looking, crescent-shaped blade.

"Just what you need," he assured me. "I'll teach you how to use it."

Jigs had taught our children to use a scythe (he had learned from an authentic Irish peasant), and they became so accomplished that when they were still in their early teens they could help mow a whole field of oats, gracefully swinging their scythes, letting the tool do the work of slicing through the stalks so they lay in neat, angled rows, the stalks cut close to the ground. I am a different matter altogether, and no matter how patiently Jigs shows me the technique—it certainly looks easy when he does it—I find it hard to get into the proper rhythm.

I discovered, however, that the long-handled brush hook is a forgiving tool. It not only does the work it was meant to do—trim the grass around the beds—but it also slices through long lovage stalks. The brush hook is more manageable for an inexperienced person than is a scythe (which will do the same job), it is far less laborious than using a scissors, and, with its long handle, it saves bending over—a definite plus. It is suitable for cutting back any tall herb you want to harvest in quantity *(see fig. 9)*. The fact that the stalks may fall in all directions doesn't matter since after they're cut I gather them all up in a wheelbarrow and chop them up—sorting out the large, hollow seed stalks—to reduce bulk and speed drying. Lovage is one of those herbs, like basil, that discolor when hung in bunches.

Fig. 9. Harvesting lovage with the long-handled brush hook

The lovage stalks are then chopped up in a hand-powered hay-chopper, circa 1920s, once popular on small farms for making chicken feed from hay and miscellaneous produce. The leafy stalks are fed into a wooden tray mounted behind geared blades whose action is set in motion by a hand-powered fly-wheel. After the initial turns on the wooden handle, the machine does, indeed, begin to "fly" on its own momentum. All you have to do is to keep turning the handle with one hand, stopping occasionally to keep the tray filled with leafy stalks (discarding leafless stalks), pushing them toward the blades with the other hand, taking care to keep your hand well away from the blades. A bucket or other suitable receptable is placed just under the blades to catch the chopped herbage.

When I first used the hay-chopper method for quickly reducing bulk, I was worried that chopping the green herbs would prematurely release lovage's strong flavor, the prime ingredient in my popular Herb Salt mix, but my fears were unwarranted. This is probably due to the fact that, once chopped, the herbs are dried in a dark place under optimum conditions.

The modern equivalent of the now extinct hay-chopper would probably be a gas- or electric-powered leaf shredder. For small amounts of herbs, a pair of kitchen scissors is adequate for roughly cutting up leafy stalks. Keep in mind that it takes 10 pounds of green herbs to produce 1 pound of dry herbs, whose bulk is further reduced by flaking or pulverizing. This ratio is not as bad as it sounds since a pound of dried herbs goes a long way (remember, flavor is intensified by drying). At the end of summer, after chopping, drying, and flaking, I'll have over 5 gallons of dried lovage—and that's a lot of lovage (about 5 pounds, which equals about 50 pounds of fresh lovage).

At the end of one particularly hectic season for Jo Ann's Kitchen & Garden, the ad hoc methods I was using to dry and process herbs had turned the whole house into a rather messy herb factory. Jigs suggested that we limit my activities to our mainly unused upstairs, which remained exactly as it was when our four children were still living with us, although now they were long gone. The impact of my consuming interest in herbs shook us out of the way we had, for many years, passively regarded our own living space.

We were exhilarated by the results of our reorganization, which gave rise to a large, airy space for packaging herbs and filling orders—my workshop—and the addition of drying racks in the loft, where I had already been drying bunches of herbs suspended from wooden beams.

Jigs's Magic Drying Racks

With his usual directness and speed, Jigs set up these racks in a few hours. They have revolutionized my drying methods, producing, as if by magic, lovely green dried leaves (even basil), gallons of pink rose petals—in fact, top-quality herbs of every kind. Although I try to remove the herbs as soon as each type is dry, they sometimes remain on the screens while I'm busy with some other activity. It's a blessing to know that there's no deterioration in quality. In the darkened loft, herbs retain their color and flavor almost indefinitely on these wondrous screens.

Jigs constructed two sets of wooden racks on either side of the chimney that passes through the loft. Each rack holds six screens that have been recycled from standard household window frames. The frames measure 32 inches long by 30 inches wide and are spread with clean screening. There is 8 inches of space between each screen on the rack. Beginning 2 feet above the floor and rising to slightly over my head (about 6 feet), the racks are just the right height for bending and reaching. The screens can be pulled forward or removed altogether, by sliding them along the grooved crosspieces that secure them in place *(see fig. 10)*.

Fig. 10. Jigs's magic drying racks allow us to dry herbs efficiently and quickly.

Fresh-cut or chopped herbs like lovage are put directly on the screens and stirred daily. When the herbs are completely dry, I slide out each screen and pour its contents onto newspaper, which is then shaped into a funnel for easy pouring into storage tubs or jars. If I need to vacate a number of screens to accommodate more fresh herbs at the peak harvest season (usually in early summer), I finish off the partially dried herbs downstairs in the gas or wood stove oven. From early to late in the season, the screens are always in use, magically turning fresh herbs into dry herbs, from the first crop of lovage in June to the last harvested spruce cones and bayberry leaves (for potpourri) in late fall.

The Riddle

This is another of Jigs's contributions, very effective in turning rough, dried herbs into a finished product, namely, uniform flakes. These flakes are easy to mix with other ingredients in my various herb blends. The riddle is a fine screen stretched over a wooden hoop, 16 inches in diameter and 4 inches deep, through which the dried herbs are rubbed *(see fig.11)*. I spread newspaper on the kitchen table, set a wide wooden bowl on top of it, then rub the herbs through the riddle and into the bowl. Any stems that don't go through the screen are pulverized in a minichop food processor (you can do three small handfuls at a time). The small stems of most flavoring herbs, except for the hard, woody ones, have flavor and should not be discarded. After flaking, herbs are stored for future use.

Obviously, not all types of dried herbs need to be processed through a riddle. It's mainly for those, like lovage, whose leaves and stems have been

Fig.11. Dried herbs are rubbed through the riddle into a bowl to make uniform flakes.

chopped together. Herbs dried in hanging bunches are more conveniently processed by stripping the leaves from their stems; I usually use this method for the tea herbs. I cut the leafy stems of basil in the garden with kitchen scissors, then cut them into smaller pieces, discarding the larger stems, before laying the chopped herbs on screens. When they are dry, they may be processed through the riddle, as I have described. Parsley is also cut with kitchen scissors, chopped up a bit, then laid on the screens, but it does not usually require processing in the riddle; it can be broken up by hand to a usable consistency. Whether or not you use the riddle for all herbs depends on your needs, as do the general techniques you use to harvest and dry herbs. Mix and match the various techniques to suit your purposes.

Herbs Suitable for Air-Drying on Screens

NAME	PREPARATION/PART OF PLANT
Basil	Cut-up leafy stems
Bergamot	Individual flower heads or leaves
Calendula	Opened, spread-out flower heads or petals
Chamomile	Fresh, wide-opened flowers (these also readily dry in a gas oven just from the pilot light)
Chives	Cut up fine; freshly opened flowers
Costmary	Leaves
Dill	Fern-leaf type, leaves on short stems
Hollyhock	Flowers, fresh or spent (rolled up)
Hops	Flower clusters on short stems
Lady's Mantle	Flower clusters on short stems
Lavender	Flower buds
Lovage	Chopped leafy stems
Marigold	Opened flowers
Mint, Apple	Whole leafy stems (then leaves can be stripped from stems)
Parsleys	Cut-up leafy stems
Roses	Petals, buds, small flowers
Sage	Leaves
Southernwood	Woody-stemmed sprays
Sweet White Clover	Leafy stems with flowering tips
Thyme	Short, leafy stems

OTHER ALTERNATIVES: MICROWAVE AND FREEZER

For those who want to try other methods for preserving herbs, the following alternatives work well.

Microwave Oven Method

Spread herbs in a single layer between paper towels and heat for 2 minutes. If, after that time, the herbs still aren't crispy dry, continue to microwave for 30-second intervals.

Freezing Herbs

Some herbs, like chervil, retain their flavor only when frozen, not dried. However, you can freeze any herb by using one of two methods.

The first method is to strip leaves from the stems and cut them up finely. Then freeze the herbs in small, labeled plastic bags, or file them in waxed paper envelopes placed in an airtight container.

The second method is to place 2 cups of herbs in a blender with 1 cup of water. Blend, then pour the mixture into ice cube trays and freeze. Remove the cubes from the trays and store them in labeled plastic bags in the freezer. To use, drop the cubes into soups, stews, and sauces.

CHAPTER THREE

Using Herbs in the Home

Take the leaves and floures of Primrose, boile them a little in fountaine water, and in some Rose and Betony waters, adding thereto sugar, pepper, salt, and butter . . .—John Gerard, *Gerard's Herball, 1597*

In this chapter you will find a general guide to using and preserving herbs as well as a glossary of popular terms whose meanings may have puzzled you. The material is organized alphabetically for quick reference. If, say, your roses produce zillions of blooms one year and you'd like to try making potpourri, just flip through the pages until you reach P, and you'll find all the information you need to proceed. If you want to know which herb flowers you can safely (and enjoyably) eat, these are listed for your convenience. I hope this handy guide will encourage you to get the most out of the herbs you grow.

AROMATHERAPY

In classic aromatherapy, essential oils—the distilled fragrance from scented plants—are rubbed into the body by massage to alleviate various physical and emotional conditions ranging from muscle ache to depression. Today, the term covers several variations: Aesthetic aromatherapy applies to skin care and relaxation; holistic aromatherapy uses massage as well as inhalation techniques; psycho-aromatherapy involves using scents to help patients recall past experiences and feelings. **Caution: Do not under any circumstances consume essential oils.** A friend of mine once thought she'd alleviate her asthma by making herself a nice cup of tea with a few drops of eucalyptus oil—which made her very sick indeed.

I am not a serious student of aromatherapy, but I certainly agree that in a general way pleasant scents give us a lift, while unpleasant ones annoy and irritate us. I love to inhale rose and lavender fragrance; I even keep a rose sachet under my pillow. I enjoy washing with lavender-scented soap; I also add lavender oil to a comfrey foot soak for its beneficial effects. (Maybe just inhaling the scent invigorates me all over, including my tired feet!) My customers buy little vials of the best oils I can find (see Source Appendix) and put a drop or two in their vacuum cleaners, rub it on light bulbs, put a few drops in the rinse water of their hand-washables, and generally find ways to envelop themselves in pleasant scents all day long, from the time they wake up to the time they go to bed. This is obviously a simplified explanation of aromatherapy. If you want to find out more, read *Aromatherapy,* by Robert Tisserand (Lotus Light Press, 1988), also published under the title *Aromatherapy for Everyone* (Penguin Books, 1988).

BATH HERBS

I make scented bath crystals by adding ¼ teaspoon of essential oil (I use rose or lavender) to each cup of coarse rock salt; then I add a few drops of vegetable coloring (use the chart that comes with the colors), stirring it in until I get the desired tint. Next I stir in some glycerine—a thick, liquid emollient for chapped or roughened skin, available at the drugstore—until it is absorbed by the salt. The mixture should be sparkling (from the glycerine), but not wet; stir in more salt if necessary.

To use herbal bath salts, add 2 to 3 heaping tablespoons to a hot bath. The glycerine will leave your skin feeling smooth, while the essential oil is both relaxing and invigorating.

Another way to use herbs in the bath is to combine oatmeal (a skin softener) with herbs in equal parts. Tie up the mixture in a piece of cheesecloth or a thin piece of material, and put it in the water; or you can add a small amount of shaved, scented soap to the oatmeal and herbs, using the bath bag as a washcloth.

- **Herbs regarded as relaxing are** chamomile, comfrey, lavender, lemon verbena, mugwort, roses, and thyme.
- **Herbs regarded as stimulating are** elderflowers, hop flowers, lavender, lemon balm, marjoram, peppermint, rosemary, savory, and yarrow.
- **Herbs regarded as soothing are** calendula, catnip, comfrey, elderflowers, hyssop, mallows, mugwort, roses, sage, tansy, and yarrow.

Note that some herbs are relaxing and invigorating at the same time, and you may know that catnip is soothing for humans and stimulating for cats. The response to herbs varies among people; try your own combinations. If you want to learn more about bath herbs and related subjects, read *The Aromatherapy Book,* by Jeanne Rose (North Atlantic Books, 1992).

BUTTERS

Herb butters are wonderful concoctions combining flavorful culinary herbs with sweet or salted butter to use on fish and vegetable dishes, as a spread on bread or crackers, or any other way you want. My approach to herb butters has always been to use real butter, because we like its rich flavor (and we do keep a small herd of Jersey cows), but margarine can be substituted in these directions. You can feel free to use any culinary herb whose flavor you enjoy.

To Make Herb Butter: Use 3 to 4 tablespoons of fresh herbs chopped finely, or half the amount of dry, pulverized herbs, for every 1/2 cup of softened sweet or salted butter. If the herb is strong (basil, for instance), cut the amount to suit your taste. Beat the herb or herbs of your choice into the butter, softened at room temperature, add 1 tablespoon of lemon juice, and salt and pepper to taste. Store the herb butter in a well-covered container (a plastic cottage cheese or yogurt container works well) in the refrigerator until needed. Herb butter can be stored in the refrigerator for about 2 weeks or in the freezer for 3 months.

Soften herb butters at room temperature, then put small amounts of different types on the table in small cups (I use custard cups) and let guests choose their own for spreading on crackers or biscuits. Following are some of my favorite herb butter combinations and the ways I use them.

* For fish (brushed on just after the fish is broiled or fried): lemon balm; fresh dill, chervil, and parsley; 1/2 teaspoon fresh basil, 1/2 teaspoon fresh chervil, 1 teaspoon parsley, and chopped chives; fresh or dried lovage (a small amount)
* On cooked vegetables or potatoes: fresh or dried parsley; parsley, marjoram, thyme, rosemary, and savory, individually or in combination
* On biscuits, thick slices of toasted Italian bread, crackers, or rolls, with or without 1 pressed clove of garlic: rosemary, sage, savory, and thyme, individually or combined.

CANDIED FLOWERS

Any culinary herb can be preserved by candying it to use on cakes or other desserts. The easiest method (see *Calendula*) is to brush freshly picked, perfect flowers—as dry as possible—with an egg white beaten with a little water. If the flowers are bulky, try to spread them out flat or pull off the petals and candy them individually. After brushing with egg white, sprinkle both sides of the flowers with granulated sugar, then lay them on waxed paper to dry, turning occasionally and changing the paper at least once *(see fig. 12)*. Store in a waxed-paper-lined container if you want, but they're best to use just after candying, as soon as they're dry. The following are good candidates for candying: calendula (small, whole flowers or petals); hollyhocks (large, perfect flowers are spectacular); marigolds (the small, signet type); mints (leaves, especially apple mint); rose petals (dark pink ones are best); and violets or pansies (*Viola* spp.).

Fig. 12. To candy flowers, brush both sides lightly with beaten egg white, then sprinkle with sugar.

CHEESE HERBS

Cottage cheese and cream cheese are wonderful mediums, like butter, for carrying herb flavors. Cheese spreads are delicious on whole wheat or rye bread, to serve on special occasions as appetizers, or to accompany soup and salad as a main course (see *Sage—Herbed Cottage Cheese*). In summer, I make a quick spread by thinning homemade cottage cheese with yogurt to a smooth consistency, then blending in fresh, minced burnet and dill to taste. When I serve this spread on thinly sliced whole wheat bread, I gently press a whole nasturtium flower onto each slice.

COOKING WITH HERBS

If your family or friends say they don't like herbs, it may be because you have been too generous in your use of them. Particularly at first, herbs should be used sparingly, and at all times discreetly. The particular taste of each herb should not be glaringly apparent in the dishes that call for such flavoring. Herbs should only enhance the natural taste of food, not mask it entirely. In other words, if you love basil, restrain yourself until you're sure others share your affection. If they don't, one solution is to get in the habit of putting pulverized or flaked dried herbs on the table—I use little containers with small spoons—so everyone can add them as desired, like salt and pepper. For a large amount, pulverize dried herbs by rubbing them briskly between your palms; for a small amount, rub the herbs together on rotating fingertips. Directions for flaking herbs with a homemade riddle are given in the previous chapter.

DECOCTIONS

This term describes a method of preparing herbs—usually hard parts such as roots, woody stems, bark, or seeds—for medicinal use: Herbs are either boiled for 10 minutes or steeped in boiling water for 30 minutes. The standard quantity is 1 ounce of dried or 2 ounces of fresh herbs to 3 cups of water. The resulting decoction is very strong and is not advised for self-medication.

DRIED FLOWERS

I use air-drying to preserve colorful flowers or attractive, scented leaves for winter bouquets. The principle is the same as for drying culinary herbs: Bunches, not too thick, are secured by strong elastics and suspended from the ceiling on hooks, away from direct light. A variety of wildflowers and cultivated flowers can be dried this way as well. The time to pick each type depends on the effect you want. If, however, you pick a flower for drying when it is fully opened, and it should have been picked in bud (these buds usually open after being picked), don't worry; it may still be usable. Dried flowers shatter easily. (The pieces can be used in potpourri.) To prevent shattering, spray dried flowers with a light mist once a week, and add a few drops of scented oil to the water if you wish. To store for any length of time, place dried flowers upright in plastic tubs, separating them by color and type for convenience later on when you want to use them. Keep in mind that aromatic herbs will release their scent in dried bouquets if they are placed in a warm, moist room, as in a bathroom or a kitchen. If kept out of indirect light, flowers will retain their bright colors longer.

The following herb flowers dry well: bergamot, chives, feverfew, hops, lady's mantle, lamb's-ears, wild marjoram, mints, common mugwort, white mugwort, pearly everlasting, blue sage, garden sorrel, sweet white clover, tansy, sweet wormwood, and yarrow. Consider also the dried leafy stalks of lemon balm, mints (in flower as well), and common sage *(Salvia officinalis)*. For complete information on the art of drying and using flowers, see *The Complete Book of Everlastings,* by Mark and Terry Silber (Knopf, 1988).

EDIBLE FLOWERS

Flowers have been used for culinary purposes for millennia, to make into wines, to flavor syrups, to garnish foods, to add to salads. The following herb flowers are not merely edible—they taste good, too.

Edible Flowers

NAME	PREPARATION AND USE
Arugula	Flowering tips and seedpods in salads
Basil	Flowering tips sparingly in salads, cheese spreads
Bergamot	Petals for salads, fruit desserts
Calendula	Petals for salads, rice dishes, cookie batter, biscuit dough
Chives	Whole flowers or petals in salads, cheese spreads
Cress	Sprigs in salads, chopped up for cheese spreads
Dill	Chopped up in salads
Elderflowers	Florets added to pancake or muffin batter (see *Elderberry*)
Lavender	Mix with savory, thyme, and fennel to use on potatoes

Mallows ....Garnish desserts

Mints ....With leaves for cold drink garnish

Nasturtium ....Whole flowers or individual petals in salads;
stuffed with cottage cheese–yogurt spread or
chicken, tuna, or egg salad

Rose petals......................Pressed into sweet butter on fancy sandwiches

Sweet cicely.....................Chopped into rhubarb or gooseberry for stewing

Sweet woodruff..............For flavoring wine (see *Sweet Woodruff*)

Violets ....Press fresh or candied flowers into frosting;
sprinkle on salads, desserts

ESSENTIAL OILS

Essential oils are the concentrated scents of various aromatic plants, usually obtained by distilling, a process that is virtually impossible to reproduce without sophisticated equipment. True essential oils are quite volatile—their scent evaporates quickly—and can be costly. It is reputed to take 250 pounds of rose petals to produce 1 fluid ounce of rose oil (rose geranium oil is much cheaper to produce and has a nice roselike scent). Fragrance oils or synthetic aromas often combine natural and synthetic scents; they are less costly than essential oils, and fairly stable. If the oils you are buying are all the same price, then they are the synthetic type, no matter how they are advertised. Either essential or fragrance oils can be used for crafts; true essential oils are used in serious aromatherapy.

FINES HERBES

Fines herbes is a French term that refers to a mix of finely chopped herbs, usually fresh, but sometimes dried, added to foods near the end of their cooking time, so the herbs' flavor is evident (see *Parsley*).

FIXATIVES

A fixative is a natural substance derived from plants or animals that is used to "fix," or preserve, the volatile oils in potpourri (though nowadays, most of the animal substances are synthetically produced). Some of these substances—like orrisroot, which is derived from certain species of iris—have a fragrance of their own, while others are odorless. However, all perform the same function: to capture scent and hold it over a prolonged period. Consult *The Pleasure of Herbs,* by Phyllis Shaudys (Storey, 1986) for a clear discussion of fixatives and a description of the types. Also see *Potpourri* in this chapter.

INFUSIONS

An infusion is made by steeping, not cooking, herbs in water or any other liquid medium, either hot or cold, as in making herb teas or vinegars. Cooking herbs in water for any length of time, however, produces a *decoction,* which is too strong to consume and is intended for external use only.

JELLIES

Making herb jellies is a wonderful way to store the flavor of herbs until they are ready to be tasted. Herb jellies can be used as condiments to accompany a main course—as with meat or fish—or used in the same way as any other jelly, on crackers with cream cheese, on buttered biscuits, or on toast. Beautiful in their glistening jewel-like colors—rose, champagne, garnet, and gold—they add a festive touch to special occasions.

To Make Basic Herb Jelly: Place 1½ packed cups of chopped herbs (the amount can vary according to the strength of the herb) in a saucepan, bruise them with the bottom of a glass, then add 2 cups of water, juice, or wine. Bring the mixture to a boil, cover, and steep for 15 to 20 minutes (a shorter time for strong-flavored herbs, like basil), occasionally bruising the herbs to release more flavor. Next, strain the herbs and reheat the resulting infusion, equal to 1½ cups, with 3 cups of sugar, 2 tablespoons of vinegar, and vegetable coloring (if desired). Bring the mixture to a rolling boil that can't be stirred down, and stir in 1 pouch or ½ bottle of liquid pectin. Bring the mixture to a rolling boil once more and boil it, stirring all the time, for 1 minute. Then pour the liquid into small, sterilized jars and seal at once. If you use pectin crystals, reverse the procedure: Add the pectin and vinegar at the beginning, bring the mixture to a boil, then stir in the sugar and boil for 1 minute.

For herb jelly recipes, see *Purple Basil, Mint, Rose,* and *Sweet Woodruff* in the plant profiles section of this book. Try using white wine for parsley jelly, apple juice with sage, and orange juice with rosemary.

In addition to using herb jellies on toast, this is the way I use them as condiments:

* Basil: on hot rolls, crackers, party sandwiches with cream cheese, any meat dishes
* Lemon balm: for fish and poultry
* Mint: with lamb, pork, ham; a little added to fruit desserts with pears or peaches
* Parsley with wine: for meat, vegetable, and egg dishes and casseroles
* Rosemary: for beef and pork dishes
* Rose petal: the ultimate flavor, added to desserts, used as a cake glaze by thinning with hot water; spread on top of butter for party sandwiches on whole wheat bread, or on top of butter on bran muffins for a holiday breakfast.

I use rose petal syrup (made by omitting commercial pectin from the basic herb jelly recipe and cooking until thick) as a delicate topping for party cakes, pancakes, waffles, ice cream, and yogurt desserts.

MEDICINAL HERBS

There is great interest today in medicinal herbs, and I hope the reader won't be disappointed that I have not delved very deeply into the subject. Since this book is first and foremost about my life with herbs, I must tell the truth: We are seldom sick and have little need for a large pharmacopoeia of any type. The sum total of our use of herbs as medicine applies to herbed China tea for relaxing; pure herb teas for alleviating minor headaches and cold symptoms; homemade horehound cough drops for sore throats; and wormwood tea for stomach complaints. We swear by the spores from mature puffball mushrooms to kill bacteria and heal wounds, even deep ones. (On a farm, wounds are more common than illness.) Herbs, in the form of plant extracts, are commonly found in the patent and prescription medicines that we may take ourselves or administer to our animals, especially to treat diarrhea, various skin conditions, and sore muscles.

Many people today mistakenly believe that plants are wholly benign and will cure all our ills. They may have marvelous properties to cure, but they also contain extremely potent substances that can kill or make you very sick. I don't endorse self-medication for serious illness. There are a number of books on the market about making home preparations to treat common ailments. Two of the best are Penelope Ody's *The Complete Medicinal Herbal* (Dorling Kindersley, 1993) and her *Home Herbal* (Dorling Kindersley, 1995).

OILS

You can preserve herb flavor by transferring it to cooking oils. Place the leaves of aromatic herbs, like basil, in a glass jar after bruising them, then completely cover the leaves with oil and cover the jar. If the jar is placed in a sunny window, the oil will be sufficiently flavored in 2 to 3 weeks. Then the herbs can be strained out and the oil refrigerated until it is needed. Gertrude Foster, in *Park's Success with Herbs* (George W. Park Seed Co., Inc., 1980), recommends adding a tablespoon of wine vinegar to the oil as a preservative when it is being infused. Unlike herb vinegars, herb oils are subject to bacteria growth, especially if garlic is used in the infusion, so be sure to keep the oil refrigerated. Use herb oils in salad dressings, marinades, added to sauces, or splashed on cooked vegetables.

POTPOURRI

Potpourri, a French word meaning literally "rotted pot," describes a method of making moist, scented cakes, whereby bushels of rose petals are fermented with salt. The resulting moist potpourri, which may last for many years, is characterized more by scent than by appearance.

Nowadays, dry potpourri, a mixture designed for both scent and appearance, is much more common than the original moist version. Dry potpourri is made from a mixture of naturally scented or unscented dried flowers, herbs, seedpods, cones—anything attractive—to which essential or synthetic oils and fixative have been added.

Little has been said thus far about the sensuous pleasure that comes merely from drying herbs and flowers—the casual combinations are often gorgeous—then mixing them together to create something that is aesthetically appealing. Making potpourri is a very satisfying experience.

Dry potpourri is easy to make, but the process is not widely understood, resulting in much disappointment for beginners. Follow the basic method described below for never-fail results.

All during the growing season, I gather materials for potpourri wherever I find them: in my garden or in the wild, in the hayfield, the pastures, the woods.

Everything is dried either on Jigs's magic drying rack or on cookie sheets in the oven of the gas stove, where the warmth from the pilot light is sufficient to dry foliage or small flowers in a day or so. (You could also use a microwave oven.) The idea is the same as for drying herbs, but now it is to preserve color and scent, rather than flavor.

As the various materials dry, I store them in labeled plastic tubs by type: rose petals in one, blue flowers in another, reds and yellows together, and so on *(see fig. 13)*. When I have at least 1 quart, I mix the materials together for eye appeal and scent: reds, yellows, white, and in-between shades suggest a citrus blend, so I add lemon balm, lemon verbena, costmary, and orange peel to the mix. With each addition, the mix takes on a different character, assuming a life of its own. I know when the mix is complete for it looks just right, a balance of textures and colors.

Once I have created the blend I want, I pour the mixture into a container that has a tight-fitting lid (crock, glass jar, plastic tub), and select a complementary scented oil. For every quart of dry blend, I use 1 teaspoon of essential or fragrance oil premixed in a small jar with 3 tablespoons of fixative (see below). The mixture is shaken well every day for 3 or 4 days until the fixative has

Fig. 13. The ingredients of potpourri, stored for later use

absorbed the scent, after which it is added to the dry blend. The container is tightly sealed, then shaken (turned upside down) every day to distribute the scent. At the end of 4 to 6 weeks, the dry blend has been transformed into a potpourri that should last several years.

To use potpourri, display it in dishes or pretty jars; cover it occasionally and shake or stir it before opening again. Do not, however, expect a small amount of potpourri to scent a large room; potpourri is most effective in a warm, moist room such as the bathroom or the kitchen. You can freshen a potpourri by adding a few drops of scent, preferably premixed with fixative.

I used to use powdered orrisroot as a fixative until I discovered cut orrisroot, which does not obscure colors by coating the dry blend with a fine powder. Orrisroot is nice because it also has scent, like a bouquet of violets, but it can cause a skin reaction. I also use corn cellulose, a relatively inexpensive natural substance with no odor but great absorbent qualities. I use 4 tablespoons of cellulose to 1½ teaspoons of scent, or 3 tablespoons of cut orrisroot to 1 teaspoon of scent (cut orrisroot is in small pieces, rather granular), for every 1 quart of dry blend. Potpourri made with celluose lasts at least 2 years. Let your imagination be your guide in creating combinations of colorful herbs and flowers.

My Christmas Extravaganza always features scented cones; bright, large flowers; lots of orange peel; and the soft silvery flower tops from lamb's-ears (*Stachys lanata*). See the *Costmary* and *Rose* entries in part II for specific potpourri recipes. For where to obtain fixatives (including cellulose) and scented oils, see Sources at the back of the book.

SACHETS

Classic sachets are pretty little cloth bags filled with potpourri, used to scent linens or whatever you want. I have been making these for years from decades worth of accumulated oddments: fabrics of all types with pretty patterns and/or soothing colors, and assorted bits of lace and ribbons. The result is very attractive and useful—miniature decorated pillow slips filled with fragrant potpourri *(see fig. 14)*.

Tea Bag Sachets

Large tea bags 4¾ inches by 3¾ inches are available from Lavender Lane in California (see Sources). To make them into sachets, simply fill them with 2 tablespoons of pre-scented cellulose (pre-scent 1 cup of cellulose with 2 tablespoons of fragrance oil, and use as needed). Tea bag sachets have many uses: to scent drawers, musty storage areas, or a box of stationery; filled with herbs they can also be used to make foot soaks (see *Comfrey*) or for moth prevention (see *Southernwood—Herb Guard*). To use as room fresheners, simmer a tea bag in 2 cups boiling water; the bags can be re-simmered for about a month.

Fig. 14. To make a scented sachet:

1. With pinking shears, trim a piece of material 8 inches by 4 inches.

2. Fold the edge of the long end, making a ¼-inch hem.

3. Pin and sew the lace on the inside of the hemmed edge just over the stitching, gathering the lace to fit if necessary.

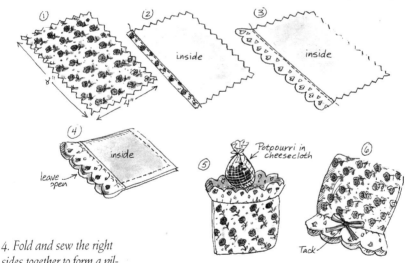

4. Fold and sew the right sides together to form a pillowcase, leaving the lace-edged end open. You should have two seams, a short seam at the top of the case and a side seam. Turn the pillowcase right-side out.

5. Place a few tablespoons of potpourri on a double layer of cheesecloth, tie it with a string, and slip the cheesecloth into the case.

6. Tack the case in the middle of the open end with a few stitches. Cover the stitches with a little ribbon tied in a bow.

SWAGS

A swag, as opposed to a wreath, is linear; that is, it hangs downward. Swags can be long and elegant, draped over a doorway, or short and simple, like a harvest swag made to hang in the kitchen. I tend to prefer the simple style.

One year I had great fun making harvest swags using cut baling twine as the base. I gathered enough twine to make three thick strands, then braided them together, securing them at the top and at the bottom with a few strands of baling twine or raffia, resulting in a 3- to 4-foot-long braid. I hung these about the house wherever I could, and as the season progressed I inserted small, live bundles of flowers and herbs in the spaces between the strands, until they were almost filled up, at which point I pronounced my swag complete. For a more sophisticated approach, see *Dried Flowers for All Seasons,* by Jenny Raworth and Susan Berry (Reader's Digest Books, 1993).

TEAS

Herb teas are sometimes called *tisanes.* If well prepared from quality herbs, they are both delicious and soothing. Many commercial herb teas have additives in the form of spices to mask the fact that the herbs have little flavor. True herb tea is made from herbs alone and has plenty of flavor, so much that only 1 or 2 teaspoons of dried herbs are needed to make each cup. Pour boiling water over the herbs (place them first in a tea ball if you have one), cover the cup with a saucer to keep the tea warm, and let the herbs steep no longer than a minute or two. You can usually get another cup out of the tea ball. If you don't have one, don't worry; the leaves will settle or they can be strained out. **Never make tea from an herb unless you are sure it is safe to use.** You can safely make tea from any of the following herbs: bee balm, calamint, chamomile, catnip, costmary, elderflowers, lemon balm, and the mints.

Lavender Lane (see Sources) also sells small tea bags (the same size as commercial ones) if you want to make your own bagged herb tea—very convenient to use.

TUSSIE-MUSSIES

It's great fun to suddenly produce a tussie-mussie for a departing guest. These are small bouquets, sometimes referred to as nosegays, of fresh or dried flowers

Fig. 15. Surrounding a tussie-mussie with a doily and ribbon makes a nice finishing touch.

and herbs that tell a story in the language of flowers (their meanings vary, depending on your source). I began my tussie-mussie education with an invaluable little booklet printed years ago by The Herb Grower Press. Those were the days when making a tussie-mussie was almost a lost art.

To Make a Tussie-Mussie: Pick a perfect, colorful flower (or several of them) for the center of the bouquet—roses are traditional—then encircle it with sprigs of foliage in groups of three, alternating with sprigs of tiny flowers, and ending with distinctive foliage, such as that of lamb's-ear *(Stachys lanata),* to frame the bouquet. It's most effective if the size of the foliage increases as you work your way to the outer edge of the bouquet. With each additional layer or circle, use strong carpet thread to draw the bouquet tightly together, close to the flower heads, to give it fullness. Keep adding layers for contrast until you have a 3- to 4-inch-wide bouquet. You can bind the stems tightly with green floral tape, then insert them through the center of a small paper doily—it acts as a ruff—in which you have cut a small opening in the shape of a cross. Tie a pretty ribbon over the thread, letting the ends hang down over the doily *(see fig. 15).* You can use either fresh or dried flowers and herbs. If a fresh bouquet is going to be out of water for some time, place a small plastic bag around the stems and insert a little moistened moss or similar material; the bag can be wrapped in foil (I use silver or gold candy wrappers).

Choose herbs and flowers based on the traditional language of flowers. Some common plants and their associated meanings are given below.

The Language of Flowers

PLANT	MEANING
Angelica	Inspiration
Basil	Love, hate
Borage	Courage
Burnet	Mirth
Chamomile	Patience
Chives	Usefulness
Coriander	Concealed merit
Costmary	Sweetness
Cress	Stability, power
Dandelion	Coquetry
Dill	Tranquility
Elderflower	Compassion
Hollyhock	Ambition
Hops	Injustice
Horehound	Health
Hyssop	Sacrifice
Lady's mantle	Comfort
Lamb's-ears	Surprise
Lemon Balm	Sympathy
Marigold	Jealousy
Marjoram	Happiness
Mint	Wisdom
Mugwort	Luck in travel
Nasturtium	Patriotism
Pansy	Sad thoughts
Pennyroyal	Flee away
Rose	Love
Rosemary	Remembrance
Rue	Grace
Sage	Esteem
Southernwood	Constancy
Tansy	Hostility
Violet	Modesty
Wormwood	Absence
Yarrow	Cure for heartache

I have given away many tussie-mussies, but have received only one. Although the bouquet itself has long departed, the little card that accompanied it is a treasured keepsake from a little girl named Veronica (whose very name is a symbol of fidelity). I still smile when I think of her so earnestly reading the Gertrude Foster booklet on the language of flowers, then quietly (and secretively) gathering her materials and composing her message:

Mr. and Mrs. Gardner, I am full of sad thoughts (pansy) because I am leaving. I find it hard to leave people who have perfection (strawberry), are full of wisdom (mint) and love as you are (basil). I wish you much happiness (marjoram).

Love (rose), Veronica

VINEGARS

There are several ways to make herb vinegars, but, basically, bruised herbs are steeped in vinegar until the desired flavor is reached. This process may take 2 weeks if the infusion is placed in a warm, sunny spot, or it could take 2 months if the infusion is placed in a cool, dark closet. If the vinegar is heated (not boiled), then poured into jars that have been filled with herbs, the desired infusion is achieved almost instantly. You can use any full-strength vinegar (5 percent acidity) that complements your herb; the choice is up to you. I use white vinegar with strong-flavored herbs like the basils, and cider vinegar for herbs that go well with its flavor, such as dill, garlic chives, and salad burnet.

The following culinary herbs—in any combination, with or without garlic—may be used: basils, burnet, chives, garlic chives, dill, lovage, marjoram, mints, nasturtium, parsley, rose, rosemary, sage, savory, and thyme.

Herb vinegars are marvelous in salad dressings; in coleslaw; egg, potato, or bean salads; on cooked broccoli, Brussels sprouts, beets, or cabbage; on poached eggs or fish; or used to marinate slices of raw carrot, cucumber, and peppers.

Using the same method, you can make floral vinegars to use on salads (especially fruit salads), or cosmetic vinegars to use as skin fresheners or to alleviate headaches: A cloth is wrung out in the solution (diluted by half with water) and placed on the forehead. (See *Costmary* and *Rose* to make skin freshener and floral vinegar.) Use the following herbs for floral vinegars: chive blossoms, elderflowers, lavender blossoms, signet marigold blossoms, mint leaves and flowers, nasturtium flowers, rose petals, thyme flowers, and sweet violets.

Use the following herbs for cosmetic vinegars: costmary leaves, lavender buds, lemon balm leaves, lovage leaves, mallow flowers, marigold flowers, mint leaves and flowers, rose petals, rosemary, and southernwood foliage.

WREATHS

Nearly everyone loves wreaths these days, for their simple beauty and decorative quality in the home. It is a passion that does not seem to dissipate, although by now you would think that even herb enthusiasts would be suffering from wreath overload. I have friends who make stunning wreaths, so I no longer make my own, but I continue to grow the plants that are most important as background for colorful dried flowers, seedpods, and the like. These include common mugwort, white mugwort, wormwood, and sweet wormwood. Of these plants, I think common mugwort *(Artemisia vulgaris)* is the most beautiful, if the stalks are picked when the buds have just formed. Then the drying leaves curl upward, revealing their soft, silver-gray undersides. I also like sweet wormwood *(Artemisia annua)* as a wreath base for its unusually sweet, citrus-camphor scent. Wreaths are usually made from fresh herbs and flowers, more flexible and easier to work with than dried material.

You can use fresh mugwort and wormwood stalks as a natural base, forming them in a circle. Wind them around a plastic tub of the desired circumference to get a perfect circle, then secure them with thin, flexible 28-gauge wire. Or you can cut 3- to 4-inch sprigs, tie these in fan-shaped bunches with thin wire, then attach them to a purchased wreath form, covering the whole circle. See *The Complete Book of Everlastings,* by Mark and Terry Silber (Knopf, 1988) for complete wreathmaking directions.

CHAPTER FOUR

The Integrated Landscape

. . . Walk in the dusk of evening, forget the weeds, the plans and the problems, and enjoy the tall spires of the artemisias; stay out until the moon touches all with quiet beauty. —Adelma Simmons, *Herb Gardening in Five Seasons*

It takes many growing seasons to learn how to create a pleasing landscape. In great measure, the land itself dictates how we will use it, and what we can do with it. Most of us bumble on, unaware of the forces shaping our choices. We plant what we like, where we like, sometimes achieving success on the first try, but more often moving things around until we are satisfied with the results. In truth, there is never an "until," for the landscape is never entirely finished. It is always changing—however subtly—based on the changing nature of our particular needs and desires, as well as natural forces over which we have no control.

Given these factors, it is really impossible to design a garden in the abstract as if that was all that mattered—as if its being were the center of the universe. This is what I object to in the barrage of garden plans ceaselessly offered from the pages of gardening publications. I call them "paper gardens," and I think they are generally worthless, because such plans exist in a vacuum. Real gardens, on the other hand, exist in a multifaceted world I call *the integrated landscape,* a creation of nature, practical needs, and aesthetic vision.

So now you know that I'm not going to offer you a blueprint to make a tidy herb garden, one of those pseudomedieval plantings laid out with timbers and filled in with gray-leaved plants. What I am going to do instead is describe how my gardens and plantings have evolved, so that in the process we might discover some of the principles inherent in successful plantings of whatever size, no matter how grand or how small.

THE STARTING POINT

When we first moved to the farm, it was quite bare, a simple farmhouse perched on a south-facing knoll with some worn-out apple trees scattered about, a tumbledown barn up the hill to the east, and beyond that a rundown hayfield, all bordered by dense woods. Over the years, the area around the house has filled in to reflect our needs. Fruit trees were planted along the approach to the farm; small fruits like currants, gooseberries, raspberries, strawberries, elderberries, blueberries, and rhubarb were established nearby. A vegetable garden occupied a south-facing stretch of ground, shrinking over the years to half its former size, with the other half eventually used for tethering young stock. Early on, we added a lean-to greenhouse at the front of the house and built one of two log cabins just at the edge of the woods. The old coal shed, right next to the house, was moved by our team of horses to the garden site and transformed into a garden shed. We built a smokehouse on the edge of a ravine, and a repair shop for our antiquated machinery and an attached woodshed rose up below the vegetable garden, which had now become a series of raised beds backed by a slab fence for protection. A turkey house and yard occupied ground that had been our first strawberry patch.

It is within this changing framework that I have established gardens of various shapes (by necessity on the small side), weaving them around and between the established network of structures, fruiting shrubs, old and new apple trees, and, not least of all, areas used to tether young stock (Jersey calves) during the summer. These leftover spaces are often problematic for growing plants: small and tight, exposed to wind, or on sod ground that is very difficult to improve.

My plantings, like the framework that contains them, have changed, too, over the years, not only because of different conditions, but because they needed improvement. As I have become surer in my knowledge about how particular herbs respond to our growing conditions, I have also become more discerning about where and how I plant them, and, as a consequence, I am better equipped to solve my particular landscaping problems. In fact, I no longer regard these problems as obstacles but instead as interesting puzzles to solve.

In the process of overcoming the barriers of cramped sites or tough growing conditions, I have learned a lot about how to get the most out of the herbs that thrive here, discovering ways to use them creatively as hedges, accents, or ground covers and—a favorite strategy—to return them to the wild. The greatest single lesson I have learned through years of trial and error (and it is a lesson that increases in value as I grow older) is how to make plants work for me to solve specific landscaping problems. I don't mean to imply that I can master nature, for no one has that ability. But knowledge does give us power of a sort, to live on more amicable terms with nature.

AN ISLAND BED

My very first garden was shaped by the remains of an old rock and wood pile, so it was roughly round *(see fig. 16)*. Since I knew nothing about garden design at the time, this didn't daunt me in the least, but, as I have since learned, the round shape is not for beginners. Unlike a standard border backed by a wall, fence, or shrubbery, an island bed stands alone, all sides fully exposed, and each plant within is seen from the back as well as the front of the garden. I often used to stare at the planted circle, trying to figure out what was wrong, which plants were in the right place and which ones needed moving. This had mainly to do with height. In a standard border, the background acts as a backstop, as it were, and in a general way provides a point of reference for all the plants in front of it—the taller ones at the back, the shorter ones at the front.

With no point of reference except for an old apple tree off to the side, I wasn't sure where anything belonged, except at the circle's outer edges. Even I, dyslexic when it comes to design, realized that a circle would benefit from some sort of edging. Establishing the low-growing common lungwort *(Pulmonaria officinalis)* as a living wall was a stroke of genius, at once enclosing and framing the planting, giving it coherence and definite form, and at the same time keeping out grass and weeds. As a bonus, the lungwort's small pink and blue flowers attracted the first hummingbirds of the season. Over the years I have found ways to use a variety of herbs to solve similar problems.

Of course it was not genius, but necessity, that was really responsible for this early success. Before we acquired a small gas-powered mower, Jigs cut the grass with the team of horses, doing a fine job, but not doing it very often, which resulted in shaggy grass around the garden. A stone wall would have been nice, but the plants were handier. An old planting of lungwort, dating back to the 1920s, was already growing lustily at the base of an old lilac shrub. All I had to do was dig up some clumps and replant them in the moist earth of

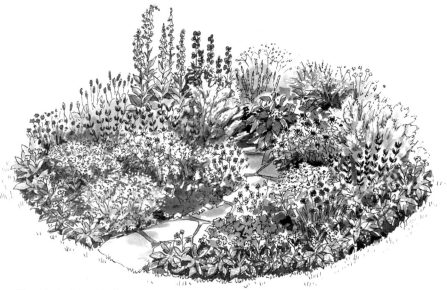

Fig. 16. An island bed
is enhanced by a curved path

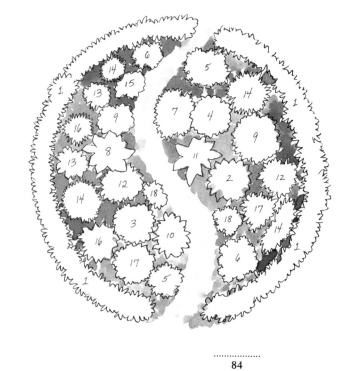

Planting Scheme
1. Lungwort
2. Bee Balm
3. Wild Bergamot
4. White Mugwort
5. Feverfew
6. Lady's Mantle
7. Hyssop
8. Foxglove
9. Southernwood
10. Dame's Rocket
11. Comfrey
12. Annual Clary
13. Bistort
14. Chives
15. Monkshood
16. Garlic Chives
17. Calendula
18. Johnny-Jump-Ups

the old woodpile, where they soon multiplied, bearing many clusters of pretty pink and blue bells—a thick azure hedge in late spring. Later, as the plants matured, they spread their spotted leaves to form an impenetrable barrier to unwanted growth from without.

Gradually, I gained control of this spot of ground, learning to plant taller herbs toward the middle—a typical island bed design—with shorter types surrounding them, until the circle was filled. The area was enlarged by the simple expedient of laying down heavy plastic in the fall (we recycled the tough black type used to wrap circular hay bales) in order to kill the weeds without having to dig—not a favorite activity in our heavy ground. The following spring we removed the plastic, then covered the area with a thick layer of composted, enriched barn manure, in which I planted more herbs, mostly hardy perennials with showy flowers.

It was evident that the area was now too large to take care of without creating a bisecting path. Jigs solved this problem in his usual, direct fashion. First, he laid down plastic grain bags through the garden from the front to the back. Next he laid an assortment of flagstones, gathered from the fields, on top of the bags, arranging them in a graceful S-curve (curved paths are more interesting than straight ones). Finally, he spread sawdust to cover the remaining spaces between the stones. The sawdust is replenished as needed; usually once a season is sufficient.

This winding path, so simply constructed, greatly improved the garden's form by breaking it up into smaller areas—separate, miniature islands, where taller, straight plants, like veronica and foxglove, are offset by lower, bushier plants like feverfew and hyssop. The path also provided an opportunity for dainty plants like forget-me-nots and Johnny-jump-ups to seed themselves between the pavings, and for scented and aromatic herbs like southernwood, dame's rocket, and the bergamots to be appreciated at closer range (my kind of aromatherapy).

The island bed is a changing scene of bloom, accented by the silvery foliage of southernwood, Roman wormwood, and horehound. Early in the season comfrey, sweet cicely, and the pastel colors of dame's rocket *(Hesperis mastronalis)* are striking among shorter herbs, whose varied forms combine well: pink-spiked bistort among mauve and white globe-flowered chives; lady's mantle, a low, chartreuse frill spilling over the pathway. All of these plants attract butterflies and other flying insects to feed on their fragrant blooms. I enjoy pausing in the path to observe the activity and the apparent compatibility of these welcome guests.

The season follows with mallows, bergamots, and double-flowered feverfew *(Chrysanthemum parthenium),* which provides a mass of white pompons almost all summer. Later, monkshood, purple-flowered hyssop, and the creamy white sprays of white mugwort—a central feature of the late summer garden—carry on the garden's raison d'être: flowers. Toward the circle's edge the elegant garlic chive finally come into their own, their straight stems topped by numerous, lightly scented white globes. Annual herbs like calendulas and painted sage *(Salvia viridis)* continue to produce colorful flowers and bracts well into late fall.

This is a different sort of herb garden, one that focuses primarily on flowering herbs for their beauty and fragrance. I pick flowers all summer for bouquets or for potpourri, and I do cut the occasional chive leaves when the clump by the front door gives way in the fall. But mainly (dare I say it?), I just enjoy this garden. There should be no "justs" about it. Gardeners, no matter how enthusiastic they are about the concept of useful plants, should not be ashamed to grow herbs solely for their beauty. The most useful among them—culinary herbs like parsley, for instance—do not always, or indeed, ever, need to be harvested. Many herb gardeners, especially in the beginning stages of adoration, suffer pangs of guilt when they think they are failing in their duty. Herbs are useful plants, but they are also beautiful to behold.

THE ART OF NATURALIZING

Naturalizing means returning a cultivated plant to its origins—woodland natives to the woods, for instance—and allowing it to grow there with minimal interference. You need two elements to succeed. First you need vigorous herbs that are close to their wild forms, plants that are either largely or wholly unimproved by human selection or plant breeding (not, in other words, hybrids or named cultivars); such plants will be able to compete most successfully with weeds. You also need a compatible habitat, one that is similar (though not necessarily identical) to the plant's native home.

Inevitably, some of the more vigorous herbs outwore their welcome in the island bed, where I had naively invited them to grow and expand at alarming rates. Unable or unwilling to control them within the confines of a small garden, I began to dig down deep and root them out. Yet I could not bring myself to discard them altogether. Tansy, after all, is handsome in the right place. Other vigorous plants, like cowslips and bistort, could be fairly easily controlled, but there were always extra divisions to be made. And what about chives? What was I to do with the bounty?

When I scouted around for alternative planting sites, I discovered that nature had already provided attractive settings. In light woodland at the top of the ravine I found a carpet of herb Robert *(Geranium robertianum)*, a pretty ground cover with ferny leaves and dark pink flowers. This was the perfect place to plant extra lungwort and bistort.

In a low, wet meadow on the way to the log cabin, clumps of wild blue flag iris *(Iris versicolor)* had established themselves amid clouds of glistening yellow buttercups, into which I merely heeled soapwort, mints, and chives, chives, chives. Before then I would never have guessed that chives—this most useful of alliums—could be so beautiful, forming drifts of rosy mauve flowers when turned out on their own.

On less soggy ground, elecampane shot up on its tall, strong stems, happily bearing its distinctive yellow, daisylike flowers and mulched by a mass of spreading white sneezewort. When I opened the door, as it were, and let these wild types of plants go from my garden, I enjoyed their freedom as much as they did. The only care these plantings receive now is a rough trim around their edges with Jigs's scythe or my long-handled brush hook.

Naturalizing fits in with our rough landscape, a balance of the sown and the unsown, encircled by woods. But you don't need a similar landscape to find wild habitats for overbearing, but handsome, herbs. If you look around your property, you'll probably discover a niche in which to fit these plants, a place where you can let nature take over most of the work.

A HARVEST BED

When I needed space for a harvest bed, one where I could freely cut herbs all season long, Jigs and I made a raised bed on an exposed, south-facing, windy site adjacent to a fenced-in turkey yard *(see fig. 17)*. I had already observed that whenever plants are grown near a fence or similar structure, they really thrive, so I decided to reap the protective benefits of this microhabitat. I only have to contend with occasional forays by the turkeys, who, as soon as they have

*Fig. 17. The harvest bed is a good place
to grow in quantity the herbs you cut frequently
for cooking, drying, and flower arrangements.*

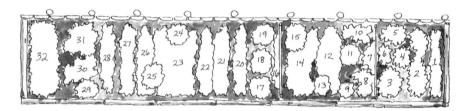

Planting Scheme

1. German Chamomile	9. Coriander	17. Sweet Marjoram	25. Chicory
2. Annual Clary	10. Sunflower	18. Chives	26. Bee Balm
3. Cooking Sage	11. Bachelor Button	19. Sweet Wormwood	27. Egyptian Onion
4. Fernleaf Dill	12. Nigella	20. Sorrel	28. White Mugwort
5. Mallow, 'Zebrina'	13. Dwarf Oregano	21. Catnip	29. Southernwood
6. Statice	14. Poppy	22. Calendula	30. Costmary
7. Nasturtium	15. Dill	23. Lemon Balm	31. Wormwood
8. Salad Burnet	16. Scarlet Runner Beans	24. Black Hollyhock	32. Lovage

slipped under or around the fence, always streak toward the chamomile, entirely stripping it of its leaves and flowers in their first giddy moments of freedom.

The long bed, enclosed by heavy logs and backed by a stockade-type fence, would appear rough and rude, out of place, in another context, but here it has become an integral part of the farm, blending in with its surroundings. Bordered on one side by the top of a steep ravine (where I naturalize herbs and flowers), on the south-facing side by a slope that leads down to our swimming pond, and on the other side by the farmhouse itself, it is a natural outgrowth of our varied activities.

Here I grow perennial herbs that like full sun, such as sorrel, chives, lemon balm, catnip, costmary, and chicory. Annual herbs may include sun-loving nigella, calendula, dill, basil, marjoram, and both annual clary and common garden sage. Up against the fence I plant black hollyhocks, tree mallow, and sweet wormwood, or garden sunflowers, 'Autumn Beauty Mix', in a bright assortment of mahogany, yellows, reds, and bicolors. From the back of the kitchen in late summer, I can just see their wonderful heads, hanging over the edge of the fence looking directly at me. A fence or wall is a great addition to any landscape, expanding possibilities, bringing unexpected rewards.

A ROSE BED

I had already been growing a few kinds of roses when rose fever struck, and suddenly I simply had to have more space to grow different kinds. With the harvest bed in place, a long parallel bed at this site, also raised, seemed quite right, especially since roses need plenty of both sun and air circulation to discourage fungus disease.

I wanted to explore the possibilities of growing a variety of hardy, long-blooming, and fragrant roses that might be suitable for a garden setting (not as vigorous, in other words, as old-fashioned shrub roses). Quite a few, I have discovered, fit these demands, among them hybrid rugosas ('Dart's Dash' and 'Jens Munk'), the Canadian Explorer series roses ('Champlain', 'Henry Hudson'), some delectable antiques ('Queen of Denmark', 'Frau Dagmar Hastrup'), and the small-flowered, classic Polyantha, 'The Fairy'.

I have exploited this site to the fullest, taking advantage of the sunny exposure and protection from the fence, to grow a variety of perennial herbs among the roses. Catmint, lavender, the thymes, veronica, hyssop, mallows, yarrow, and feverfew are apt companions for wide, bushy roses in the pink and scarlet shades. The annual sweet alyssum cascades over the sides of the logs, softening their edges.

As I walk down the middle of these parallel beds, which are separated by about 4½ feet, it is quite natural for me to reach from one side to the other to pick herbs for one purpose or another. I grow roses to grow roses. They need no justification, but I do regard them as herbs and harvest their flowers accordingly for potpourri, jellies, sauces, and cosmetic and floral vinegars.

GARDENING AT THE EDGES

What I have described above are my major plantings, but at their edges are important design elements that connect the various plantings, linking them to create a harmonious landscape.

Ground Covers

Ground covers are invaluable plants, growing where others would be discouraged: in tight corners, among and between rocks and pavings, in shade, at the base of trees or shrubs, or wherever the mower cannot conveniently reach. Ground covers smother weeds (and anything else that gets in their way), so they should never be planted in the garden proper, although there are a few exceptions.

Basically, any vigorous and spreading plant, of whatever height, qualifies as a ground cover. Many of the low-growing, carpet-forming plants are Old World astringents, used for drying up or healing wounds, such as creeping Jenny *(Lysimachia nummularia),* bugleweed (*Ajuga* spp.), and dead nettle (*Lamium* spp.). I use them to fight weeds in paved walkways, in obscure, tight corners, and at the edges of garden beds, where they form an impenetrable, tight-knit cover. They themselves are not a problem because they are easily contained by mowing, even the redoubtable variegated goutweed (*Aegopodium podagraria* 'Variegatum'). I use plants of varied height and habit, depending on the problem area: I plant silvery lamb's-ears to keep out weeds on a bank below a hedge of roses, lungwort to keep weeds at bay at the edges of a garden. I plant sweet violets to transform a weedy spot of ground adjacent to a garden. Here it serves as both a glossy-leaved ground cover and an accent plant, especially when it is in full, dainty bloom.

Accents

"Accent" is often used to describe a plant or planting, but what exactly does it mean? I think of an accent as a single plant or a striking combination used to draw attention to a particular feature in the landscape, or to hide it from view. Accents may also embellish or enliven a dull area, adding distinction to an otherwise uninspired situation. One of the most memorable accent plantings I ever saw was at the head of a driveway: tall, branchy Russian sage *(Perovskia atriplicifolia),* with mounds of the tiny-flowered sweet alyssum at its feet, white and violet, the violet echoed in the numerous branches of the sage itself.

Growing in Containers

Container-grown herbs perform the same function as accents in my landscape. I may place them singly, if they are growing in a large container (a halved cider barrel), or group smaller ones together for maximum impact (and for convenient watering). I grow bright nasturtiums, purple and green basils, tangerine signet marigolds, and the bright red Texas sage *(Salvia coccinea)* in containers, extending the herb-filled landscape right to my door.

HERBS FOR LANDSCAPING

See the individual plant portraits in part II for information about each herb. If an herb is listed in the plural (for example, Mints, Yarrows), read about the various kinds, then select the one most suitable for your situation.

The following lists are intended as a starting place for readers who are looking for herbs well suited to a particular kind of area, growing conditions, or landscape use. For complete information, consult the individual plant entries in part II.

- **Herbs for Dry, Sunny Locations:** borage, burnet, calamint, chamomile, chicory, costmary, feverfew, lavender, rosemary, sages, southernwood, thymes, wormwoods, yarrows.
- **Herbs for Moist Conditions:** angelica, bee balm, bistort, elecampane, lady's mantle, lovage, mints, soapwort, sweet rocket, valerian, violas.
- **Herbs for Shade/Partial Shade:** angelica, bistort, chervil, comfrey, feverfew, lungwort, mallows, mints, parsley, sweet cicely, sweet rocket, valerian, sweet woodruff.

- **Herbs for Container Growing:** basil (dwarf), burnet, calendula (dwarf), chamomile, dill (fernleaf), lemon balm, mints, marigold (signet), marjoram, nasturtiums, parsley (curled), rosemary, thymes, viola (Johnny-jump-up), za'atar *(Majorana syriaca)*.
- **Herbs for Edging:** basil (dwarf), burnet, chives, lady's mantle, lungwort, parsley, winter savory, thymes.
- **Flowering and Fragrant Herbs:** These flowering plants will all attract bees, butterflies, or hummingbirds. Scented ones appear in italics. *Purple basil, bergamots, bistort,* borage, *calamint,* calendula, *chamomile,* chicory, chives, *garlic chives, clary sage,* annual clary, comfrey, *elderberry,* elecampane, feverfew, hollyhock, *hops, hyssop, lavender,* lungwort, mallows, *marigold (signet), wild marjoram, white mugwort, nasturtium,* nigella, pearly everlasting, *roses,* sages, rue, *savories, soapwort, sweet cicely, sweet rocket, sweet woodruff, tansy, thymes, valerian, violas, yarrows.*
- **Herbs for Ground Covers:** bergamots, bistort, calamint, hops (without support), lady's mantle, lamb's-ears, lungwort, wild marjoram, ginger mint, sweet woodruff, creeping thyme, violas, yarrow (common).
- **Herbs for Hedges:** basil, hyssop, lady's mantle, lungwort, roses (apothecary, rugosa, Virginia), southernwood, Roman wormwood, yarrow *(Achillea millefolium)*.
- **Herbs for Naturalizing:** angelica, wild bergamot, bistort, elecampane, hops, lungwort, mallows, wild marjoram, mints, mugworts, pearly everlasting, roses, soapwort, sweet cicely, sweet rocket, sweet woodruff, tansies, creeping thyme, valerian, wormwoods, yarrow (sneezewort).
- **Herbs for Tall Accents or for Background:** angelica, elderberry, elecampane, hollyhock, lovage, mugworts, rugosa rose, tangerine southernwood, tansy, wormwood, sweet wormwood.

Part II

CHAPTER FIVE

The Herbs in My Life:
74 Herb Portraits

"Behold, I have given you every seed-bearing herb . . . "—Genesis 1:29

Plants on the following pages are listed alphabetically by common name. Each capitalized name in the list below represents a separate entry. Since some species or varieties within the same genus are significantly different, they have a separate entry; others can be grouped together (the mints). Recipes are indented under each entry.

Angelica 99
    Angelica Candy 101
Arugula 101
Basil (Common) 103
    Jo Ann's Quick Pesto 106
Basil, Purple 106
    Purple Basil Vinegar; Purple Basil Jelly 108
Bee Balm 109
Bergamot, Lemon 111
Bergamot, Wild 113
Bistort 114
Black Currant 116
    Dried Black Currants; Black Currant Juice 118
Borage 119
Burnet 121
Calamint 123
Calendula 124
    Candied Calendula Flowers 127
Catnip 127

Chamomile (Annual) 129
 Tea 131
Chervil 131
Chicory 132
 Jo Ann's Breakfast Mocha 134
Chives 134
 Chive Blossom Vinegar 137
Chives, Garlic 138
Clary 140
Clary, Annual (Purple-Top, Painted Sage) 141
Comfrey 143
 Jo Ann's Kitchen & Garden Herbal Foot Soak 145
Coriander 145
Costmary 147
 Herbal Skin Freshener; Orange Blossom Potpourri 149
Cress (Garden and Upland) 150
Dandelion 152
 Spring Salad; Wilted Dandelion Salad 155
Dill 156
 Jigs's Dill Crock 157
Elderberry 158
 Elderflower-Mint Tea; Elderflower Pancakes 160
Elecampane 161
Feverfew 163
Hollyhock, Black Hollyhock 165
Hop Vine 167
Horehound 169
 Jigs's Horehound Candy 170
Horseradish 171
 Jigs's Mother's Sauce 172
Hyssop 173
Lady's Mantle 174
Lamb's-Ears 176
Lavender (English) 178
Lemon Balm 181
 Herbed Tea 183

Lovage 183
    Jo Ann's Kitchen & Garden Herb Salt 186
Lungwort 187
Mallow, Common 189
Mallow, Musk 191
Marigold (Signet) 193
Marjoram 195
    Herbed Lamb Chops 196
Marjoram, Wild 197
Mints (Apple, Ginger, Orange, Peppermint) 199
    Mint-Blend Tea; Iced Herb Tea; Iced Tea Deluxe;
    Cold Beet Salad; Mint Jelly 202–4
Mugwort (Common) 205
    Bob's Tussie-Mussie 207
Mugwort, White 207
Nasturtium (Climbing, Semi-Trailing, Dwarf) 209
    Nasturtium Sauce; Summer Salad Extravaganza 211
Nigella 212
Parsley (Curly, Hamburg, Italian) 214
Pearly Everlasting 217
Rose (Apothecary, Rugosa, Virginia) 219
    Rose Petal Jelly; Rose Petal Sandwiches;
    Rose Petal Vinegar; Rose Petal Potpourri 223–4
Rosemary 225
Rue 227
Sage (Common) 229
    Jigs's Barbecued Chicken; Herbed
    Cottage Cheese Spread 231–2
Sages, Tender (Mealycup Sage, Texas Sage) 232
Savory (Summer, Winter) 235
    Soup Seasoning 238
Soapwort 238
Sorrel 240
Southernwood 243
    Herb Guard 244
Sweet Cicely 245

Sweet Rocket 247

Sweet White Clover 249

    Simmering Sweet White Clover Room Freshener 251

Sweet Woodruff 252

    Wendy's May Jelly 254

Tansy 254

Thyme (Common, Creeping) 257

    Herb Rolls 260

Valerian 261

Viola (Wild Pansy, Sweet Violet) 262

Wormwoods (Wormwood, Roman Wormwood,

    Sweet Wormwood) 265

Yarrow (Common Yarrow, Sneezewort) 269

Za'atar *(Majorana syriaca)* 272

    Jo Ann's Favorite Pita Bread 275

ANGELICA

Angelica archangelica
Apiaceae (Celery Family)
Type: Biennial
Height: 6 feet
Site: Partial shade
Soil: Moist
Growing Zones: 3–9

Angelica archangelica

In its first year of growth, angelica is an inauspicious mound of broad divided leaves that gives no hint of the drama to come. By its second season, angelica sends up a hard, hollow-stemmed stalk that reaches upward to the sky, unfurling chartreuse umbels of flowers atop its side stems and at its masthead—altogether a spectacular show in early to midsummer. The umbels gradually darken as the oblong seeds develop, ripen, and drop to the ground. The whole plant is strongly aromatic, with a clean, sharp scent of celery and gin, sweetened with a dash of licorice. A native of northern Europe, angelica is best known for flavoring gin and liqueurs, but it also has an ancient history as a medicinal herb for treating digestive disorders and coughs.

Angelica was one of the first herbs that I noticed in Jigs's little herb collection by the back door when we lived in northern Vermont. Since he didn't know it is virtually impossible to raise angelica from stored seed (information about growing herbs was hard to come by in the early 1960s), that was the way he grew it. In fact, it was not the first time in our various moves that he had raised it successfully from seed, just the first time I took note of it. I could hardly ignore its dramatic presence, rising up and towering over all the other clumps of herbs, few of which I remember now with such clarity.

Even in the days when I did little to preserve herbs, other than drying bunches of culinary herbs from the vegetable garden, I made angelica candy. This was my first foray into more sophisticated herb use, and it became associated with early summer, when the angelica stems were still young and succulent. Then I would take a little basket and scissors to the backdoor garden and harvest enough stems to use during the winter months for eating out of hand (for their pleasant taste and digestive properties) and for decorating cakes (these would have been an extravagance in those very lean days).

When we moved to Cape Breton and I became seriously involved in raising and using herbs, I naturally wanted to duplicate the angelica of my memories, but it was not easy. I don't know what magic Jigs used to get his dried seed to germinate, but I had no luck, and only managed to establish the plant from a purchased root.

Because of its size and cultural requirements it has been a challenge to incorporate angelica successfully into a garden setting, to find just the place where it is most happy and shows off to advantage. I have grown it in a variety of places: in the partial shade of an old apple tree; by the damp ground of the compost heap, where it self-seeded among sweet rocket; and even in a container to dwarf its stature. Here it looked quite elegant in an urn-shaped rubber tire turned inside-out (the rim becomes its pedestal), ringed by bright yellow fern-leaved signet marigolds *(Tagetes tenuifolia)*.

Growing: We now know that angelica is one of those plants whose seeds germinate best when they are fresh, before they have been dried and stored. Some growers store seed in moist conditions before sowing to simulate freshness, but I prefer to let nature do the job for me, to allow the plant (established from a piece of root) to ripen and cast its seeds to the ground, where they germinate when conditions are right, in early spring here. If you cut back angelica before it goes to seed, this will prolong its life another year, and new plants can be grown by detaching shoots, which form at its base. Unless you plan to manufacture Angelica candy in a big way, one plant is sufficient for household use. If you have the room, several plants can add distinction to the landscape.

Using: Angelica candy may sound like a lot of work, but it's really very easy, and if you follow these directions carefully and store the candy in a jar in a cool, dry place away from light, it will last for years and years. Use the stems to decorate cakes or eat them following a meal, like after-dinner mints, to aid digestion. They have a sweet and clean taste. The leftover syrup is delicious in summer fruit cups or over ice cream.

Angelica Candy

Harvest ½-inch-round young stems from a second-year plant. Cut them up into 2-inch pieces and boil them in salted water until tender. Drain the stems and scrape off their outer skins so the stems are bright green. Weigh the stems and make a syrup of the same weight (2 cups of sugar equals 1 pound), using 1 cup of water for every 1 pound of sugar. Let the stems sit in the syrup for 3 or 4 days, and twice a day bring the syrup to a boil and pour it over the stems until the syrup is nearly absorbed. Drain the stems and dry them on paper, turning them often until they feel absolutely dry.

ARUGULA (Rocket, Salad Rocket, Roquette)

Eruca vesicaria var. *sativa*
Brassicaceae (Mustard Family)
Type: Half-hardy annual
Height: 2 feet
Site: Sun
Soil: Well drained

Eruca vesicaria var. *sativa*

The name *arugula* is an Italian corruption of the Latin word *eruca,* or "colewort," and reflects this herb's Mediterranean origin. Its pungent, garlic-flavored leaves, green and wavy-edged, grow in neat clumps at first. As the plant matures, the older leaves get rougher and turn a darker green. The seed stalks rise to a height of 2 feet or more, and bear small, attractive, creamy white, purple-veined flowers that bees love. Arugula, or rocket, as it's sometimes called, should not be confused with sweet rocket *(Hesperis matronalis),* also a member of the mustard family, which is grown for its sweet-scented flowers (see *Sweet Rocket*).

Over 30 years ago, friends from the city brought us a small bunch of wilted greens they called "arugula." The leaves, they assured us, would add a marvelous tang to our salads. In the city, they said, arugula was highly prized and very expensive, available only in out-of-the-way food shops specializing in Italian or gourmet foods.

We were impressed. More than that, once we had refreshed the leaves in cold water and torn them into our salad, we became arugula fans, too. Since then, we have planted arugula in the garden wherever we have lived, no matter now inhospitable the climate and soil. It has always thrived.

The flavor of the leaves is hard to describe. Depending on their maturity, they are nutlike, peppery, spicy, and always garlicky. Jigs is such an admirer of this interesting green that he often picks the young seedpods in early fall to toss into the salad. These can be eaten separately, too, as a peppery relish.

Growing: Sow seeds early in the growing season, when you plant lettuce. Arugula thrives in cool weather. Two sowings will ensure a longer season of young, tender leaves, since plants grow so fast to maturity. Eat the thinnings. If left undisturbed, arugula will self-seed prolifically.

Harvesting: Even though arugula seeds are available nowadays (look for arugula or rocket listed under Gourmet Vegetables or Herbs in seed catalogs), I like to harvest them to share with friends and to sell under my own label, "Jo Ann's Kitchen & Garden." I cut down the stalks in the fall before the dry pods have discharged their seeds. Then I put them upside down in a large paper bag and leave it in a sunny, dry spot in the house or in our lean-to greenhouse. When the stalks are crisply dry, the small, oblong seedpods are easy to detach and press open. I can harvest enough arugula seeds in a few minutes to satisfy a small army of enthusiasts, eager to add this herby green to their salad patch.

Using: I pick arugula leaves (as well as flowers and seedpods) all season long, no matter how mature, since we enjoy their flavor, even when strong, in salads with our homemade cottage cheese and mayonnaise. Their distinctive flavor also adds dash to cooked greens, but don't overdo it—a couple of handfuls in the pot is sufficient.

The dried stalks, with their bullet-shaped seedpods pointing upward on both sides of the stem, like little rockets, are nice in dried bouquets. Could this be the origin of the plant's other name, rocket?

BASIL
(Common Basil,
Sweet Basil)

Ocimum basilicum
Labiatae (Mint Family)
Type: Tender annual
Height: 8 inches to 2 feet
Site: Sun
Soil: Well drained, warm

Ocimum basilicum
'Minimum'

'Sweet Genovese'

A native of the tropics, this is the herb that comes to mind whenever basil is mentioned: broad, shiny, almond-shaped leaves, slightly crinkled, with a strong clove scent, on branching stems. Of somewhat mounded habit, it bears a cloud of tiny white flowers in whorls late in the season. Differing in leaf size, habit, and scent, this ordinary cooking basil has many interesting forms, among them the dwarf variety known as bush basil or Greek basil, *O. basilicum* 'Minimum', a compact plant with a multitude of small, sharply pointed leaves.

In the old days, growing basil was simple. We ordered seeds labeled BASIL, planted them outdoors when the soil had warmed, and harvested bushels of leafy stems by late summer or early fall.

So when we moved to Cape Breton, and I had sole charge of the herbs, I grew basil the way we always had, with disastrous results. Here, the plants were puny, stunted by cold soil and unfavorable growing conditions (wind, for instance). And I began to notice variations in the plants from year to year, significant differences in leaf size and habit.

Gradually, I became more discerning when choosing seed, always ordering the basil with the largest advertised leaf size and with a recognizable cultivar name, from a specialty seed house. This was to increase the chances of getting the large-leaf type I preferred, the one that would yield the greatest amount of leaves for preserving. That's how I discovered 'Sweet Genovese', a large-leaved Italian selection introduced in 1985. It is very productive and vigorous, with intensely scented, elongated leaves.

I was inadvertently introduced to the small-leaved bush basil when I ordered an anonymous basil advertised as the "large-leaf type." Although it didn't yield quantities of leaves for preserving, I discovered that it is especially suited to wintering-over indoors, where it provides enough fresh basil for salads and general flavoring all winter long. It's cheering to see basil, even a miniature version, growing on a windowsill during the northern winter. Bush basils are also fine landscaping plants, creating a low, compact hedge for the front of the garden.

It's quite likely that there were variations in the basils we grew in Vermont, but since our harvests were always large, we never noticed them. The Basil Revolution of the last decade—and the introduction of many basil types and named cultivars—has, in any case, improved the quality of seed offerings, so it is more likely today that what you order in the basil line is really what you get.

What about the growing problems in cold-climate or short-season areas, though? After all, of what use are fancy cultivars if you can't grow them well?

Growing: I have devoted a lot of thought and energy to solving The Basil Problem. My strategies are quite simple, yet effective. Six to 8 weeks before the last frost, I sow seeds indoors in the usual way (see chapter 1) in a Styrofoam cup placed on an old heating pad set to medium. With this bottom heat, germination takes about 3 days (14 days is standard for seeds without the added warmth). Seedlings are very carefully transplanted to plastic plant cells about 2 inches square and set under two 40-watt fluorescent growing tubes. If the room temperature in our leaky old farmhouse is under 70 degrees, I continue to provide plants with bottom heat in the form of an old heating pad. (With two bad backs in the family, one accumulates old pads.) When the plants are growing well and the temperature in our greenhouse is steadily warm, then and only then are the basil plants transferred there, moved again when one of our two hotbeds has a vacancy. Used primarily to raise vegetable seedlings (tomatoes and other heat-loving plants) in the early spring, the hotbed later provides ideal conditions for growing basil plants all summer. There they are transplanted from their cell-packs, about 12 inches apart, into the kind of warm environment basil must have, at all stages of its growth, to develop plentiful leaves and to avoid the fungus disease known as powdery mildew. The soil of the hotbed is rich and conducive to the production of leaves, especially after I pinch off the top growth once the plants are reestablished and 5 to 6 inches tall.

I usually grow a few plants outdoors in pots just by the front porch for quick picking, but these stay in the greenhouse until outdoor temperatures are up to 70 degrees, below which basil seems to shrink back into the soil from which it came. If you live in an area where tomatoes grow well and ripen before frost, you can sow basil seeds outdoors when danger of frost has past, covering them with ¼ inch of soil, and thinning plants to 12 inches apart.

Once plants are established, you can propagate them by putting a few stems in a glass of water, where they will quickly form roots. I discovered this when I included a few springs of purple basil in a bouquet.

Harvesting: Cut basil sprigs all summer as needed; this will encourage bushiness and leaf production. If the whole plant is cut back before blossoming—to the cleanest set of lower leaves—it will grow more leaves, which can then be harvested until frost. The amount of regrowth depends on the climate. Where I live, basil does not usually set seed and continues to grow until killed by freezing temperatures. In warmer regions, plants mature quickly, stems become woody, and leaf production is sparse. In such conditions, you can sow successive crops for cutting all summer.

Drying: Despite everything negative you may have read about preserving basil by drying, I still think it's worthwhile. I've tried other methods (freezing, for instance) and find that I prefer the texture of the dried product. Dried basil is easy to use in all dishes and, if properly done, the herb's flavor is preserved remarkably well. The secret is to reduce the vegetative mass so that the leaves will dry rapidly, retaining both their green color and their flavor. Nothing is more dispiriting than having your entire basil crop turn brown. To achieve the desired results, I discard all of the larger stems, cut up the basil leaves, and lay them one layer deep on cookie sheets, drying them in a just-warm oven (below 150 degrees F). Stirring the leaves occasionally helps speed up drying. For larger amounts, I use Jigs's magic drying racks, described in chapter 2.

Preparation and Storage: Pack the whole, dried leaves into wide-mouthed glass jars and store away from light in a cool, dark place. Carefully dried and stored, basil will keep its color and scent for more than a year.

Using: Fresh basil goes into salads of all kinds, embellishes tomato dishes and pastas, is steeped in vinegar, flavors jellies, and turns my morning scrambled eggs and cottage cheese into gourmet dining. Dried basil can be used in much the same way as fresh leaves, even for vinegars and jellies, and for the ultimate in Basilmania, pesto. Pulverize the broken leaves of dried basil between your fingers so that their flavor will be more quickly released.

Jo Ann's Quick Pesto

Into a small bowl, squeeze as much garlic through a garlic press as you have patience for (the cloves should be skinned first). This probably won't be enough, so shake in some garlic flakes or garlic powder. Now, add a handful of grated Parmesan cheese of the highest quality, with a sharp, well-aged flavor. (Our homemade cheese is at least 10 years old.) Stir in olive oil with a sturdy fork until the dry ingredients are well blended; then add a handful of pulverized dry basil or twice the amount of chopped or crushed fresh basil leaves. This is your starter, to which you keep adding grated cheese, garlic, and basil until you have the flavor you like. Preparation time is 5 minutes if you use dried basil. We like using this pesto to "gild the lily," as it were, on our homemade spaghetti sauce. A few dollops are also delicious on baked potatoes, string beans, or in minestrone (a thick meat-vegetable soup). I've never had the traditional pine nuts around to use in pesto, but we find it very tasty anyway.

PURPLE BASIL

Ocimum basilicum 'Dark Opal';
O. basilicum 'Purple Ruffles'
Labiatae (Mint Family)
Type: Tender annual
Height: 18 inches
Site: Sun
Soil: Well drained, warm

Ocimum basilicum
'Dark Opal'

Ocimum basilicum
'Purple Ruffles'

'Dark Opal' is the original variety of purple basil, developed in the 1950s. It is less robust than ordinary green basil and more slender in form, with deep purple leaves and pink rather than white flowers. The cultivar 'Purple Ruffles' is a sturdier plant with purple, deeply cut, ruffled foliage and lavender-rose flowers.

I don't know precisely when I became aware of the Basil Revolution. It was a gradual realization that while I had been struggling to grow plain old cooking basil, herb enthusiasts had been trying out more than a dozen varieties I'd never heard of, with names like 'Lemon', 'Cinnamon', 'Camphor', even 'Holy Basil', as well as the purple types. I was reluctant to try them because I'd heard they are even more demanding in a cold climate than ordinary basil. But with a well-thought-out battle plan, one that involved providing plenty of additional heat, from seed to harvest time, I decided to venture into the unknown with the purples.

The first one I tried was 'Dark Opal'. I had been cautioned that up to 30 percent of the seedlings might not be all purple, so when these sports appeared among the purple seedlings—either streaked or well on the green side—I pulled them out. I kept the plants in pots in the greenhouse until the outdoor temperatures were warm, then placed them in a sunny, sheltered spot to show their stuff.

I was enchanted with 'Dark Opal's looks: slender, pink-flowered wands above purple foliage, a striking contrast of colors. Unlike the regular cooking basil—grown for its green leaves, with its flowers pinched back to encourage bushier plants—flowering of the purple type is encouraged to show off the plant's beauty. But was purple basil good for anything besides show?

The answer is yes! 'Dark Opal' turned out to be great in salads, though it is less perfumed, and with a sharper, spicier flavor than regular green basil. It is also delicious in jelly, and absolutely unrivaled for making beautiful and flavorful vinegar.

So the next season I tried 'Purple Ruffles' at the same time as 'Dark Opal' to compare the two. The problem was that I loved them both. Although authorities tell us that neither variety is what it used to be, that both 'Dark Opal' and 'Purple Ruffles' have lost their looks—the one its purpleness, the other its ruffles—growers I know are still delighted with them. Perhaps we just don't know what we're missing. The recently introduced 'Red Rubin', which I haven't yet tried, is supposed to be an improved version of 'Dark Opal'. It is the result of seed reselection (an improvement in the seed stock).

Growing: I grow the purple basils the same way as I do the green type, starting them indoors a little earlier (eight weeks before the last frost) to encourage earlier blooming. The purple types are also supposed to make fine houseplants on a sunny windowsill and I intend to try growing them indoors someday. For this purpose, you should sow some seeds later in the season and pinch off the top growth to encourage bushiness as well as to delay flowering until after the plants come inside.

Using: The purple varieties can be used fresh, just as you would green basil. Their unique flavor is best preserved in vinegars and jellies.

Purple Basil Vinegar

Pack clean stems with leaves (adding flowers is okay, too) into a sterilized, wide-mouthed jar. The size is up to you, depending on how much vinegar you want to make and how much purple basil you have on hand. The jar does not need to be tightly packed since the herb's flavor is strong. I use 1 cup of herbs to 2 cups of vinegar. Fill the jar with white vinegar, making sure the basil is covered. Place the jar on a sunny windowsill or in a greenhouse (a good way to make use of surplus solar heat during the summer months). Depending on the intensity of the sun, the vinegar may be sufficiently flavored in two weeks. Strain out the herbs through a double layer of cheesecloth and pour the lovely rosy pink liquid into a narrow-necked vinegar-type bottle, one that is easy to handle. You will be using the vinegar quite often for making your own salad dressings: Use ¼ cup of vinegar to ½ cup olive oil. Shake before pouring.

Purple Basil Jelly

Place 1 packed cup purple basil leaves in a saucepan and bruise them with the back of a sturdy spoon so they are crushed. Add 2 cups of water, bring the mixture just to a boil. Simmer for a few seconds only, then turn off the heat and let the herbs steep, covered, for no more than 10 minutes (longer steeping will give the jelly a rank flavor). Strain, saving the liquid (there should be 1½ cups), to which add 2 tablespoons cider vinegar, 3½ cups sugar, and a pinch of salt. Bring this mixture to a hard boil and, when it can't be stirred down, stir in 1 pouch of liquid pectin. Bring to a hard boil again for 1 minute.

Remove the pot from the heat, let the mixture subside, skimming if necessary, then pour it into small jelly jars, leaving a ½-inch headspace. Seal immediately with sterilized vacuum-sealed lids, or cover the jars lightly with newspaper, wait until the jelly has cooled, then carefully pour about a tablespoon of melted paraffin on top of the jelly, rotating the jar to seal the edges. Repeat once.

Try this beautiful and tasty jelly as a spread with cream cheese.

BEE BALM (Bergamot, Oswego Tea, Red Bergamot, Scarlet Bee Balm)

Monarda didyma
Labiatae (Mint Family)
Type: Perennial
Height: 3½ feet
Site: Sun/Partial shade
Soil: Moist
Growing Zones: 4–10

*Monarda
didyma*

Bee balm, like all the bergamots, is native to North America, where it grows in moist woodlands and bottomlands from New England to Georgia and Tennessee. A vigorous plant that spreads by creeping underground roots, it produces striking blooms of tubular, scarlet flowers in whorls—sometimes two-tiered—atop stems that grow from the axils of pointed, slightly drooping leaves and red-tinged bracts. The whole plant exudes a sweet, citrusy aroma, released when lightly brushed. This is the species of *Monarda* most attractive to hummingbirds. Native Americans used bee balm to flavor meat dishes, relieve bronchial congestion, and for tea. Named after the Oswego tribe, Oswego tea became famous as a substitute for imported tea in the American colonies following the Boston Tea Party.

Many years ago, I began growing bee balm. At least that's what I thought I would be growing when I ordered seeds listed as bergamot under Herbs in the seed catalog. I had visions of the gorgeous, showy scarlet flowers I had admired in pictures. Today I would know, even without the Latin name as a guide, that any bergamot sold as seed could not be the species form of *Monarda didyma* (the one with the bold red flowers), since that rarely produces seeds. Despite its common name, bees have little use for the plant, because its deep-throated flowers are difficult for them to enter and, thus, pollinate.

So, after carefully planting seed of what I thought was bee balm, and nursing the plants through the summer, the following year I was disappointed to find a more subdued plant than I had anticipated, with less spectacular blooms in the mauve-purple-pink line. As I soon learned, this plant was wild bergamot *(M. fistulosa)*. The only way I could acquire my heart's desire was by begging a chunk of true bee balm from a gardening friend. It seems hard to believe now, with herbs so popular and accessible, but 20 years ago this was not the case, and I was thrilled to finally establish a planting of bee balm, which I then considered to be the only type of bergamot worth growing.

The only problem I've had with this delightful herb over the years is that I'm incapable of throwing any away, even onto the compost heap, where, presumably, it would always be with me in the form of soil. But I just can't bring myself to do it.

Why do I love bee balm so? First of all, it is beautiful. Its mass of shaggy, vivid flowers enhances the general landscape. Second, I enjoy being in its vicinity and basking in the delicious fragrance it wafts my way as I weed or just walk through the garden. Finally, I take pleasure in watching hummingbirds in action, zooming in and around the flowers. So for all these reasons, I have established plantings of bee balm in virtually every one of my 10 gardens, and naturalized them in a light woodland setting in our ravine, in a wild meadow planting, and on the north side of our house, so I can watch the hummingbirds from the back kitchen window when I pass by in the morning or late afternoon (their favorite times for nectar-sipping). Considering bee balm's vigor and the need to split up plantings every few years, it is no small claim to report that I have never thrown a plant away, unless it was a worn-out, hardened mass that even I could not regard as viable plant material.

In my gardens, bee balm blooms the whole month of August, glorious everywhere, by itself or combined with the herbs and flowers of high summer: bright yellow and orange calendulas; tall, shaggy yellow elecampane sunflowers; sprays of white mugwort; and phlox. In the wild, bee balm is complemented beautifully by dusty pink Joe Pye weed, fluffy near-white boneset, and the yellow-buttoned tansy.

Growing: Grow bee balm from clumps set in rich, moist soil in sun or shade. Flowers are more long lasting and brighter in dappled shade. Blooming can be extended by cutting stems of spent blossoms at the leaf axil, which encourages the production of new flowering stems. Clumps should be broken up and divided every 3 years, or when the center of the planting becomes hard and unproductive. It's possible to grow hybrid forms from seed. 'Panorama Mix' offers a range of colors—pinks, reds, mauve-purple, white—but in my experience these plants are invariably prone to powdery mildew, a fungus that attacks bee balm when it is grown in shady, moist conditions. If you must have colors other than the vivid scarlet ('Croftway Pink' is nice), buy plants. None of these, however, will be as popular with hummingbirds as the red-flowered form.

Using: I mark the passage of summer with the midsummer appearance of bee balm blossoms to pick for our deluxe salad productions. The petals are plucked from the flower head and sprinkled as a garnish, with nasturtium flowers and a variety of herbs, over our many colorful and beautiful varieties of looseleaf and butterhead lettuces. Bee balm leaves are added to the teapot, either fresh or dried; the dried flower heads and leaves are major ingredients in Jo Ann's Kitchen & Garden Christmas Potpourri. Fresh leaves can be cut up and added to fruit cups; fresh or dried leaves can be used to flavor tomato dishes. The flowers and leaves, either fresh or dried, have a sweet, fruity flavor with a hint of minty sharpness.

LEMON BERGAMOT
(Lemon Mint)

Monarda citriodora
Labiatae (Mint Family)
Type: Annual
Height: 2 feet
Site: Sun/Partial shade
Soil: Well drained

*Monarda
citriodora*

Lemon bergamot, another species native to North America, grows wild in the Appalachian Mountains and bears its characteristic whorled blooms in shades of rose-lilac and sometimes white. About 3 inches high, appearing at the top third of each stem, the flowers grow from chartreuse bracts that have a lilac tint. The small, narrow leaves, set at intervals along the stem, have a lemon-mint scent, although some gardening authorities describe it as camphoraceous. The most striking thing about this plant's appearance is that the flower heads are stacked on top of one another—two to four of them on each stem—with the largest at the bottom of the pile, making for a spectacular show. Bees love lemon bergamot's loosely open, clawlike florets.

I ordered seeds of this bergamot on a whim and I was not sorry. Lemon bergamot is a desirable herb, useful and beautiful, but seldom grown, at least in the Northeast. Here it must be grown as an annual, but this is not really a drawback, since the plants are easy to raise and they bring much satisfaction over the summer.

I like to plant lemon bergamot in an old sap bucket by the kitchen door. The piled-up flowers show themselves to advantage against the gray, weathered clapboards. Every time I pass this planting—many times a day—I stop to admire and sniff the blossoms and pick a few leaves for the teapot.

Growing: I sow seeds 8 to 12 weeks before our last frost, just covering them with soil. Seeds germinate in 5 days at 70 degrees (the expected days to germination for most monardas is usually 10 to 40). Growing information for this herb is hard to come by. At first I had no idea if lemon bergamot was an annual or a perennial. In fact, *Hortus Third* lists it as an annual or biennial. In warmer regions, lemon bergamot self-seeds in the fall; in the Northeast, seeds may germinate outside in the spring from last year's plants.

Using: Add the fresh or dried leaves to China tea—use a small handful of fresh leaves or 2 tablespoons of dried leaves per quart of boiling water. I use 1 to 2 teaspoons of dried leaves to make a single cup of herb tea. The fresh or dried leaves can also be used to flavor fresh fruit desserts. The dried leaves and flowers go into potpourri. Lemon bergamot makes a good cut flower, fresh or dried.

WILD BERGAMOT

Monarda fistulosa
Labiatae (Mint Family)
Type: Perennial
Height: 2½ feet
Site: Sun
Soil: Well drained, on the dry side
Growing Zones: 3–10

Monarda fistulosa

Wild bergamot is no more and no less wild than the other *Monarda* species, but it must have some name to distinguish it from the others—hence, this one is known as the wild one. It favors sunny sites from New England southward, growing best in dry soil. A more slender plant than bee balm but taller than lemon bergamot, it too bears tubular flowers in whorls, growing from lilac-tinged bracts, on stems with sharply pointed leaves, smaller than bee balm's. The flowers vary in color, from pale lilac to rosy mauve. Wild bergamot has been crossed with bee balm to create hybrid monardas.

I've made my peace with this bergamot. Yes, it isn't the showy one, but I've come to appreciate its subdued beauty and learned to use it to advantage in the landscape by naturalizing it—returning it to the wild whence it came. It is one of the first plants I used to try to hide the ugliness of the old glass-fronted meat cooler we salvaged and transformed into a hotbed. The ground around the hotbed was the perfect location for this species: exposed and south-facing.

Early in the season wild bergamot's mound of leaves is handsome, more attractive than its showier cousin, bee balm, and it always elicits interest from plant customers at this stage of its growth. In bloom, it is the perfect meadow flower, its soft pastel hues blending with those of wild marjoram (*Origanum vulgare),* just as it does in its natural habitat. Blooming a little earlier than bee balm, wild bergamot can be cut back to the ground after flowering to grow another attractive mound of foliage for late-season interest.

Growing: Sow seeds as for lemon bergamot and plant seedlings outside in early summer. Once established, wild bergamot will be around as long as you want it, and probably longer than that. The plant mounds are composed of a network of roots, easily moved if you have a good, sharp spade and a strong back. Chop them up in smaller pieces to propagate.

Using: Wild bergamot has a sharper flavor than that of bee balm. I like to dry the flowering stems for winter bouquets and I add the dried flowers and leaves to potpourri.

Polygonum bistorta

BISTORT
(Snakeweed)

Polygonum bistorta
Polygonaceae (Buckwheat Family)
Type: Perennial
Height: 2½ feet
Site: Sun/Shade
Soil: Moist
Growing Zones: 3–8

Bistort is an Old World herb that has literally taken root in the New, from the wet meadows of Nova Scotia to New England. It grows from a twisted root (the meaning of its species name, *bistorta*) that produces an attractive wide mound of large, tapered leaves with a reddish tint. In early summer here, the tall, knot-jointed stems, characteristic of the Buckwheat Family, are topped by fluffy, soft, pink flower heads, densely packed with tiny florets that attract bees and butterflies. Their scent is lightly sweet. Bistort has a long and venerable history as a medicinal herb and food. As an astringent, it was used to dry up wounds and stop diarrhea. As a food, it was featured in a dish known as Bistort Pudding, traditionally served in spring as a restorative.

I acquired bistort from a remote hillside garden on the mainland of Nova Scotia, drawn there by the gardener's reputation for having a large collection of unusual plants. It was a veritable botanical garden, cultivated all alone by a woman in her 60s. She was rather mad, driven to grow every single plant she had ever read about, in every color. "I have the white," she would say, "but need the blue," and so on and on. The result was an astonishing diversity of plants in varied forms: many of them old-fashioned types from local gardens; others, rarities she had raised from seed or bought from out-of-the-way nurseries. Among these was bistort, in the form known as 'Superbum', an apt description for this magnificent cultivar.

Bistort and its new owner (me) came in for a lot of ribbing from Jigs, who these days regards arcane herbs as little more than weeds. But when the pink pokers bloom in early summer, they are always very much admired by all the visitors to our farm. Weed or not, they make a big splash in the landscape. In the shade of an old white lilac, bistort is flanked by the arching stems of Solomon's seal, with its dangling ivory bells, and buttercup yellow globeflowers (*Trollius* sp.). In full sun, it grows very well backed by pastel-flowered sweet rocket (*Hesperis matronalis*) with the spreading 'Johnson's Blue' hardy geranium at its feet.

On a fine day in mid-June I love to observe the fritillaries, bees, and all sorts of other flying insects work over bistort's fluffy pink heads, each on a different stalk. In the early evening when I return to the garden, all have left except a lone bumblebee, still plying his trade, methodically going from flower to flower to collect more nectar.

Even Jigs has to admit that bistort has some merit, but he can't resist asking, "When are we going to have some Bistort Pudding?"—referring to a ghastly concoction made from young bistort shoots mixed with nettles and similar greenery, then cooked up for hours with barley. Bistort is one of those herbs I don't do much with but enjoy for their beauty and for the varied and beneficial life they bring to any planting.

Growing: Any little piece of bistort's creeping root will grow into an attractive mound in one or two seasons, depending on conditions. For best results it should be grown in moisture-retentive soil, whether in full shade or full sun. After the mound is established, new plantlets will develop around the mother plant. I have never found any difficulty in finding new homes for these. This is one vigorous plant whose rambunctious habits I cheer on. It can be dug up at any point in its growth cycle and replanted without sulking, a quality that I find especially endearing. As if this weren't enough to recommend it, bistort blooms again in the fall if the stalks are cut back after their first flowering.

Using: The fluffy, lightly scented flower heads can be dried for potpourri. Bistort is a wonderful and long-lasting cut flower.

BLACK CURRANT

Ribes nigrum
Saxifragaceae (Saxifrage Family)
Type: Perennial shrub
Height: 5 to 6 feet
Site: Northern exposure
Soil: Moist
Growing Zones: 3–9

Ribes nigrum

Ribes nigrum is the European species of the black currant from which most garden cultivars are bred. A mature shrub is 6 feet tall and 8 feet wide, quite ornamental in bloom, when it is covered with small white blossoms and three-lobed, miniature, maplelike leaves. By late summer, the stems arch toward the ground, laden with round, black berries. They are rather unpalatable for eating out of hand, but the pectin-rich fruits can be turned into tasty preserves. During the 1920s, black currants were banned from cultivation across the United States because, as a carrier for the white pine blister rust fungus, they posed a threat to commercially valuable white pine plantations (the fungus does little damage to the black currant itself). With the development of fungus-resistant white pine cultivars, as well as the decline of the white pine lumber industry, black currants are once more being grown in the United States. There are also fungus-resistant black currants, often bred in Europe or Canada, where the black currant is a traditional and important small fruit.

U.P. Hedrick, the great American horticulturalist, lamented the absence of black currants from American gardens in 1944 in his classic work, *Fruits for the Home Garden* (Dover reprint, 1973): "The black currant, so greatly prized in all other northern countries, is hardly known on this side of the Atlantic."

We knew nothing about them when we ordered six bushes of the rust-resistant cultivar 'Consort', after we moved to the farm in Cape Breton more than 25 years ago. Over the years Jigs and I had honed our skills in gathering from the wild, but we yearned to grow a variety of cultivated fruits.

We grew black currants because Jigs had always been interested in them. We planted them on a northern slope and watched with pleasure as they grew to maturity and began to bear fruit. And what fruit! Each bush was so full of berries that it took several adults *all day* to pick them. Then the question arose: What to do with the bountiful harvest?

Of course, I had been anticipating the day when I would have to do something with black currants, even though I had had no idea of the size of the yield. Without a freezer, moreover, the small, perishable fruit would have to be speedily processed. I looked over my cookbooks, some of them going back to the 1890s. There were no recipes that dealt specifically with black currants, but I was able to adapt some for other bush fruits, among them directions for drying the berries for the winter (like raisins). A by-product of this process was a syrup that we used as a base for juice, high in vitamin C and quite delicious. (I didn't know it then, but the syrup I learned to make is called Ribena in England, where it has long been valued as a staple juice as well as a nutritious substitute for orange juice.) This single method of preserving thus provided us with fruit to eat out of hand as well as a breakfast juice that lasted throughout the winter and into the spring. This is in addition to the jam, jelly, and wine that we learned to make from each season's harvest.

Eminently suited to the northern climate, the black currant bush is both decorative and useful. Growing it forced me to learn how to deal with an unknown fruit, and the knowledge I gained became the basis for my first book, *The Old-Fashioned Fruit Garden* (Nimbus, 1989). That book was, and remains today, the only source of detailed information on growing and preserving black currants.

Growing: Plant nursery stock in the spring. One bush may yield as much as 4 or 5 gallons of fruit, so plan accordingly. The best site is a slope with northern exposure to provide cool conditions. Black currants thrive in fertile, clay loam. Trim plants to about 6 inches and put them in a bucket of water while preparing the planting holes, spacing them 6 feet apart. Add a shovelful of well-rotted compost to each hole and water it. Then build a little mound of earth in the hole and set the roots over it, tamping the soil around the plant. In a dry spell, water the plants regularly until they show signs of new growth.

Black currants benefit from mulching, which not only keeps the plants cool, but also prevents competition from weeds. We use a three-layer system: First we set down a 2-foot-wide, 6-inch-thick ring of well-rotted manure or compost; this is followed by a layer of heavy paper, cardboard, or worn-out nonsynthetic carpet; the top layer consists of hay, straw, or eelgrass harvested from the nearby shore. Whatever materials are used, they should be renewed once a year in the spring or fall. These organic materials will break down from one season to the next, producing rich, loose soil, but—be forewarned—also a crop of lush weeds. The weeds are easy to pull out, however. All things considered, we find this method of mulching worth the extra weeding, and I never fail to be thrilled by the new soil that is created in just one season.

When the plants are dormant in early spring, remove any dead or broken stems and thin out any overcrowded or old ones, so the center of the plant is open to light. Black currants readily propagate themselves by self-layering, from branches that dip to the ground and take root. These can be separated from the mother plant and replanted where you want them.

Using: Black currants, high in pectin, can be used to make fast-setting jams and jellies. I use ripe and overripe berries for juice. Jigs makes gallons of wine every summer. This recipe makes dried berries and juice at the same time.

Dried Black Currants

Layer ripe black currants overnight in a large enamelware or stainless-steel pot, adding 1 cup of sugar for every 3 cups of berries. In the morning, bring the resulting fruit and juice to a boil. Reduce the heat and, stirring occasionally to make sure the berries don't stick to the bottom of the pot, simmer gently for 15 minutes. Strain the berries, reserving the juice. Spread the berries on a wax paper–lined pan and set them in a sunny spot to dry, stirring the berries—now quasi-raisins—so they don't stick together. Change the paper after the first day. Drying may take several days, depending on conditions. I use the intense heat from our greenhouse, which helps speed the process. Use these dried currants as you would raisins: to eat out of hand, to add to bread and cake dough, or even to flavor tea. Black currant tea is an old-fashioned cold remedy.

Black Currant Juice

Bring the strained and reserved currant juice, now a thick syrup, to a boil and cook for 5 minutes. Pour into scalded canning jars and seal at once, or freeze in plastic containers. To make juice, add ¼ cup of syrup per cup of water or to taste. I usually dilute 1 quart of syrup with 3 quarts of water to make 1 gallon of juice.

Borago officinalis

BORAGE

Borago officinalis
Boraginaceae (Borage Family)
Type: Annual
Height: 1½ to 3 feet
Site: Sun
Soil: Well drained

Borage is native to southern Europe and North Africa, where it grows in optimum conditions—light, dry, infertile soil—producing deep, vivid blue flowers (in North America, they are usually described as sky blue). These blossoms are in the shape of small stars, about ¾ inch across, and are borne in nodding clusters that protect the flowers' nectar from rain. Like other members of the family to which borage gives its name—comfrey, lungwort, forget-me-not—the blue flowers may begin life as pink buds. The epithet *officinalis*, 'from the apothecary', reminds us that borage was once considered an official healing herb, useful for its soothing properties. Because of its widespread use in imparting its cool cucumber flavor to alcoholic beverages, it became associated with courage, as in the ancient motto, "I borage, bring always courage." The flowers' appeal to bees earned it the common name of bee bread.

I had been growing borage for many years (or allowing it to self-seed with abandon), when I saw it, as if for the first time, growing in the Jerusalem Botanical Garden. The nodding clusters were a brilliant blue under the equally brilliant Mediterranean sky, nodding down from a stony cliff so that I, looking up, could fully appreciate the exquisite beauty of the blue stars. In my own garden, in rich, moist soil, borage had become top-heavy, so bent over that there was no way I could admire the flowers unless I got down on the ground to peer up at them.

This was an important lesson, not only about borage, but about other herbs as well, plants whose specific growth requirements I had never really tried to meet. I had assumed that it would be enough to give such plants well-drained soil and sun, but "well-drained" (where water easily passes through the soil) is not synonymous with "light" and certainly not with "infertile." It is hard for the well-intentioned gardener to really believe that a certain plant prefers to grow, and even thrives, where the soil lacks the various nutrients that give it fertility. However, as I have seen on several trips to Israel, many plants, including a variety of attractive herbs, are well adapted to growing in stony ground, in what we would regard as poor, thin soil.

Since borage revealed its inner soul, so to speak, by showing me how it prefers to live, I now try various strategies to make up for the fact that my landscape does not include a Mediterranean-type habitat—no stony cliffs, no brilliant blue sky (only occasionally), no dry, infertile soil. On the contrary, soil conditions in our gardens are generally fertile (we strive to make them so) and moist. I try to plant borage on an incline so the nodding, curly clusters—beautiful in their own right—reveal the flowers' faces, rather than just their backs. And I ruthlessly cut back top-heavy plants to encourage more flowers on shorter stems.

I have heard of an all-white variant of borage, but I have no desire to grow it. White flowers are fairly common, but borage's blue stars are distinctive, in a class by themselves. In my garden they are more sky blue than the vivid blue I remember in Jerusalem, but they combine well near the back of the garden with orange and yellow lilies early in the season, and with purple coneflower and phlox in the fall.

Growing: You can start borage from seed indoors, where it germinates fast at 70 degrees, but I'm in no rush. I know that if I seed borage outdoors in late spring or early summer, it will also germinate readily: Cover the black seeds with ½ inch of soil. I also know that, once sown, I will not have to sow it again unless I want to establish it elsewhere. Borage is tricky to transplant (only try it in its very young growth) because of its deep taproot. Self-sown plants, having an earlier start, are coarser in stem and leaf, with a more spreading habit than first-year plants, and need to be cut back once or twice during the season to maintain upright growth and flower production.

Using: Borage adds a blue accent to fresh bouquets all season long. I enjoy candying the flower heads, which look lovely when paired with calendula flower heads or petals on a buttercream frosting. I add the flowers to salads and cold summer drinks as an edible, cucumber-flavored garnish.

BURNET
(Salad Burnet)

Poterium sanguisorba
Roseaceae (Rose Family)
Type: Perennial
Height: 1 foot
Site: Sun
Soil: Well drained
Growing Zones: 4–9

Poterium sanguisorba

Burnet is an herb of Mediterranean origin that later spread throughout Europe. In the Northeast it grows as a biennial, the first year producing a low mound of long, wavy-edged leaves arranged ladderlike, close to the ground. In the second year thimble-shaped flowers—green with reddish pink tufts—appear atop wiry stems, making an attractive addition to the basal rosette of leaves that spreads to a 24-inch mat in maturity. Although now restricted to culinary use, at one time burnet was considered an important medicinal (to treat infection and gout) and was one of the first herbs the colonists brought to their new home.

Jigs grew this dainty herb off and on for several years, beguiled by its looks as well as the cucumber-like flavor of its leaves (its main claim to fame nowadays). When I took over the herb growing, I quite naturally included burnet because I was already familiar with it, and soon discovered why growing it is an off-and-on affair. Although described as perennial, it's a short-lived one, so if it fails to seed itself you must do without it until the next season, when you raise a fresh crop of plants.

Burnet leaves lend their subtle cucumber flavor to sour cream dips, spreads, salad dressing, herb vinegars, and salads—a little goes a long way—

until the real cucumbers finally make their late-season appearance here. Burnet must be used fresh since it loses its flavor in drying.

Why bother with an herb that one must raise from seed virtually every year to be assured of its presence? Why bother with an herb whose only use is seasonal? Because it's a pretty sight that gladdens the heart, a green ruffle that dresses up the plainest of plantings. I love the way the new leaves, a soft green, appear in the middle of the clump, tightly pleated. But I also enjoy its mature appearance with its wands of pretty thimble flowers.

I grow burnet in tubs with purple basil, in an old wooden chest with cascading white petunias, and as an edging plant that is always attractive. Wherever it grows, I always snatch a few of the youngest leaves (the tastiest) to add to our salads. Burnet leaves have the added value of remaining green and tasty throughout the fall into early winter, a decided bonus for us, since all our salad material comes from what we can grow here on the farm. The second-year plants are strictly ornamental.

Growing: Start plants indoors 4 to 6 weeks before the last frost. In my experience germination is very quick (2 days) if light is excluded—cover the planting medium with a piece of paper—and seeds are not more than 1 year old. The expected germination for burnet is 8 to 10 days. I grow the seedlings under lights in 2-inch plant cells to encourage the formation of a solid block of roots. This helps when transplanting burnet outside since it resents being moved. Plants should be spaced 12 inches apart to give the spreading leaves the room they need. Mature plants develop a taproot and cannot be moved.

Soil must be well drained to ensure that burnet will survive the winter. Excess moisture around the root crown is a major cause of premature death in the spring. If burnet has a favorable site—one that's sunny and well drained—it should return for many seasons by self-seeding.

Using: Steep handfuls of burnet leaves in cider vinegar until it is the desired cucumber flavor, then drain and use for salads. Add finely cut fresh leaves to sour cream dips, cottage cheese, cream cheese, or yogurt cheese spreads, and to salad dressing along with finely cut basil, dill, and garlic.

CALAMINT
(Showy Calamint,
Showy Savory)

Calamintha grandiflora
Labiatae (Mint Family)
Type: Perennial
Height: 14 to 24 inches
Site: Sun
Soil: Well drained
Growing Zones: 5–9

*Calamintha
grandiflora*

Calamint, originating in Europe and Asia, is one of seven aromatic herbs in the genus *Calamintha,* of which it is the showiest. Its leaves are similar to those of catnip—soft, light green, and serrated—but much smaller. By midsummer these leaves form a mat from which grow many square-sided stems bearing bright pink or magenta tubular flowers in 6-inch spikes. The plant exudes a fruity scent with the somewhat camphoraceous note of thyme and pennyroyal. Calamint was used as a medicinal tea in the Middle Ages to induce perspiration and loosen coughs and bronchial infections. Its Latin name is derived from *cala,* meaning "beautiful," a very apt description.

This delightful, little-known herb was sent to me by a woman in her 80s, a gardener of choice plants. I had no idea how to grow it—there is little information about it in herb books—but realizing it was a mint, I put it in the shade of my herb garden. Here it lingered for several seasons before joining all those ghostly herbs, the ones I have killed, in herb heaven. I now know with the wisdom of hindsight that calamint is a sun-loving herb from the sun-baked, rocky areas of southern Europe. The moral of the story is this: Just because an herb is a mint (or belongs to the Mint Family), do not automatically put it in the shade. In fact, in my experience, most mints thrive in sun.

While the calamint was with me, I thoroughly enjoyed it: an attractive leafy mound early in the season, a striking mass of bright bloom in mid- to late summer. For several seasons, I always potted up a few plants to winter-over indoors. Calamints make fine houseplants and provide enough fresh leaves for a very pleasant tea.

I know I shall grow calamint again, and this time around I'll give it the conditions it prefers so it will be always with me. I cannot think about my beautiful calamint without a twinge of regret.

Growing: Both seeds and plants are available, but sometimes hard to find. Among other sources, Well-Sweep Herb Farm in New Jersey and Nichols Garden Nursery in Oregon sell plants to US gardeners. Richters in Canada sells the seeds, which can be shipped to the United States. The seeds should germinate readily at 70 degrees in 7 to 10 days. Once the plant is established you can propagate calamint by making stem cuttings (see chapter 1) early in the season. Space plants 1 foot apart in sharply drained soil in full sun. Calamint is a short-lived perennial, but if growing conditions are favorable (dry and sunny) it should reseed itself. Cut the plants back during the season if they become leggy. Pot up a few plants to winter-over. This is best done 6 weeks before the first expected frost.

Using: Calamint is lovely in fresh or dried bouquets or dried for potpourri. To make tea, use 1 to 2 teaspoons of dried leaves per cup, or more for fresh leaves.

CALENDULA (Pot-Marigold)

Calendula officinalis
Asteraceae (Aster Family)
Type: Annual
Height: 1 to 2 feet
Site: Sun
Soil: Well drained

Calendula officinalis

Calendulas have been valued for their medicinal and culinary properties since at least the 13th century. Native to southern Europe, these are cheerful daisylike flowers, in colors ranging from pale yellow to deep orange, some with dark centers. The blossoms are borne on sturdy yet brittle stems with long, pale green leaves mostly at the bottom of the plant. A favorite of the cottage garden because of its ease of culture, beauty, and usefulness, it was called pot-marigold in the 19th century to distinguish it from the then newly introduced *Tagetes* genus that we now call marigold. Calendula flowers were steeped or dried to use in healing ointments and the dried petals sold by the ounce from barrels to flavor soups and stews. (Their sweet, salty flavor is enhanced by drying.) In pioneer times in America, the bright orange petals were used to color cheese and butter. The flowers yield a yellow dye.

Calendulas were among the few herbs that made an impression on me in the days when Jigs was growing them. They were planted by the back door and I couldn't help noticing them every day, so colorful against the white clapboards. But back then I did nothing with them.

When we moved to Canada and I began to grow herbs in earnest, I added calendulas to my plantings, but still I did nothing with them except to enjoy the sunny-faced flowers in fresh bouquets. It was not until I began creating herb products to sell under my "Jo Ann's Kitchen & Garden" label that I was motivated to explore their many uses: I add the dried petals to my popular Herb Salt and Herb Blend mixes (see *Lovage*); I use the dried flowers with stems in dried posies; the colorful small flower heads and petals go into potpourri; and I use the fresh flowers at workshops to demonstrate the basic process for candying flowers.

I also appreciate the landscaping value of calendula, a colorful and dependable flower that will bloom without interruption from early to midsummer (depending on when you sow it or if it has self-seeded) well into fall. The plants are remarkably frost-resistant.

I have tried several cultivars and have never grown one I didn't like. My favorite is the tall (18-inch) 'Pacific Beauty' with its large 3-inch flowers in a range of shades from the lightest and softest of yellows, through bright gold and apricot. Some flowers have a nice brown eye, barely noticeable in the more fully double blooms, but quite pronounced in the semidoubles (my favorite). I grow these elegant calendulas in my ornamental herb garden, a mixed planting of perennial herbs and flowers. I've grown the dwarf type in containers: 'Bon Bon', 'Patio Mix'. 'Touch of Red' comes in the exquisite 'Pacific Beauty' shades with the addition of an orange-red tinge on the reverse of each petal that also outlines the front of each petal, in striking combinations. For herbal uses, I grow 'Orange King' because of its large, double, deep orange flowers, and because it has so many petals on each bloom.

But there's nothing at all wrong with the little cottage-garden calendula: a more modest flower, to be sure, usually not much more than 1 foot tall, with pale orange- or yellow-petaled flowers about 2 inches wide, some with brown centers. If the named cultivars sometimes self-seed over many years, the cottage-garden type inevitably reasserts itself. There is a place for this calendula, too—useful as well as beautiful—in any garden.

Growing: The large, boat-shaped seeds readily germinate indoors or outside. For earlier bloom I sow seeds indoors 4 to 6 weeks before the last frost, where they germinate in 3 to 4 days at 70 degrees. (The expected time for germination is 4 to 14 days.) I sow the seed outdoors only when the soil has warmed, about the same time Jigs sows beans, and thin the seedlings 9 to 10 inches apart. In the fall, I save seeds of favorite types, usually the brown-centered ones, to ensure their reappearance next season. Calendulas will produce more flowers if the spent blossoms are kept picked, but leave some of the old blooms if you want to harvest seed or allow the plants to self-seed.

Harvesting: I pick flowers for drying all season, picking small, fresh flowers for drying whole, and older blooms for their petals, which are more easily removed at this stage. Whole flowers or petals can be dried on cookie sheets in a just-warm gas oven, occasionally stirred to prevent the petals from sticking together. When fully dried, I keep the petals in glass jars stored in a cupboard away from light. The whole flowers usually go right into potpourri, either my Orange Blossom mix or my Christmas Extravaganza. (See chapter 3 for basic potpourri instructions.)

Using: I mix dried calendula petals into herb seasonings for color and flavor, and into potpourri for color and texture. I use the fresh petals as an edible salad garnish, and the candied flowers and petals to decorate cakes, especially striking when combined with candied blue borage star flowers.

Candied Calendula Flowers

Pick fully opened fresh flowers after the dew has dried. Small flower heads can be left whole; otherwise, carefully pull petals apart. Brush flowers or petals with an egg white beaten with a little water, being careful to only cover, not saturate, them on both sides. Then sprinkle the flowers or petals with granulated sugar and set them on paper, turning several times until they are completely dry. Store dried flowers or petals in a waxed-paper-lined tin or box. It's advisable to use them soon after drying for best appearance and flavor.

CATNIP
(Catmint)

Nepeta cataria
Labiatae (Mint Family)
Type: Perennial
Height: 3 feet
Site: Sun
Soil: Well drained
Growing Zones: 3–8

Nepeta cataria

Catnip is native to Europe and Asia but has been naturalized in North America since colonial times. Before it blossoms it is a mound of soft, light green, scalloped leaves. As it matures and produces spikes of small white flowers, the leaves are more sparse, the plant dominated by the flowering stems. The soothing, calming effect of catnip on humans has long been recognized. The essential oil, nepetalactone, is very attractive to cats, who are excited by eating and rolling on the plants, thus releasing the aroma that intoxicates them.

We began growing and using catnip years before we moved to Cape Breton and I took over the herb growing. It has always been one of the three dried herbs we add to China tea (the others are lemon balm and mint), so naturally I raised it from seed our first growing season more than 25 years ago.

    For several years we enjoyed huge harvests, so large that I didn't have room in the house for all the drying bunches, so Jigs put up nails on one of our guest log cabin rafters and I hung some there. It was a mistake to take growing catnip for granted, though, because one spring it didn't return and that's when my troubles began.

You've probably heard the old saying, attributed to William Coles in his 17th-century work, *The Art of Simpling*: "If you set it, the Catts will eat it / If you sow it, the Catts can't know it." Well, Mr. Coles is wrong. I have sown it, I have set it, and it makes no difference. Our resident fleet of cats (8 to 10) always find it and destroy it. The male cats are the worst offenders. I've tried growing it in pots in the greenhouse all summer, but the temperatures are too warm and the resulting harvest too small.

Lately, I've had some success in establishing a few plants by placing some old rolled-up chicken-wire fencing (small mesh) right on top of them when they're small. They grow up right through the fencing and can be cut without disturbing the wire. So far, the cats have not found a way to get at the catnip, and we are enjoying moderate harvests once more.

I have always been attracted to the catmints, and one year I ordered the dwarf type, *N. mussinii,* for its aromatic mound of leaves and bright blue flowers. But my joy didn't last long. The plant was soon discovered by the cats and rolled on and chewed up. I have actually read that catmint isn't attractive to cats (which is why I thought I could establish it), but I can assure you, our cats thought it was dandy. I recently acquired the cultivar 'Dropmore Blue', which produces a mass of flowering blue spikes virtually all summer long. Having learned to foil our cats with wire fencing over the catnip, I applied the same technique to the mound of catmint, with great success. It is a lovely aromatic ground cover in sun or partial shade, among roses or in a bed of pastel annuals and perennials such as pinks, veronica, and hardy geraniums.

Growing: Catnip is easily raised from seed sown 6 to 8 weeks before the last frost at 60 to 70 degrees. The seeds should germinate in 7 to 10 days (mine take 3 with new seed). Outdoors, space plants 12 inches apart when transplanting. You can also sow the seeds outside, but since they won't germinate until the soil is warm, plants will have a late start. The catmints (except for named cultivars) can be grown from seeds like catnip.

Harvesting: Cut the plants back about 6 inches from the ground when flower buds are just forming. This way you'll get the cleanest leaves and leave something for regrowth. If the soil is rich and plants grow quickly, you may get a second harvest, but it's important not to cut back the plant severely late in the season, since it may not winter-over as well, or at all. This was probably why I lost my catnip planting years ago.

Processing: Catnip leaves contain a lot of oil, so they don't dry as readily if tied up in large bunches. Make the bunches smaller or, if the amount to dry is not very great, pull the leaves off the stems and dry them on cookie sheets in a just-warm oven. When the leaves are crispy dry, strip them off the stems (if dried in bunches) by running your hand vigorously down each stem. Store them in a jar away from light.

Using: We like to add dried catnip leaves to China or black tea in equal proportions with dried mint and dried lemon balm, about 2 tablespoons of dried herbs per quart of tea. These herbs, all calming, counter the stimulative effect of regular tea, creating a refreshing yet soothing drink.

CHAMOMILE
(German Chamomile, Annual Chamomile)

Matricaria recutita
Asteraceae (Aster Family)
Type: Annual
Height: 1 to 2 feet
Site: Sun
Soil: Well drained

Matricaria recutita

Annual chamomile, native to Europe and western Asia, is a sprawling plant with twice-divided, ferny leaves and masses of small, daisylike flowers— hollow, conical yellow centers ringed by numerous white petals. The characteristic pineapple flavor is most noticeable in the dried flowers. Both the annual and perennial chamomiles have been used medicinally for their sedative properties, mostly in teas to treat digestive problems, headaches, and insomnia. The perennial, or Roman, chamomile *(Chamaemelum nobile)*, was used in southern Europe, while the annual or German chamomile—so named because of its widespread use in Germany, where it grows as a wildflower—was used in northern Europe. When Roman chamomile was first introduced to the North, it temporarily supplanted the annual type, which has since become the medicinal herb of choice in Europe. It is probably the annual type that Mrs. Rabbit gave to her naughty son, Peter, after he had gorged himself in Mr. MacGregor's garden.

I don't remember when I first started growing chamomiles—both the annual and the perennial types. But I do know that I gave up on the perennial after several years of raising the plants without ever successfully overwintering them. Perhaps today, when I am a more careful gardener, I could better accommodate perennial chamomile's need for a sunny, well-drained site, but the annual type is easier to grow and often self-seeds. In any case, since I want chamomile primarily for tea, the annual has better flavor. If, on the other hand, I had any highfalutin notions about establishing a chamomile lawn or seat, I should certainly try the perennial form once more—but I don't.

I like to grow annual chamomile in the very front corners of my long harvest bed, where it can sprawl over the edges. The masses of little flowers have an ornamental value that is not diminished in the least by intensive picking during their season of bloom, because the more you pick, the more new flowers come right along. Self-sown plants are more substantial and bloom earlier than first-year plants (in mid- to late June here), but they also mature sooner and go to seed.

Growing: The dustlike chamomile seeds germinate in cool conditions, around 50 degrees, in 10 to 12 days. If I use fresh seeds, they usually germinate in 3 days indoors. I transplant the seedlings by small clumps since they are fragile and hard to handle when tiny. I thin them out as the plants grow on, and plant them out in the garden, either in small clumps or individually, spaced about 6 inches apart. Since I like to have a long period of harvest, I usually raise plants every year to extend the season with any self-sown plants that might be around. You can also sow seeds outdoors on the soil surface, but in my experience, these don't always germinate readily.

Harvesting: Harvesting chamomile flowers (without stems) is a ritual I associate with high summer and bright sun. I go out to the harvest bed about twice a week, or more if I can manage it, and gently pull off the flower heads—they snap off—and place them in my basket. The flowers should be dry, of course, and the petals just beginning to droop. Then I spread out the flowers on cookie sheets placed in a just-warm oven—if you have a gas stove, the pilot light is warm enough. Flowers dry in a day or so, after which they are poured into glass jars and stored in a cupboard away from light. To pour neatly, dump the flowers off the cookie sheet onto a half-sheet of newspaper, then form it into a funnel along the fold-line; in this way, the flowers will easily pour into the neck of any jar.

Using: It may seem as though you're getting very little for your efforts, since the flowers are so small, but a little bit of chamomile goes a long way. I mix 1 part dried chamomile flowers with 3 parts dried lemon balm for very nice flavor and a relaxing, soothing tea.

CHERVIL

Anthriscus cerefolium
Apiaceae (Celery Family)
Type: Annual
Height: 1 foot
Site: Partial shade/Shade
Soil: Well drained

Anthriscus cerefolium

A native of Europe and western Asia, chervil is a dainty plant with lacy green leaves and clusters of tiny white flowers. Under optimum conditions—cool shade—plants may spread out twice their height, to 2 feet wide. Chervil is associated with French cooking, especially in the combination of finely chopped green herbs known as *fines herbes,* traditionally used in egg dishes, soups, and in sauces for fish. The leaves have an anise-licorice flavor similar to that of sweet cicely.

Chervil is one of those herbs that I can live without, but every once in a while I remember that I haven't been growing it and I sow some seeds early in the season under the old apple tree near the pansy patch. It grows well there and is attractive in this setting. The only problem is that I have limited use for the fresh leaves (they doesn't preserve well), because Jigs hates anything that tastes like licorice except licorice.

One year someone from down-country gave us a packet of seeds for the latest in gardening fashions, called mesclun—a mix of lettuces and other greens that one sows thickly and eats in the baby stage. The idea didn't come as a revelation to us; we've been growing mixed greens like that for over 35 years.

Anyway, I gave Jigs the packet and he sowed the mesclun seeds with all of the other many lettuces we grow. Nothing came up, and we forgot all about it until the fall, when we discovered a thick row of dainty greenery, quite noticeable now with some of the other lettuces gone by. One snippet of leaf was enough to tell me that our fall lettuce crop was dominated by chervil, alias mesclun. Apparently, the chervil was the only kind of seed in that mesclun mix that was viable or vigorous enough to grow and thrive in our gardens. We had a good laugh over it, and I picked a little now and then to add to my morning eggs or, in small amounts, to our fall salads.

Growing: Sow seeds outdoors early in the season, just covering them with soil; chervil does not transplant well. Seeds germinate in 14 days at 55 degrees. Thin plants to 9 to 12 inches apart so they can spread their lacy leaves.

Using: Combine chervil with marjoram and chives or with parsley and chives to make a classic *fines herbes* seasoning, or use any similar combination of fresh herbs. Cut these up fine and add to soups, sauces, and butters. The butter is nice spread over fish while it is cooking or just after it is done.

CHICORY

Cichorium intybus
Asteraceae (Aster Family)
Type: Perennial
Height: 3 to 5 feet
Site: Sun
Soil: Well drained
Growing Zones: 4–10

Cichorium intybus

Although native to Europe and Asia, chicory has long been naturalized at North America's roadsides and in waste places, where it sometimes makes great stands of porcelain blue. An ungainly plant until it flowers, the stems are stiff with coarsely toothed leaves, sparse as they progress upward. The flowers are daisylike in form with ragged-edged, somewhat overlapping petals that give them a fringed appearance. Chicory has been used for food for millennia. The roots are used to make a coffee substitute; the greens are eaten both fresh and cooked; and special types known as witloof chicory or Belgian endive have been bred for indoor forcing. Chicory was one of the plants in Linnaeus's famous "clock garden," because its flowers predictably open in the morning and close in the afternoon.

Chicory has a very special place among my herbs, not because it is the most useful or even the most beautiful—although I do love its ragged blue flowers— but because it is one of the herbs that Jews are supposed to eat at the Passover Seder as a reminder of the bitterness of slavery in Egypt. It is also the only one of the five plants mentioned in the Talmud that is available to me in the season of Passover. At that time I go out to my harvest bed, sometimes pushing aside a layer of late snow, and look for the tiny, emerging, semifrozen leaves. The fact that in Israel the same plant is transformed in appearance from its early close-to-the-ground greenery to a hard stalk bearing tiny, bitter leaves—thus graphically illustrating to those who pick it the whole Exodus experience from sweet to bitter—does not detract from its importance for me. By eating a small amount of chicory, even in its early stages, I am linked to a tradition that grew from the land, that was created by the teachers of the time for ordinary people who could easily understand a lesson based on the growth habits of common weeds in everyday use. If you associate the phrase "bitter herbs" with horseradish, as I used to, please read the Horseradish entry for enlightenment.

On a more prosaic level, I have roasted chicory roots to use as a coffee substitute or coffee extender. Chicory gives a strong, pleasantly bitter taste to coffee without additional caffeine (in fact, it may even have a mild sedative effect), but preparing the roots is a lot of work. I have also forced the roots indoors for early greens. But the main reason I continue to grow chicory, aside from its role at Passover, is because of its pretty blue flowers, open every morning, closed by early afternoon or later on cloudy days. The flowers combine well with the scarlet bee balm in my harvest bed.

Growing: Sow chicory at the same time as lettuce, early in the season, and thin plants to 1 foot apart. The soil should be friable and deep if you intend to harvest the roots to make the coffee substitute. Such conditions will produce the desired long, thick white root, which looks like a fat, white carrot. The best variety for root growth is 'Magdeburgh'. Once established, chicory will self-seed from year to year.

Harvesting: To make a coffee substitute, harvest roots of first-year plants (older roots are woody and twisted). Scrub them clean and scrape them as you would carrots. Cut them into small to medium-sized pieces with a sharp, hefty knife (watch your fingers!) or use a food processor. Next, place the pieces on a cookie sheet and roast them in a slow oven (325 degrees F) until they are dark brown, not black. The last step is to grind the pieces to the consistency of coffee.

Using: I have no fancy ways to make coffee, but I think the following method makes a very tasty brew.

Jo Ann's Breakfast Mocha

Bring 2 cups of water to a boil in a covered pot. I use a small old-fashioned enamelware coffeepot, the kind used for camping. When the water boils, I throw in 1 coffee-scoop (3 tablespoons) measure of fresh-ground coffee beans, then generously top with ground chicory (a heaping teaspoon). The second the water comes to a boil again, I remove the pot from the heat. To serve, fill a cup with two-thirds brewed coffee-chicory and one-third rich cocoa (non-instant, made with creamy milk). This amount will make enough for 2 cups of Breakfast Mocha.

CHIVES

Allium schoenoprasum
Liliaceae (Lily Family)
Type: Perennial
Height: 1 foot
Site: Sun
Soil: Well drained, damp
Growing Zones: 3–10

Allium schoenoprasum

Chives, almost always referred to in the plural, are native to Europe and Asia. One of the most popular of all herbs, they are instantly recognizable even to those who are not herb enthusiasts. A mature plant is an impressive clump of numerous hollow green spears or leaves, among them stiff flowering stems topped by decorative mauve balls of tightly packed florets. The flower heads are visited by many bees in early summer. Chives have long been valued as a dependable bit of early-season onion-flavored greenery after the long winter.

Chives were one of the first plants to go into my Cape Breton herb garden. They were from stock we had originally obtained from a friend's garden in Vermont, and who knows where he got his? Extra clumps always abound wherever they are grown. I know very few people who actually raise chives from seed.

In Vermont, where garden crops thrived, I took chives for granted, allowing them to swell and increase as they liked, picking a few spears now and then to flavor salads. It was in Cape Breton that I first took serious notice of chives—not, however, as a useful or practical plant. I had set my heart on creating my first flower garden, but knowing little about growing ornamentals—especially in a harsh climate—I had dismally failed in my first attempt. The only plants to survive winter were the sturdy herbs, among them chives. Although disheartened by my failure, by the bare piece of ground where I had fondly imagined I would find a wealth of floral treasures, I was cheered by the early signs of emerging growth in the bright green tips that pushed through the cold soil. I kept my eye on the chives (not hard, since there was little else to observe) and saw them as if for the first time. I was thrilled and impressed when they bloomed—such delicately colored little globes atop blue-green foliage.

I haven't changed my mind about chives' ornamental value, but I have learned, through necessity, to exploit their other uses. Both leaves and flowers are picked early and often to flavor salads and my delicious homemade cream cheese; I also use the leaves and flowers in my Herb Salt and Herb Blend products. Fresh chive flowers go into our salt shaker to make an onion-flavored salt as well as into vinegar to make a beautiful rosy pink infusion; dried flowering stems are great for winter bouquets.

Chives abound in our landscape, but they are not superfluous. When clumps become too wide and unproductive, I chop out the extra growth and naturalize the clumps in our wetland area (formerly known as boggy ground).

There they enjoy the extra moisture, producing plentiful flowers with a rosier hue than those grown in drier ground. I always have some growing right outside the front door in a sunny corner garden, handy for quick picking. The rare, elegant white form—a natural variant given to me by Bernard S. Jackson when he was curator of the Newfoundland Botanical Garden—enjoys a prominent spot by a large rock in my ornamental herb-flower garden (former site of my first failed flower garden), backed by the taller, shrubby hyssop. I wonder now how I could ever have taken the useful and beautiful chives for granted.

Growing: I don't recommend growing chives from seed because it may take three seasons or more to get a reasonable harvest, and plants are widely available. Space plants 1 foot apart; divide every 3 years or as necessary, in spring or fall. If you harvest chives on a regular basis, be sure you enrich the soil with compost to encourage the production of many succulent leaves.

Harvesting: Cut small bunches of chives for daily use, close to the ground to stimulate new growth. Trim the ends and rinse the bunch before using. I usually pick from the back of a clump if it is in the front of an ornamental planting; in my harvest bed, created specifically for the purpose, I harvest from any part of the plant. If you want to use just the leaves, avoid the flower stalks; they are hard and undesirable for cutting. If I'm early enough, and flower stalks haven't yet formed, I cut the clumps to the ground, putting the leaves in a basket, and go from plant to plant on a sunny day until each one is entirely cut back. If I'm too late and the stalks have already formed, I include them in the cut bunches and sort them out later. Flowers for salad garnish or for making a cream-cheese spread are picked throughout the season, left whole or separated for salads, and always pulled apart for the cream-cheese spread. Flowers for drying (for bouquets) are picked when they are freshly opened, gathered into medium-sized bunches, secured with an elastic band, and hung upside down to dry. Flowers for flavoring vinegar are picked when freshly open.

On a nice sunny day in June I sit on an ancient steamer trunk on the front porch, and, while Jigs is mowing the front field with the team, I sort my basket of chives. First I gather up a good handful of leaves and trim off the ends so they are even and clean. I discard any damaged or discolored leaves, and if the flowering stems are included I pull these out by gently tugging on the flower heads with my free hand. As each bunch of leaves is sorted, it is cut up in small pieces with a kitchen scissors into a large bowl or pot. Eventually, all the cut-up chives will be transferred upstairs to drying racks where they dry in two days, retaining their green color and onion flavor (contrary to the negative views about drying). Eight plants yield about a gallon of dried chives, which are stored away from light in glass jars until mixed in with the other ingredients for Herb Salt (see *Lovage*).

After cutting up the leaves, I then turn back to the growing pile of flowering stems. Half of these are divided into smallish bunches (a small handful), bound by elastic bands, and suspended from the kitchen ceiling, where they are most decorative. They are dry when the stems are straw-colored, at which time some of the bunches are taken down and stored away from light in boxes until needed for dried bouquets or small nosegays. The mauve flowers dry to an attractive lilac color and blend well with other pastels as well as with the silvery leaves of lamb's-ears. The flowers from the remaining bunches are pulled apart (and the stems discarded) and stored in glass jars, as for cut chives, for later blending with other dried herbs. It's important to make sure the blossoms are thoroughly dried before storing or they'll mold in the jar (I speak from experience).

The other half of the flowering stems are used to make chive vinegar (see the following recipe).

Using: Chives, either fresh or dried, including the flowers, can be used lavishly with omelets, potatoes, soups, and stews. Add fresh chives (including flowers) to potato and egg salad (or any salad) and to cottage cheese. Fresh cut-up chives and broken flowers can be worked into cream cheese at room temperature, then chilled. This spread is delicious on whole wheat or rye bread. The fresh flowers can be broken up or left whole as a salad garnish. For a quick onion-flavored salt, put two or three fresh flowers into a salt shaker; these will very soon lend their oniony flavor to the salt. We keep a shaker on hand just for breakfast use with eggs.

Chive Blossom Vinegar

Pull flower heads from stems, inspecting them first for insects and shaking them out if necessary (I rarely find any). Place several good handfuls in a wide-mouth glass or plastic jar and pour white vinegar over them to cover. The ratio of blossoms to vinegar is not critical. The flowers quickly turn the vinegar a beautiful rosy hue and begin to transfer their delicate onion flavor to the vinegar. Adding more or less vinegar or chive blossom will determine the strength of the infusion. I have found that it is not necessary to entirely fill a container with flowers, as generally recommended, before pouring the vinegar over them, since this makes too oniony a vinegar. I use two good handfuls of blossoms to 3 quarts of vinegar.

I place the containers in our greenhouse, where they remain for about 2 weeks. Then I strain the infusion through two layers of cheesecloth into a wide-mouth stainless-steel pot and jar the vinegar in an assortment of clean, sterilized, narrow-necked bottles (salad dressing jars work well), which friends and neighbors save for me. The vinegar should never be in contact with metal lids, which will rust. I add a dash of Chive Blossom Vinegar to potato salad or use it instead of apple cider vinegar in my homemade mayonnaise or in salad dressing (½ cup olive or vegetable oil to ¼ cup vinegar).

GARLIC CHIVES (Chinese Chives, Oriental Garlic)

Allium tuberosum
Type: Perennial
Height: 2 to 3 feet
Site: Sun
Soil: Well drained
Growing Zones: 3–9

Allium tuberosum

Unlike regular chives, garlic chives are relatively unknown, both as an herb and as a landscaping plant. Native to Asia, it is called gow choy and widely used in cooking. The leaves of garlic chives are flat, wider than those of chives, and not hollow. The plant forms an attractive arching mound that sends up tall stems in late summer, each bearing umbels of white, star-shaped florets with a sweet, rather than garlicky, scent.

Garlic chives do not abound in gardens. I have never known anyone who had any to spare. In fact, I've seldom met anyone who grew them at all. When I decided to investigate garlic chives they were just a name, a reference, a picture in a gardening or herb book. I grew them from seed and waited impatiently for the plants to grow into a significant mound, to bear their lovely flowers. That took several years, but I was finally rewarded with a late-blooming herb that I would not want to be without. The low, arching, green-leaved mound is attractive all summer at the front of mixed plantings of flowers and herbs—even with low-growing hardy roses like the white-flowered 'Henry Hudson' (a rugosa hybrid)—where they rise up in late summer to make an impressive accent when one is least expected. Garlic chives are always greatly admired when they bloom. What are those pretty flowers? everyone wants to know. The question is, why aren't they grown more often?

I don't really know the answer, but it may be because they fall between being herbs and being perennial flowers. As the former, their virtues are not widely known, overshadowed as they are by common chives, which were introduced to North America from Europe in colonial times. Perhaps the modern interest in Oriental cooking will rescue garlic chives from obscurity. As perennials, they belongs to that large group known as "ornamental onions." Here, too, they are overshadowed by the more dramatic types with huge flowering globes, such as *Allium christophii,* with its 10-inch-wide head.

Wherever they are grown, garlic chives extend the blooming season, adding fresh flowers in late summer or early fall when they are most wanted. I value garlic chives more for their ornamental value, though, than their herbal uses. Perhaps I need to take a course in Oriental cookery.

Growing: Sow seeds indoors 6 to 8 weeks before the last frost; seeds germinate in about 2 weeks at 60 to 70 degrees. I set the seedlings in a coldframe, planted in small bunches about 6 inches apart. The next season, I plant the clumps out in the garden, spaced 1 foot apart. Garlic chives grow more slowly than chives in my experience. If you want to raise more seedlings, let some of the stalks go to seed; otherwise, cut them back after flowering.

Using: I occasionally use the leaves in salads for their garlicky flavor. The freshly opened flowers are cut for dried bouquets. The green seedpods are used in place of garlic, especially to flavor vinegars (no peeling necessary). But the truth is, I hate to disturb my plants at all. The answer is to grow a few in the harvest bed.

CLARY
(Clary Sage)

Salvia sclarea
Labiatae (Mint Family)
Type: Biennial
Height: 3 to 5 feet
Site: Sun
Soil: Well drained
Growing Zones: 5–9

Salvia sclarea

Clary, native to southern Europe, is a distinctive member of the extensive *Salvia* genus. The first year it produces a rosette of large, textured leaves up to 9 inches long, covered with a silky down. The following season the plant flowers in midsummer, sending up tall plumes of small two-lipped blossoms—white tinged with lilac—growing from rose-colored bracts. The whole plant exudes a strong, musky aroma. Clary's grape-scented essential oil is used in perfume, where it is a fixative for other scents. The seeds are mucilaginous when soaked in water and were once useful for treating sore eyes, hence the common name clary, shortened from "clear-eye."

Clary is a beautiful plant that comes and goes in my garden. Such is the nature of biennials if you don't keep a close watch on them—in other words, if you fail to raise new plants every season and if the second-year plants don't reseed themselves. Sometimes seedlings succumb to winter and there follow two years without any clary in bloom. Then how sorry I am that I didn't take precautions and raise another generation of first-year plants.

Although I don't do very much with clary, I like having this plant around. I enjoy its odd, musky aroma while I'm working in the garden, brushing against its tall plumes and releasing their strong scent. It is a magnificent flowering herb for landscaping, with beautiful leaves all season long—in first- and second-year plants—and its wonderful musk-scented flowers in high summer. Clary makes a dramatic statement wherever it is grown, either as a solitary accent against a large rock in full sun—in imitation of the way it grows in its native habitat—or as part of a border planting of mixed herbs and flowers, among soft pink mallows and purplish pink wild bergamot. Clary's downy leaves give it resistance to drought, an asset in dry conditions.

Growing: Seeds germinate readily indoors 10 to 12 weeks before the last frost date at 60 degrees in 4 to 5 days. The furry seedlings should not be overwatered or they may rot. Plant seedlings outside just after the last expected frost, spacing them 1 foot apart or more, since clary is a substantial plant in maturity. The site should be in full sun with sharply drained soil that is on the dry side. Such conditions will encourage clary to raise another generation on its own.

Using: If I can bring myself to do it, I sometimes harvest some of clary's flowering stalks to add to potpourri. The musky scent is not overwhelming. In fact, it blends the other scents together and helps to prolong the combined aromas.

ANNUAL CLARY (Painted Sage, Purple-Top)

Salvia viridis
Type: Annual
Height: 1 foot
Site: Sun
Soil: Well drained

Salvia viridis

Like its biennial cousin, annual clary is native to most of the Mediterranean region, but it is quite different in appearance. A slender, vertical plant with showy, veined top bracts—usually dark purple, but sometimes pink or white—it bears tiny, insignificant flowers that grow from the leaf axils. Annual clary has no scent and is valued today mainly as a dried flower. At one time its seeds were used in the same way as the biennial clary, hence its common name.

I first grew annual clary from seeds of Park Seed's pink cultivar 'Pink Sundae', sent to me by Gertrude Foster, the well-known herb authority and author of *Park's Success with Herbs* (Geo. W. Park Seed Co., Inc., 1980). I used to be a regular contributor to her magazine, *The Herb Grower,* which at one time was the only source of information in North America about herbs. Any recommendation from Bunny, as she was known to her friends, was enough to stimulate interest in a plant, so I sowed the seeds with great confidence in the outcome. But I was not yet a seasoned gardener and I squandered the seedlings, virtually sentencing them to death among the rich growth of my herb and flower garden, where they were overshadowed by vigorous neighbors. Because the plants did not receive the sun they need to thrive, they failed to reproduce themselves by casting their seeds on the ground for the next season; thus 'Pink Sundae' joined many other worthwhile herbs in my own herb heaven.

It was not until my first trip to Israel, several years later, that I was inspired to try growing annual clary again. There I saw annual clary in its native habitat, growing among the brilliant flowers of the annual spring carpet: deep orange calendulas, blue and violet anchusas and bugloss, rosy flax, bright yellow crown daisies, and chamomile.

My first attempt at growing it again, from seeds sent to me from Israel, was unsuccessful. As I recall, the seedlings did not thrive and were plagued by slugs. Next, I ordered seeds and began to have great success once the seedlings were planted in a drier, sunnier, exposed situation, like that in my harvest bed, where they began to self-sow from year to year. I suspect that the commercial seeds I bought were the result of selection of the wild purple type and its pink and white variations, and better suited for North American gardening conditions than were the Israeli seeds.

Although still not widely available, seeds of annual clary are not as rare as they once were. (Thomas Jefferson grew this plant, so it has been around a long time.) I've grown the tricolor mix and the white cultivar 'White Swan', as well as 'Claryssa', a shorter, more compact form with broader bracts. I grow the purple or blue type in my harvest bed so I won't mind cutting the top bracts for drying (they dry to a navy blue). I grow the pink and white types up front in my herb-flower garden, where they fill in empty spots left by spring tulips, and where they are not overshadowed by taller plants. For best effect, annual clary should be grown in groups of at least five plants, where they will give a bright spot of color and interest all summer and well into the fall.

Growing: Seeds should be sown indoors 10 weeks before the last expected frost at 70 degrees, when they will germinate in 4 to 12 days. I sow seeds close to the surface, just covering them. Plant out the seedlings 6 inches apart after the last expected frost. Once you have found the best place for them—in full sun with well-drained soil—they will self-seed from year to year, but only if there is sufficient bare ground in their vicinity. I save seeds of the pink and white annual clary since these are not as vigorous as the purple type. In any mixed planting, this color form always dominates and crowds out the others.

Using: I cut the stems when the tops have their brightest color, gathering them in bunches bound with an elastic band. These are hung from the kitchen ceiling, decorative before they are even added to winter bouquets, where they are very striking when used with pastel tones. I also add the dried purple tips to lavender potpourri for their color.

COMFREY
(Blue Comfrey, Knitbone)

Symphytum caucasicum
Boraginaceae (Borage Family)
Type: Perennial
Height: 3 feet
Site: Sun/Partial shade
Soil: Damp
Growing Zones: 4–9

Symphytum caucasicum

Two species of comfrey are most often grown in herb gardens. Both are native to Russia and the Caucasus and both are vigorous plants that develop deep root systems. Their leaves are hairy and rather coarse, the main stems quite large (as thick around as your thumb), succulent, and lax. The flowers—especially those of blue comfrey—are very showy, typical of the Borage Family: pink buds that open to a multitude of dangling blue bells. The flowers of the other comfrey, *Symphytum officinalis,* are dusky rose, and the whole plant is rangier in appearance. Comfrey was most commonly used to help heal broken bones, hence its old folknames, knitbone and boneset. It was the center of controversy several years ago when it was discovered to be carcinogenic if taken in large amounts, so its internal use (as in teas) has since been discouraged.

Just before we left Vermont to move to Cape Breton, the herb writer Adele Dawson stopped by to return a favor. We had given her a root of Jigs's elecampane and now she was giving us comfrey, the blue-flowered type, to take to our new home. It was a wonderful present, an enduring beautiful herb that always elicits favorable comment, usually along the lines of "I didn't know comfrey was so pretty." (It isn't if you grow the dusky rose one.)

The late Mrs. Dawson's comfrey was an early resident of my herb-flower garden. A vigorous plant, as wide as it is tall, it has to be controlled, not only because it crowds out smaller plants but also because it sprawls in a great arc, bent from the weight of its many bell-laden stems. I prefer control to banishment, however, for it is so beautiful in early summer under the old apple tree, paired with the white-flowered sweet cicely, and attracts the attention of hummingbirds and butterflies.

Comfrey provided me with one of my first lessons in naturalizing. This is the art of returning plants to their favored habitat to grow more or less without human interference. Comfrey enjoys growing in moist conditions, so I chopped out extra growth in early spring and soon established attractive clumps in wet areas where nothing else would grow (though over the years I've discovered other showy herbs and flowers that thrive under these conditions). Jigs once planted my extra roots in the turkey yard for feed (some types of comfrey are used as fodder) but the turkeys ate them to death. This must be the first time in recorded history that comfrey met its match and succumbed. Apparently the deep roots that would have ensured its survival had not yet developed.

Of all the herbs we have fed to our livestock (surplus and cut-back plants), comfrey is the overwhelming favorite. Animals don't really go for highly aromatic plants. Sweet cicely leaves are trod upon, releasing their refreshing licorice aroma, but they are not eaten. But comfrey, harvested in great quantities after its month or more of bloom, quickly disappears in the chicken coops and pigpens, causing the animals no discernible ill effects.

We have never consumed comfrey ourselves, even in its heyday as a miracle cure for what ails you, but we do add heaps of it to the compost pile, where it adds nutrients and minerals.

Growing: Start with a piece of root. You'll probably only need one, for very soon you'll have more than you need. Plant it in moist, even damp soil, in sun or partial shade. Mature plants in rich soil will need to be staked. For this reason, try to keep plants manageable by chopping out unwanted growth every other year or even every year if necessary.

Sometimes, plantings need to be drastically reduced. To do this, take a sharp spade, place it alongside the plant, and jump on it with all your might. Do this around each side of the plant, making a square. Pull out all the growth you can. You may not get the entire root—it is very deep and becomes woody—but you will get enough to tame comfrey for the season. Discard woody roots and replant the youngest growth. After flowering, cut plants back to the ground. Soon new growth will appear, an attractive mound of tapered, fresh green leaves.

Using: Add comfrey to the compost pile and use as a mulch (remove any seed heads first). I have developed a foot soak featuring comfrey, a popular item at craft sales and in gift stores.

Jo Ann's Kitchen & Garden Herbal Foot Soak

Combine 1 part dried comfrey stems, leaves, and flowers; ½ part dried mint leaves; and ½ part dried mugwort leaves and flowers. Put 2 tablespoons of the herb mixture into a large tea bag, open at one end. (Tea bag and cellulose suppliers are listed in the Sources section at the back of this book.) To each bag, add 1 teaspoon baking soda and ¼ teaspoon lavender-scented cellulose (see chapter 3). Iron the open ends of the bags together using the COTTON setting of your iron.

Use one bag to a foot tub of water. Pour boiling water over the tea bag and let the water cool to very warm. In my experience, this combination of dried herbs, baking soda, and lavender oil relaxes and soothes sore muscles. Adding dried and ground comfrey root to this mixture makes it even more attractive.

CORIANDER
(Cilantro, Chinese Parsley)

Coriandrum sativum
Apiaceae (Celery Family)
Type: Annual
Height: 1½ to 2½ feet
Site: Sun
Soil: Well drained

Coriandrum sativum

Coriander, which is native to southern Europe and Asia, has been known since ancient times. It's a sun-loving, graceful plant with lacy foliage and dainty, light pink flowers borne in small umbels. The distinctive seeds—round, ribbed, or striped, and drying to a beige color—mature quickly on the rapidly growing plant. The whole plant has a pungent aroma; when crushed, the seeds have a sweetly spicy scent that comes from the inner heart of the husk. In warm-climate countries, the young leaves are traditionally used for flavoring, while in the north, the seeds are more frequently used. The seeds are also reputed to have digestive properties when infused in teas. "Coriander" describes the whole plant and its seeds; "cilantro" refers specifically to its leaves.

Since I only need a few tablespoons of coriander seeds to flavor our homemade pastrami (we only make it when we've raised a steer), I don't always plant it. But it self-sows easily, and I am always pleased to notice the little lacy-leaved seedlings. Coriander grows on its own with virtually no attention, very happy as long as it is in full sun. It is a pretty plant, especially when its dainty, clustered flowers are all in bloom, appearing as if from nowhere, fast-growing and -ripening. The large seeds dry on the plant and are easy to harvest.

Gradually, I have found more uses for coriander seeds: I crush some for potpourri and I gather enough to sell under my "Jo Ann's Kitchen & Garden" label. Coriander is a great plant for the novice herb grower because its seeds are easy to handle, germinate well, and virtually never fail to produce fast-growing seedlings.

I have to admit that I haven't joined the ranks of cilantro-lovers. I don't find the leaves pleasant smelling and, with so many choice flavoring herbs around, I haven't been motivated to explore their culinary possibilities. In those cultures where cilantro is highly valued, the young leaves are pickled, stir-fried, and used in soups. In Thai cooking, even the roots are used. Friends talk knowingly about adding cilantro to salsa, though I have to admit that I have never made salsa.

Still, I enjoy what coriander offers me—an attractive flower for the front of the harvest bed and seeds for the taking.

Growing: Coriander must be one of the few seeds planted with their husk. Plant in ½-inch-deep holes in early spring when temperatures are still cool, when, say, you plant lettuce. Thin plants to 3 to 4 inches apart. If you intend to use the leaves, you'll need to make successive sowings, since plants grow fast and quickly go to seed in warm weather.

Using: Add leaves to dishes shortly before they are done cooking, since the flavor quickly dissipates. Add the seeds, crushed or whole, to meat dishes, sauces, and curries, as well as to potpourri.

COSTMARY
(Bible-Leaf, Alecost)

Chrysanthemum balsamita
(also *Tanacetum balsamita*)
Asteraceae (Aster Family)
Type: Perennial
Height: 3 feet
Site: Sun
Soil: Well drained
Growing Zones: 4–9

Chrysanthemum balsamita

Costmary is a seldom grown aromatic herb native to southern Europe and western Asia. It was once highly regarded for its medicinal properties in treating liver and stomach disorders and for flavoring, clarifying, and preserving ale (the origin of one of its folknames, alecost). Costmary grows from a creeping root that produces pointed, tapered leaves up to 12 inches long—apple green and edged as if with a pinking shears—with a refreshing balsam, lemon-mint taste and scent. Leaves decrease in size and quantity as the stem grows up during the summer. In areas where the growing season is long enough, small buttonlike yellow flowers, ½ inch across, appear at the top of the plant. The folkname costmary comes from the Latin *costus,* meaning "fragrant root," combined with Mary, a reference to the herb's use in easing childbirth. The colonists used it both for a tea they called "sweet Mary" and as an aromatic bookmark in church, from which use it gained the name bible-leaf. Some authorities say the leaves were chewed in church to keep the parishioners awake.

I got a root of costmary from Henry, a man in his late 70s who briefly lived on our backland peninsula several years ago. First he established himself in a shack by the roadside, then he planted a series of raised beds that contained a magnificent collection of old-fashioned flowers and herbs. These, Henry said, were his friends, the plants of his New England youth, the very same plants his parents and their neighbors had grown in the early 1900s. He called costmary by the New England colonists' name, "sweet Mary," but he no longer remembered what it had been used for.

Costmary is one of those herbs that fell out of favor in the modern era because their uses were tied to a vanished age. Nor is it particularly valued for landscaping. Since there is little reliable information about growing costmary, it took me a couple of seasons to figure out its needs. I learned that in rich soil and less than full sun, its growth is confined to a multitude of leaves on a sprawling plant. In full sun, it's more upright in habit. I have not yet learned how to use it to advantage in the landscape, so I confine its growth to the harvest bed, where I can pick its leaves as I need them, and where they make a pleasant mound of soothing greenery. I have heard that costmary makes a distinctive fall flower if massed against a fence, but this will occur only if the site is in full sun, the soil lean and dry, and the growing season fairly long (Zone 6 southward).

Once I realized what costmary had to offer, however, I did not worry about its inability to flower in my landscape. What I want are the leaves, lots of them, especially the young, fresh ones early in the season that grow close to the ground. These are the largest, most unblemished ones, and they lie perfectly flat, just right for aromatic bookmarks. Costmary leaves are an important ingredient in my herbal skin freshener, a product I developed after reading about the reviving properties of aromatic vinegars in Gail Duff's *Natural Fragrances* (Storey, 1989).

Since I always try my products before I sell them, I have had ample opportunity to prove its efficacy. I use my costmary skin freshener at haying time when we are working in the hayfield, usually under very hot, humid conditions. Who do you think is atop the load—pitchfork in hand, protected by a large straw hat, rising higher and higher toward the sun? I keep a little bottle handy, and after each load is stored away in the haymow (my job is to drive the horse who powers the old pitching machine), I dab myself with Herbal Skin Freshener before we head out to pick up another load. Just as the old-timers drank the vinegar-based drink, switchel, to revive them in the field, I am renewed by the judicious application of aromatic vinegar scented with Henry's old-fashioned "sweet Mary."

Growing: Costmary is grown from rhizomes spaced 1 to 2 feet apart in late spring or when the soil has warmed. For leaf production, plant in enriched, well-drained garden soil in full or partial sun. Aphids may appear in midseason, but their damage is mainly cosmetic. If necessary, use a soap-based spray: 1 teaspoon dish detergent and a few drops of oil (I use vegetable oil) to 1 quart of water. If the stems are kept cut back for leaf production, there is less chance of infestation.

Using: Although I mainly use costmary leaves to scent skin freshener, I also add dried leaves to a potpourri I call Orange Blossom (see the recipe below), the fresh or dried leaves to tea (either with China tea or infused alone—1 to 2 teaspoons dried or a small handful fresh for 1 cup), and pressed leaves to scent letters and notes.

Herbal Skin Freshener

Put the following in a wide-mouthed glass or plastic jar: 1 part each costmary, mint, and southernwood sprays (trim these with a small clipper, since branches become woody), plus ¼ part citrus-scented marigold flowers and leaves. Pour cider vinegar over the herbs and set the covered jar in the sun for at least 2 weeks to allow the herb scents to be infused in the vinegar. Strain through two thicknesses of cheesecloth and pour into narrow-necked jars, *diluting half and half with water,* and taking care not to let any metal cover come in contact with the solution. Use plastic wrap under the lid if necessary. I like to add a perfect costmary leaf, upside down, to each bottle of freshener. To use, pour a little on a cotton ball and dab behind the ears, on the forehead, or on the wrists; or add 2 tablespoons to a basin of warm or cold water, dip a facecloth in the solution, wring it out well, and apply to the forehead, being careful to keep the freshener away from your eyes; or add ½ cup freshener to bath water.

Orange Blossom Potpourri

1 cup daffodils (mixed types, yellow and white)
1 cup calendula flowers and petals
1 cup costmary leaves
1 cup scraped and dried orange peel, coarsely broken
4 tablespoons corn cellulose or 3 tablespoons orrisroot (cut, not powdered)

1 to 2 teaspoons essential oil (mixed or alone, as you prefer): lemon, sweet orange, and/or sandalwood. Use the larger amount of oil with the cellulose.

Flowers and leaves must be crispy dry. Prepare quartered orange skins by scraping all the white pith from the skin; place the scraped skins on a cookie sheet and dry in a just-warm oven (under 200 degrees F). When dry, break up into smaller pieces as desired. Add the essential oil to the fixative (cellulose or orrisroot) in a jar that is large enough to allow you to shake the mixture vigorously at least once a day for three days to blend. Put the dried flowers, herbs, and orange peel in a 2-quart container with a tight-fitting cover (a crock or plastic tub), add the fixative-scent mixture, cover securely, shake well, and let stand for at least 2 to 6 weeks before opening. Every other day, gently shake the container, turning it upside down, then right side up to help distribute the fixative-scent throughout.

GARDEN CRESS (Peppergrass, Curled Cress)

Lepidium sativum

UPLAND CRESS (American Cress, Scurvy Grass)

Barbarea verna
Brassicaceae (Mustard Family)
Type: Annual/Biennial
Height: 16 inches to 2 feet
Site: Sun
Soil: Well drained
Growing Zones: 3–9

Lepidium sativum

Garden cress and upland cress are fast-growing greens alike in both appearance and flavor: slender and sprawling, with finely divided, spicy or peppery-tasting leaves, similar in taste to watercress *(Nasturtium officinale)*. Widely distributed throughout Eurasia and naturalized in North America, both types are used in many countries for their edible leaves, seeds, and roots.

We have grown cresses ever since we had a vegetable garden, since Jigs likes to try new salad-type plants. Along with our ever-expanding lettuce patch—up to 27 varieties each season—we have always had a row or two of the cresses, usually planting two crops a summer, since the plants quickly go to seed. When I make my salad selection among the rows of beautiful and varied looseleaf and soft butterhead lettuces, I always pick a small handful of cress—usually thinnings, since virtually every seed germinates.

Garden cress, the more popular of the two plants, is available in two forms, one featuring curly leaves ('Fine Curled', 'Extra Curled'), the other flat leaves ('Reform Broadleaf'). While their flavor is identical, the curled type is faster growing, ready to harvest in 25 days or earlier from planting time; broadleaved cress is ready for picking in about 32 days.

The advantage of upland cress is that it is somewhat slower growing (35 days from seed to harvest), can be grown indoors as a potted plant, and in some areas it winters over. Both types readily self-sow.

Growing: Sow seeds outside early in the growing season when temperatures reach 60 degrees, just covering them with soil; the seeds germinate in 7 to 10 days. The cresses quickly bolt in hot weather, so make successive sowings every 10 days for a continuous supply of young leaves all season. Mature leaves, not as desirable, have a stronger, hotter flavor. To enjoy salad sprouts all winter, sow seeds thickly on a well-moistened paper towel folded in half and placed in a pan or dish, then covered with plastic. Seeds will germinate in about 2 days, after which uncover the sprouts and move them (still in their dish) to a sunny window and keep them moist. Eat them when they are about 2½ inches long.

Using: Cut young leaves all season for salads, garnishes, and sandwiches (great stuffed into pita bread), or to use as a substitute for parsley. The small, white, peppery-tasting flower heads can be harvested, too. Add stems of the finely cut leaves to fresh bouquets; add the dried, straw-colored stems with their emptied seed disks to dried bouquets, either combined with other everlastings or—most striking—by themselves.

DANDELION

Taraxacum officinale
Asteraceae (Aster Family)
Type: Perennial
Height: 6 inches to 1 foot
Site: Sun
Soil: Well drained
Growing Zones: 2–9

Taraxacum officinale

The familiar dandelion, native to Europe and Asia, is naturalized throughout the temperate regions of the world. Growing from a hard taproot, its leaves are long and jagged, from which characteristic comes the French folkname, *dent de lion,* or "lion's tooth"—hence, dandelion. All parts of the plant are edible and have been used as a source of food for centuries, especially the young leaves, which were thought to be a restorative (they're high in vitamin A). The bright yellow-rayed flower heads are made into wine; the roots, when roasted and ground, are used as a coffee substitute (like chicory); the juice of the root has been used to treat diabetes and liver diseases.

The humble dandelion, bane of the suburban lawn-tender, has had a major role in my life. It was the inspiration for my first article, "Spring Salad," published in *The Herb Grower* magazine in the late 1970s, then the only source of information about growing and using herbs. Edited and published by Gertrude and Philip Foster, the magazine was a labor of love for all concerned. There were no ads and none of the contributors was paid, but for me it was a priceless education. In becoming a regular contributor, I strove to find something new and interesting to say about useful plants. Not easy when Gertrude Foster—a highly respected herb authority—had already covered so many of them and always from a different perspective. Her writing was based on keen observation of the plants from seed to maturity, combined with a wide knowledge of herb history. She also maintained a large and varied correspondence with other knowledgeable people all over the world, who contributed articles, too. These articles are well worth rereading today for their wealth of reliable information and insights. The basic *Herb Grower* approach to the subject of herbs was characterized by a sober, earnest, high-minded seriousness, qualities that soon became obsolete in the swinging decades to come.

"Spring Salad" told precisely how to find, harvest, clean, and prepare dandelion greens. This may seem unexceptional, but in the wake of Euell Gibbons' *Stalking the Wild Asparagus* (Alan C. Hood & Co., 1984), there was a spate of articles conveying the idea that food-gathering is a lark. Perhaps it is if you do it once and don't have to depend on it for feeding yourself or your family. Specific directions in these odes to "the supermarket of the swamps" were glaringly absent. My knowledge about harvesting food from the wild was hard earned, based on necessity. I was well aware that readers of, say, *The New York Times* were not about to forage for their food, but I thought that if they ever did attempt to gather dandelion greens, it would be a more enjoyable experience if they went about it the right way. This first article was later reprinted under the title "Dandelion Times" in a back-to-the-land publication. With the *Herb Grower* contribution, it launched my entirely unforeseen career as a writer.

In the late 1960s in northern Vermont, digging for dandelions was still a spring ritual, motivated by the age-old longing, in countries where winter is severe, to add a bit of fresh greens to the table after a prolonged diet of stored vegetables. In our area, women could be seen in the green fields in classic images of harvesting, their bodies bent, their arms reaching down to the earth. The greens they dug with a sharp knife and carried home in paper bags were boiled with a piece of salt pork, a dish savored by country folk. This tradition—with deep roots in the past—has now vanished along with the world that gave it life.

For us the spring ritual of digging for dandelions is still very much alive, providing us with something green and fresh after the stored cabbages give out in late spring. We have no greens or salad material from the garden until sometime in June, and then not in any great amounts. Dandelion greens, by contrast, are reliable—there's never a crop failure—and always abundant.

Like most weeds, dandelions flourish in rich soil. I look for them wherever the ground is deep, porous, and humusy: among the mulched rows of cultivated berries, and in all of the gardens—vegetable and flower—in early spring before they are weeded for the first time. If we find a good patch in a garden area, we sometimes cover it with a basket to blanch the leaves (this makes them less bitter).

Some years, for one reason or another, I find myself still gathering dandelion greens late in the season when most plants have developed a flower bud;

this is usually the time to stop harvesting them because they are too bitter (after all, there's a difference between piquantly bitter and unpalatably bitter). At this time of year, I look for plants among the lush growth of grass or weeds in neglected areas. Dandelions growing in these conditions are less mature and slower to develop buds because of competition from the surrounding vegetation. When you have unexpected guests for dinner, only a small amount of garden or hotbed lettuce ready to pick, and no store handy, you learn to make do with what's at hand. And discovering just what is "at hand," even in the familiar confines of your own backyard, can be a lifetime's work.

Even if we did not depend on them to supplement our diet, I suspect I would go in search of dandelion greens anyway, eager to taste again the bittersweet fresh leaves that we have come to associate with the flavor of spring.

Harvesting: Take a stout, sharp butcher's knife and plunge it straight down next to the young green leaves until you reach the crown of the plant. Cut across, slicing the crown from the root, but leaving the dandelion bunch intact. It is very important to harvest dandelions in bunches in order to facilitate cleaning. Shake out each bunch as you cut it to loosen dirt and debris. Now you will have a dandelion head, joined at the crown with a little tip of root. You'll be surprised how much of the bunch is growing just beneath and in the soil. A few green shoots might be part of a large bunch, half buried in the loose soil. Harvested in this way, it should not take more than 5 minutes to gather enough heads for a good bowl of salad, with enough greens left over for another meal or two. If you find a lot of desirable bunches and want to preserve them for a week to 10 days, place them—with a bit of root and the soil that clings to it—in a bucket, stored in a cool cellar. After being freshened by soaking in cold water, the wilted leaves will be ready to use.

To harvest greens in late season among grasses and other weeds, gather together in one hand the long leaves of a single plant and cut them off from the crown with a sharp knife. An abundance of these leaves can be stored in the refrigerator for about a week.

Using: Trim off roots, and brush off excess dirt and dead leaves. Submerge bunches in a dishpan of cold, clean water. Swish each bunch vigorously through the water and transfer them to clean water, swishing each bunch again; repeat the process twice more or until the wash water is clean. Trim off crowns and transfer leaves to clean water. Taking several leaves at a time, swish and transfer to the last clean water. Drain. This whole process should not take more than 5 minutes. The long leaves cut off the crowns late in the season are cleaner and only require a few washings. This is easiest to do by submerging hand-held bunches in clean water, repeating as necessary.

To prepare for eating, trim off stem ends and squeeze, then shake, handfuls of leaves to extract all the water. Don't be afraid to squeeze hard; they're quite resilient. Cut the leaves in bite-sized pieces.

Spring Salad

SERVES 2

This is a zesty salad with pronounced flavors that go very well
with our homemade cottage cheese.

To 3 or 4 handfuls of prepared dandelion leaves add the following: a small handful of sorrel leaves (the cultivated type), a small handful of young lovage shoots (the red tips just emerging from the ground), a few sprigs of chervil and parsley (potted from last winter), and onion slices in desired amounts. Serve this with cottage cheese and a simple oil-and-vinegar dressing: ½ cup olive or vegetable oil mixed with ¼ cup vinegar (homemade dill vinegar is nice).

Wilted Dandelion Salad

SERVES 2

When the leaves are too bitter to eat fresh, we always make this delicious main-course dish. Fry several slices of bacon; drain and dice when they're cooled. Fry 3 or 4 medium potatoes, boiled and cut into bite-sized pieces, in the bacon fat (as much as needed). When the potatoes are browned, stir in 2 cups prepared dandelion greens, 2 tablespoons chopped chives, 1 tablespoon vinegar, 2 hard-boiled, chopped eggs. Serve at once.

DILL
(Dill Weed)

Anethum graveolens
Apiaceae (Celery Family)
Type: Annual
Height: 3 feet
Site: Sun
Soil: Well drained

Anethum
graveolens

A European native and a familiar plant in North American gardens, dill is synonymous with "pickles." It also has a long history of use, especially in seed form, in settling digestive problems. A tall, rather gawky plant with thin, hollow stems and feathery foliage, dill bears 6-inch-wide umbels of tiny, bright yellow flowers in midsummer, followed by numerous flat, ribbed seeds. The mature plant in bloom has a certain grace and striking presence. All parts have the characteristic dilly flavor so prized for flavoring foods. When the leaves are called for in any recipe, they are referred to as "dill weed."

I can't recall any of our vegetable gardens, spanning almost 40 years, that did not have at least one row of dill. We add the thinnings to salad, and as the plants grow up and up, we snatch handfuls of flowers with stems and leaves for the first dill pickle crock of the summer—always Jigs's great moment in the kitchen. It was he who sought the best recipe from among many and tested each one over several seasons. It was he who, with characteristic panache, packed the stubby pickling cukes in one of our old crocks, adding spices and garlic with great flair, topping off the whole with fresh grape leaves, and adding a stone weight to press the cukes into the brine.

But it is I who still hold the record for dill pickle production. Faced with an enormous harvest of small green tomatoes many years ago, I canned them all in one afternoon, jar after jar—50 half-gallons—each with a healthy sprig of dill.

When I began making herb products for sale, I became more interested in growing and preserving dill. While we still maintain a row in the large lettuce patch, I now grow two kinds in the harvest bed, so I can dry quantities for use in my Herb Salt (see *Lovage*). I grow the familiar tall 'Mammoth', which self-sows from year to year, as well as the relatively new dwarf 'Fernleaf', 18 inches tall and slow growing so the leaves can be harvested over a long period. An All-America Selection winner, 'Fernleaf' dill is an attractive, dark green bushy plant that forms flowers late in the season. Just as the traditional tall type in bloom makes a handsome accent in the garden, dwarf dill is an attractive edging plant.

Growing: To get dill started in the garden, sow seeds outside after all danger of frost has passed, just pressed into dampened soil about 6 inches apart or closer. Pull the young plants to use in salad until the remaining plants are spaced about 8 inches apart. If you're cramped for space, grow the dwarf type, which takes up less room. Make another sowing in midsummer for fresh dill into the fall.

Using: Chop the green leaves into salad, or work a small handful into creamed butters to pour over cooked fish, potatoes, and peas. To make the all-purpose dill vinegar, fill wide-mouthed jars with leafy stalks and flowers and cover with cider vinegar. Let steep for several weeks or longer until the desired flavor is achieved. Strain and bottle.

I cut handfuls of green leaves all season and dry them on screens out of direct light. When crispy dry, I stuff the dried dill weed in jars and store them in a dark cupboard. To use, grind the dill weed to a powder (this is a top note in my Herb Salt) or rub between your palms and use the resulting flakes just as you would fresh dill weed.

Jigs's Dill Crock

One 4-gallon stone crock or plastic pail (nothing metallic)
1 bunch dill, as big around as your forearm and about as long
3 tablespoons mixed pickling spices
3 to 4 large grape leaves, plus additional to cover crock
1 pound salt
1 pint cider vinegar

Spread 3 or 4 grape leaves in the bottom of the crock, cover with dill, and sprinkle with the pickling spices. Fill the crock with 3- to 4-inch-long cucumbers (or small green tomatoes), putting in whatever quantity you have. Cover with a brine made by dissolving 1 pound of salt in 2 gallons of water and 1 pint of cider vinegar. Do *not* heat the brine.

Cover the contents of the crock with more grape leaves and set a weighted plate on the surface to keep the cucumbers submerged. Place the crock in a warm kitchen and skim off any fermentation scum daily. The pickles will be ready to eat in about 2 weeks.

ELDERBERRY
(American Elder)

Sambucus canadensis

Sambucus canadensis
Caprifoliaceae (Honeysuckle Family)
Type: Perennial shrub
Height: 8 to 12 feet
Site: Sun/Partial shade
Soil: Prefers well-drained loam
Growing Zones: 3–10

The native elderberry is very adaptable, growing from Nova Scotia to Florida and Texas under very different conditions. Long, arching, green-leaved stems give it an attractive vaselike shape, adorned by midsummer with wide clusters of tightly folded, tiny white flowers that sweetly scent the air. By late summer the fruits are mature—small, round, and dark purple—and very attractive to local birds. The name "elderblow," often seen in older recipes, refers to the elderberry's blossoms. Both the native American and the European species *(S. nigra)* have a long history of use. Virtually every part of the plant has at one time been used: to treat a variety of ailments from dropsy to dog bites, to yield dye, to flavor wines and jellies, to supply wooden taps to catch maple syrup, or to make wooden whistles to amuse children.

We established a bank of elderberries adjacent to the farmhouse 25 years ago. I soon learned to turn the fruit into jellies, jams, and sauces (a favorite on pancakes). With the development of Jo Ann's Kitchen & Garden, I found even more uses for this accommodating, old-fashioned shrub. I began with the sweet flowers, using them first to lighten pancake batter and to flavor gooseberry jelly. Then I began drying the blooms for tea. Elderflower-Mint Tea, one of my most popular herb teas, is a traditional home remedy to treat colds.

Most recently, I discovered that the old, dry stems can be easily broken off to use as a gentle prop for weak-stemmed, floppy garden flowers. Branchy stems are best—unobtrusive, yet effective in their support when simply thrust into the ground where they are needed. I also use the supports to keep vigorous plant growth at bay when it threatens to overshadow more delicate types, for instance, long monkshood stems shading lilies. When they are no longer wanted, the elderberry props are broken up and added to the kindling box. The shrub used to be called "nature's medicine chest," in reference to its wide-ranging healing attributes, but I call it "the everything plant" because it supplies just about everything I need from its flowers, fruits, and wood.

Even if it were not so useful, I value the elderberry's decorative form in the landscape. One of the most attractive plantings was sown by the birds: an arching shrub that rises every year by the side of the barn, the white flowers brilliant against the aged gray barn boards. Along with the birds, we rush to gather the fruits as summer draws to an end.

Growing: Although elderberries will grow under almost any conditions, they thrive in well-drained, loamy soil. A single shrub is attractive in a garden setting; a massed planting on a southern slope is beautiful, especially in bloom. Dig holes deep enough to accommodate the roots, which should be presoaked in a bucket of water before being planted. Water each hole, then place the plant in the center, spreading out the roots. Fill and cover the hole with soil and tamp the earth firmly into place. Water again slowly. Next, lay down a thick ring of mulch at the base of the plant: first a layer of compost; then a layer of paper or cardboard; finally, a top layer of straw or rotted sawdust. This mulch will give the plant a good start in life, and it need not be renewed if the soil is fairly fertile. To maintain fertility, add a bushel of rotted compost or manure around the bush at its drip line (where the branches extend) every season. Every few years, or as necessary, the whole shrub should be cut back almost to the ground to encourage fresh, vigorous growth.

Harvesting: Pick the umbels when most of the flowers are open to flavor wines and jellies, or to use as a flour substitute. For tea, pick the umbels with a little stem when most of the flowers are open, but still fresh. Lay them out on a screen away from direct light and turn occasionally until crispy dry. You have done a good job if the florets have retained their creamy white color. Strip the flowers from their stems and pack away in containers placed in a dark cupboard.

Harvest the berries to make jellies, jams, and wine when the clusters are dark purple. Using a pair of kitchen scissors, cut the clusters, along with about 3 inches of the main stem; or snap off the clusters from the bush by hand. The berries are easier to remove from the clusters after they have been frozen.

Elderflower-Mint Tea

This is a soothing drink for relief from cold symptoms—or just nice to have on a cold winter afternoon.

1 heaping teaspoon dried elderflowers
1 heaping teaspoon dried mint (peppermint, spearmint, or apple mint)
1 cup boiling water

Put the dried elderflowers and mint leaves in a tea ball and place it in a teacup. Add boiling water to cover and let steep only a few minutes. The herb mixture can be used again. Sweeten to taste with honey if desired.

Elderflower Pancakes

Elderflowers, when combined with buttermilk, make melt-in-your-mouth pancakes, delicious with fruit sauces or maple syrup. You can lighten any bread, roll, or muffin recipe with elderflowers by substituting 1 cup of florets for 1 cup of flour. The flowers are delicately sweet.

1/2 cup fresh elderflowers
1/2 cup unbleached all-purpose flour
1/2 teaspoon baking soda
2 tablespoons sugar
1/2 teaspoon salt
1 tablespoon cornmeal
1 egg
2 tablespoons melted butter
1/2 to 1 cup buttermilk

Shake off florets from the elderblow (flower heads) into a container and set aside. Sift together the flour, baking soda, sugar, salt, and cornmeal. In a bowl, beat the egg well and stir in the melted butter and ½ cup buttermilk, mixing only until the flour is blended in; do not overstir. Gently stir in the elderflowers and add more buttermilk until the batter reaches the desired consistency, like thick cream. Ladle batter onto a hot greased griddle and cook the pancakes until nicely browned, turning once.

ELECAMPANE (Horseheal)

Inula helenium
Asteraceae (Aster Family)
Type: Perennial
Height: 6 feet
Site: Sun
Soil: Moist
Growing Zones: 3–8

Inula helenium

Elecampane is an Old World plant known since Roman times and used to treat both humans and animals, especially horses. In the New World it was also prized as a medicinal. Before 1914, the United States imported 50,000 pounds of elecampane roots annually, principally to use in veterinary products. An odd-looking plant with enormous downy basal leaves—light green and tapering—by midsummer it is transformed. No longer an ugly duckling, it has become a striking plant, with thinly rayed, golden yellow sunflowers blossoming atop its tall, stout stems.

This memorable herb was one of the first that Jigs grew many years ago, attracted, no doubt, by its odd name and later by its odd appearance. Our plantings today are all descended from the original seed-grown plant.

Although I don't use it, except to add the flowers to potpourri for texture, it would be unthinkable not to grow elecampane. Any herb garden worth its name must have at least one specimen to honor its place in herb history.

For many years I grew it in my herb-flower garden, just under the old apple tree, but as it slowly expanded it got in the way of the redesigned garden.

Now it grew just at the point where the new path gently rounded the bend, and by midsummer it obstructed all movement in and out of the garden. It had to be moved.

If you have never moved a deep-rooted, woody plant that has been in place for many years, be forewarned: It's a difficult job and hard on the back. I became so annoyed by the obstinate roots that I swore elecampane would be banished forever. I threw the hardened mass behind the house, where I temporarily store plants with no home. It continued to sprout leaves and grow, and, what is more interesting, the roots exuded a sweet, heavenly scent. How could I bring myself to throw away this plant?

All the lore I had read about elecampane root—its use in treating wounds in humans and horses (it has proven antiseptic qualities), its use as a cough medicine and a candy—came back to me in the sweet, overpowering smell of the roots. This was a new dimension altogether of a plant I thought I knew. And all this time, its claim to herbal fame was resting beneath the soil.

Needless to say, I did not allow the roots to die. I chopped off a few eyes (pieces with growing shoots) and replanted them by the bridge that leads to one of our log cabins. It thoroughly enjoys growing on its own, putting down its deep roots in the damp soil, sending up its stout stems unimpeded, blooming freely in midsummer with the wild, tiny, white-flowered sneezewort (*Achillea ptarmica*) in billows at its feet.

Only lately have I noticed that there are tamer *Inula* types for the garden, and I mean to try them, especially *Inula orientalis*—which grows to only 2 feet, with the same spidery yellow flowers that I like. Sounds more tractable, but it will never entirely supplant the real thing.

Growing: Place elecampane where you're sure you want it, so you won't have to move it. It will grow in dry soil, but grows best in deep clay loam on the moist side. Where summers are hot, it's best to provide partial shade. Plant 2-inch roots that have a bud or eye, covering with soil and watering until new growth is apparent. In the right place, it can be left indefinitely. In my experience, elecampane does not need staking, despite its height.

FEVERFEW

Chrysanthemum parthenium
(also *Tanacetum parthenium*)
Asteraceae (Aster Family)
Type: Short-lived perennial
Height: 2 to 3 feet
Site: Sun/Partial shade
Soil: Well drained
Growing Zones: 3–9

Chrysanthemum
parthenium

Feverfew is an Old World herb at home in the New World as a roadside weed. At first glance it bears a striking resemblance to chamomile, but on closer inspection there are several differences. Like chamomile, feverfew produces masses of bloom, but in sprays rather than as individual flowers. Although feverfew flowers are also daisylike, the white rays are short and stubby, the golden centers wide and flat. The whole plant—even the tiny seeds—has a medicinal, though not unpleasant, scent. The name feverfew is a corruption of the French *febrifuge,* from the Latin *febris,* meaning "fever," and *fugere,* meaning "to chase away." Feverfew has a long history in treating fevers and headaches, and was once known familiarly as "the housewife's aspirin."

I became interested in feverfew when Bernard S. Jackson, now retired curator of the Newfoundland Botanical Garden, sent me the seeds of the double white version, a natural variant of the single daisy form. This one came with the description 'Flore Pleno', signifying an old-fashioned, fully double flower. Unlike the modern types bred to grow as dwarf, compact bedding plants— these are usually listed as annuals under *Matricaria* in most catalogs—the old-fashioned double feverfew is a rangier plant that can grow to 3 feet, is smothered in pure white pompons for most of the summer, and is always listed as a perennial, under either *Chrysanthemum parthenium* or *Tanacetum parthenium,* in herb sources. The plant is available from Well-Sweep Herb Farm and Nichols Garden Nursery. Seeds or plants of the single, daisylike form are more widely available from herb nurseries.

Contemporary research suggests that feverfew can reduce certain kinds of migraine headache. There are pill preparations available and, of course, there is the living plant, whose leaves are said to be effective if nibbled every day (one or two). Since I don't suffer from migraines, I've never been tempted to try this prescription, but I do find feverfew, both the single and double types, soothing in the landscape. They fill in after spring bulbs leave bare spots; they look lovely under old roses; and they blend clashing colors, reds and orange, creating harmony from strife. In this sense, feverfew is very much "the gardener's aspirin."

Growing: There's a trick to growing feverfew, since it's a short-lived perennial. Unless adequate drainage is assured, it may disappear over the winter. On the other hand, it can become a pest, self-sowing with abandon where conditions are encouraging: dryish soil, warm temperatures. I never take feverfew for granted, so I raise a new crop of the single- or double-flowered form almost every season. Extra plants are easy to give away, sell, or grow for Jo Ann's Kitchen & Garden seeds. Sow seeds about 8 weeks before the last frost indoors at 70 degrees. In my experience germination occurs—even with old seed—in 4 days or less. Where summers are very hot, give seedlings a little shade, space plants 1 foot apart, and cut back after the first bloom to encourage another round. Take divisions or root cuttings in the fall or spring by cutting off new basal growth with a little heel from the main stem, and replanting it in well-drained soil. After two seasons the mother plant becomes woody and will probably die of old age. Look for seedlings in its vicinity.

Using: Cut fresh flowers for bouquets all summer; this will spur the production of more flowers. One of the most charming bouquets I ever saw was Olive Jackson's combination of the double white form with deep orange calendulas, a pairing worth repeating in the garden. The double white feverfew also dries well for use in winter bouquets.

HOLLYHOCK, BLACK HOLLYHOCK

Alcea rosea; A. rosea nigra
Malvaceae (Mallow Family)
Type: Biennial
Height: 6 to 12 inches
Site: Sun
Soil: Well drained
Growing Zones: 3–10

Alcea rosea

The giant single-flowered hollyhock, a fixture of the classic cottage garden, arrived from the East centuries ago. A true biennial, it forms a mound of lobed green foliage the first season, and a tall, stout stalk the second season that bears many five-petaled, trumpet-shaped flowers in a range of colors: pinks, purples, white—some with darker eyes. The reds and yellows are the result of hybridization with other species. Like other members of the Mallow Family, the hollyhock plant contains mucilaginous substances in all of its parts, preparations of which were once used to prevent miscarriage and dissolve coagulated blood. The black hollyhock, *A. rosea nigra,* was once used as a food dye, to color wines and teas.

Once upon a time, many years ago, we rented a hillside farm in northern Vermont for $10 a month for two years. It was here that I first saw true, old-fashioned hollyhocks, growing in the rich ground below the old barn, against a stone wall. I vowed then that when we owned a farm, I would grow hollyhocks just like that.

Fate decreed that I should live on a remote peninsula, where the winters are long and rough and the soil is heavy and cold—not promising conditions to grow hollyhocks, or much else, for that matter.

My first attempts ended in failure; plants did not reappear the second season. I gradually learned that this was due to the collection of moisture on their root crowns, which caused the fleshy taproots to rot. This is the most common cause of failure in growing hollyhocks. In my explorations of old gardens in the area, though, I got used to finding stands of hollyhocks growing on their own, long after they had been abandoned. This is because they were planted in a favorable habitat, often near a house foundation, on a dry slope, or anywhere the soil provided proper drainage.

Having thus learned their growing secret from the hollyhocks them-selves, I achieve success by always providing them with the right conditions, either in raised beds or in areas where I know the soil drainage is better than usual.

Tracing local plants back to the early 1900s, and collecting their seeds, I discovered the black hollyhock as a stunning variant that turned up one year from some of the plants I raised from these seeds. I soon noticed that the black hollyhock was being offered by a few seed houses as a new discovery, and today, while still not common, it is being grown across North America. It was, in fact, introduced about 1850 and, according to her own plant lists, it was grown in Celia Thaxter's island garden (made famous by the paintings of Childe Hassam) off the coast of New Hampshire.

One day, while carrying the flower heads indoors to dry for potpourri, I saw that the color, a very dark purple, was bleeding from the damp flower. I began adding it to herb teas, where it not only lends its rich wine color, but also seems to make a more soothing blend.

Lately, I have begun to explore the landscaping possibilities of the black hollyhock in particular. (Wherever the other hollyhocks are planted, they create an instant cottage garden.) I have been working on a black garden by the front door, where the tall towers of wide-open shiny black ruffled flowers (deep maroon, truth to tell, but black in bud) provide a background for tubs of "black" basils ('Dark Opal' and 'Purple Ruffles') as well as green, with the charming black *Viola* 'Black Crystals' adding a diminutive counterpoint. Add a few shades of pink and rose to this mix (poppies, yarrow) and you have a satisfying, not at all depressing, black garden.

Growing: Sow seeds in the summer in prepared ground, thin the seedlings to 1 foot apart, and then, in the early spring of the following year, move them to their permanent quarters, spacing them 2 feet apart. Hollyhocks self-sow with abandon, but if you want to preserve certain colors and not be overrun with the dominant pink, take root cuttings in the fall by cutting a daughter plant from the base of the mother and replanting it where you want it to grow. I do this as a matter of course each year with the black hollyhocks, to ensure their dark color has not been altered by bee activity. Seed-sown plants tend to be variable.

Using: I pick hollyhock flowers for potpourri for their pastel shades, laying them out on a cookie sheet and drying them in a just-warm oven. I store the black flowers separately to add to herb teas. I created a sensation at a late-summer herb workshop by serving a chocolate-frosted cake decorated with candied hollyhock flowers, pinks and white. Use the same process as described for calendulas, candying individual petals, then reassembling them in flower form, or candying the whole flower, being sure to press it flat.

HOP VINE
(Hops)

Humulus lupulus
Moraceae (Mulberry Family)
Type: Perennial
Height: 20 feet
Site: Sun/Partial shade
Soil: Well drained
Growing Zones: 3–9

Humulus lupulus

The fast-growing European hop vine is widely naturalized in North America, having been brought by the early settlers, who used it not only for preserving and flavoring beer, but also for making barm to raise bread. A vine that grows by twining, it virtually leaps up before your eyes from ground level each season. Even without flowers it is decorative, especially when draped over an arbor. Plants that produce female flowers, as distinct from those that produce male flowers, are most desirable. The cone-shaped blooms appear first in light green clusters, gradually turning chartreuse, then bronze, at which point they open partially. This is when they contain the greatest amount of orange powder—the hops for flavoring—deep within the flowers' papery layers. Hops are said to have a soporific effect and are used to stuff "sleep pillows."

The hop vine was originally of interest to me as one of the plants grown by the Scottish settlers on our peninsula. As Ann Leighton observed in writing about the American settlers, "Hops would seem to rank somewhere with the domestic cat as an indispensable adjunct to any household" (*Early American Gardens;* University of Massachusetts Press, 1986). I found ample evidence of this phenomenon here, where one hop vine has been traced back 120 years, having originated in Cape Breton and survived a move to Newfoundland.

We became attached to hops when we grew it up an old World War II parachute line by our repair shop. The vine is taller than the shop wall, so when it hits the end of its support it grows sideways, framing the door with graceful abandon. The showy flower clusters are an added bonus. Although the hop vine was supplanted in the 1920s by tamer climbing plants, such as clematis, its ease of culture and value in beermaking and crafts continue to recommend it to gardeners interested in vigorous and useful plants.

Growing: Hop roots producing female flowers (these are the type usually sold) should be planted in the fall or early spring in well-drained, enriched soil, spaced 1½ feet apart. Give the vine support in its early growth by training it to an arbor, high trellis, or post—the way it was traditionally grown here. Without support it makes a fine ground cover for waste places in the landscape. Cut it down in the fall and clean up all the debris (it makes good compost) to discourage insects from overwintering. The hop vine is sometimes afflicted with spider mites and other chewing insects. Try a strong hosing of the foliage regularly, or spray once a week for three weeks early in the season—when damage is apparent—with an insecticide.

Using: To use hops in beermaking, gather the flowers when they begin to open and you can see the orange powder at the base of the petals. Any book on beermaking will give you directions, but they are unnecessarily complicated and may discourage the novice. For a 5-gallon batch of beer, Jigs makes an infusion as follows: In a 1-gallon pot, cover 2 quarts of fresh hop flowers with water. Cover and bring to a boil, and simmer for 10 minutes. Pour the liquid and boiled hops through cheesecloth into the wort. Then tie the cheesecloth into a bag around the remaining hops and let it float in the beer while it is fermenting. The dried flower clusters, in their light green stage only, dry well without shattering. These are very attractive in dried bouquets and wreaths.

HOREHOUND
(White Horehound)

Marrubium vulgare
Labiatae (Mint Family)
Type: Perennial
Height: 2 feet
Site: Sun
Soil: Well drained, dry
Growing Zones: 4–9

*Marrubium
vulgare*

Native to Asia and Europe, horehound has become naturalized in dry, warm areas of North America. The stems and curled leaves are covered with down, which gives the plant a somewhat fuzzy and gray-green appearance. Flowers are small and nondescript, growing in whorls at intervals along the stem. The whole plant exudes a bitter, aromatic odor when crushed. At one time, barrels of dark brown horehound cough drops were commonly sold in drugstores, but if you want to experience their soothing properties today, you must make your own.

Horehound is an old resident of my gardens and one of those herbs that Jigs grew first. He is still the one who makes horehound candy, an operation he undertakes at least once a year. I continue to grow horehound for use as well as delight—I like the wrinkled, downy, silvery green foliage, and I keep the plants trimmed and bushy. It provides a handsome accent at the front of a garden, a counterpoint to bright, colorful flowers.

When I was first in Israel, overwhelmed by all the beautiful herbs I saw growing there as roadside weeds, I noticed other downy-leaved plants similar to horehound and learned that they were species of *Ballota,* the false, or Greek, horehound. Some *Ballota* species have been introduced to North America in recent years. All of these types thrive in dry, rocky soil, protected from drought conditions by their wooly stems and foliage. It's a wonder that I can grow even the common horehound, considering that I live in such a cool, damp climate with heavy, cold soil.

I have never grown silver horehound, *M. incanu,* which is reliably hardy to Zone 5 or 6 with protection. Silver horehound is considered a more orna-mental plant than the common type, with similar medicinal properties. It was introduced to North American gardens by the late Helen Fox, a pioneer in growing and using herbs. This type is highly sought for dried flower arrangements, because of its showy green calyces.

Growing: Plants are easily raised indoors from seeds sown at 70 degrees about 8 weeks before the last frost. I have not found it necessary to stratify (prechill) seeds, as is sometimes recommended. Plant seedlings 10 inches apart in full sun and sharply drained soil. Horehound will not survive the winter if the ground is the least bit soggy.

Harvesting: Cut back stems before they flower. Hang up bunches to dry, then strip off the dried leaves and store away from light in a jar until needed.

Using: Horehound cough drops are soothing for bronchial congestion and sore throats, but we enjoy them even when we're feeling fine. The following directions are adapted from the well-worn pages of Euell Gibbons' classic *Stalking the Wild Asparagus.*

Jigs's Horehound Candy

Jigs doesn't change the proportions even when using the stronger-flavored
dried leaves because he really likes the candy's bittersweet flavor.

Simmer 1 cup fresh or dried leaves in 1 cup water for 10 minutes; strain out the leaves. Add 2 cups of sugar to the infusion and boil, uncovered, until the mixture spins a thread when dropped into a glass of cold water (the hardball stage in candymaking). Immediately pour contents into a buttered pan and cut into small squares before it hardens. Store the candy in a covered jar. If moisture condenses, remove the cover. The candy can also be used in tea in place of sugar.

HORSERADISH

Armoracia rusticana
Brassicaceae (Mustard Family)
Type: Perennial
Height: 2 to 3 feet
Site: Sun
Soil: Moist
Growing Zones: 4–10

Armoracia rusticana

Horseradish refers to the root of a homely herb that is native to colder regions from eastern Europe to western Asia. Until the Middle Ages it was primarily regarded as a medicinal plant to use in compresses for relieving pain and to treat kidney complaints. It is better known today as a pungent condiment, preserved in vinegar and eaten with meat or fish, or added to salad dressings and sauces.

Horseradish literally led me down the garden path to discover the fascinating world of biblical flora. As a returning Jew, a *ba'alot teshuva,* I began to celebrate Passover again after a lapse of many years. With my interest in herbs, I naturally focused on the bitter herbs of the Passover Seder, eaten in memory of the bitterness of slavery in Egypt as recorded in the Book of Exodus.

I wasn't satisfied with using horseradish, which is pungent rather than bitter, and does not accord with the phrase "bitter herbs," suggesting green, leafy plants. My quest to find the true bitter herbs, *maror* in Hebrew, led me to the work of Nogah Hareuveni in Israel. His parents, early pioneers, had set out to find the identity of many plants that had eluded scholars over the centuries. They determined that the bitter herbs are five common weeds whose growth cycle mirrors the Children of Israel's experience in Egypt. The weeds, among them common chicory, emerge in the winter as soft green leaves growing close to the ground, but by Passover in Israel they are transformed in appearance, with a hard central stalk from which sprout a few small, very bitter leaves. This is the time—when they are virtually inedible—that they should be eaten at the Seder. The Hareuvenis relied on the observation of the ancient Jewish sages to unravel the mystery of *maror:* "See this bitter herb, whose beginning is sweet, whose end is bitter, thus were the Egyptians . . ." (Talmud, Pesachim 39, 1). Here we have the whole Exodus experience compressed in a few words, five common weeds that tell the same story.

With this insight from the Hareuvenis' work, from my isolated farm in the wilds of Canada I traced the history of the bitter herbs, inseparable from the history of European Jews. Living in cold, northern climates, they could not find the required bitter lettuces and greens, and so, over many decades and centuries, adopted an herb that brings tears to the eyes, is always available, and is indestructible: horseradish!

We did plant horseradish roots once upon a time, but after a session of hand-grinding them to use, we neglected the plants, which nonetheless persist to this day. (Be forewarned: Horseradish is vigorous and invasive.) If we wanted larger roots, we would have to cultivate them again, giving them richer ground. But we prefer to take our chances, digging up roots from "the wild" (at the edges of the garden) as we need them, from late summer through fall, mainly to make Jigs's wonderful sauce.

Growing: Work organic matter into the soil and loosen it well to encourage the growth of long, straight roots, just as you would for growing carrots. In the spring, plant 1/2-inch-thick roots, cut in 6-inch pieces, 2 inches deep. Thin plants to 12 inches and harvest the first-year roots in the fall.

Using: Wash and peel the roots; cut them into small pieces and chop them in a food processor, adding a little white vinegar to help get the procedure started. I use a Cuisinart minichop, both the sharp and blunt blade, and the slow and fast speed in short pulses, processing a handful of cut roots at a time—whatever it takes to chop the horseradish to the desired consistency.

Pack 1/2-pint jars two-thirds full, add 1/2 teaspoon salt, and just cover with white vinegar. The ground horseradish sinks in the jar, and you may find you have added too much vinegar. Just pour off the excess when you want to use the ground root or pour it off after the mixture has settled.

Jigs's Mother's Sauce

Jigs never had a recipe for this, concocting it when need arose from memories of his mother's sauce for shrimp and other shellfish.

1 to 2 cups catsup, preferably homemade
1/2 cup fresh or preserved horseradish
Dash of tabasco sauce (or to taste)
Juice of 1/2 lemon

Stir all the ingredients together, season to taste, and let the mixture blend for an hour before using. Serve as a dip with shellfish or on salad, bread—just about anything.

HYSSOP

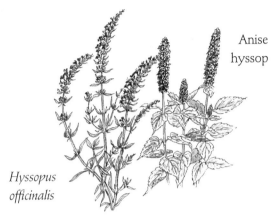

Anise hyssop

Hyssopus officinalis
Labiatae (Mint Family)
Type: Perennial
Height: 2 to 3 feet
Site: Sun
Soil: Well drained, dry
Growing Zones: 4–7

Hyssopus officinalis

Hyssop is a plant of European origin, despite being routinely confused with the Middle Eastern Bible hyssop (*Majorana syriaca;* see Za'atar), a species of marjoram. European hyssop is a subshrub with numerous slender stems and small narrow leaves, covered with small, dark, purple-blue flowers in midsummer here, very attractive to bees. The whole plant has a pungent aroma, once described as mildly skunky, an apt association. It has a history of medicinal use to treat coughs.

Hyssop is one of Jigs's early discoveries and I took it with me when we moved to Cape Breton. It was one of a handful of plants that survived my early efforts to grow "all flowers," and convinced me, by its splendid show of striking flowering spikes, of the ornamental properties of many herbs.

One of the most interesting aspects of hyssop is its strange history as the false hyssop. It is symbolic of the Westernization of the Bible, that is, identifying biblical flora in Western terms. Once I became involved in studying biblical flora, I realized that each plant or group of plants mentioned in the Bible lives in a context that is grounded in the daily life of the ancient people and the ecological relationship between and among growing things. Every time I see a reference to European hyssop as the hyssop of the Bible, I am reminded of how casually we dismiss this rich literature, not realizing it has a connection to a living land and a living people.

Despite its being an interloper among plants of the Bible, I admire this hardy shrub with its odd scent, and use it mainly for landscaping. I grow it at the front of my herb-flower garden by a large rock, a remnant from the old rock pile on which this garden was built. Ironically, the biblical hyssop also "grows from the rock," or between the sides of rocks, where it finds enough moisture to thrive even in the desert—thus its origin as a symbol of modesty, requiring little to survive. European hyssop also enjoys its rock in my garden, where it benefits from the stored heat as well as extra moisture, especially in periods of drought.

Growing: You can grow hyssop from seeds or roots. Barely cover seeds with soil and keep temperatures at 60 to 70 degrees. Germination time in the literature is 14 to 42 days, an assertion I can't verify, having always grown hyssop from rootstock. Space plants 2 feet apart or closer to make a striking hedge. (This is a good idea, especially if you have a hard time growing lavender.) In hot climates, provide hyssop with partial shade. Even in the hotter summers in our northern climate, hyssop looks very unhappy and produces fewer flowers. If clipped back it may bloom again in the fall. Hyssop will survive harsh winters provided good drainage is assured. Clip back woody stems in the spring to encourage fresh growth; divide plants in spring or fall. Several worthy cultivars are available with pink and white flowers, as well as a dwarf form.

LADY'S MANTLE

Alchemilla vulgaris
Roseaceae (Rose Family)
Type: Perennial
Height: 1 to 2 feet
Site: Sun/Partial shade
Soil: Moist
Growing Zones: 3–9

Alchemilla vulgaris

This native of Europe is an elegant plant, beautiful in foliage and in flower. Leaves are cloak-shaped (hence the common name) and softly pleated, catching glistening dew and raindrops in their central folds. Flowers appear in loose, delicate clusters, creating clouds of frothy chartreuse nearly all summer. Lady's mantle was once widely associated with female disorders and is still highly regarded by contemporary herbalists. The Latin name, *Alchemilla,* meaning "little magical one," is apt, whether describing the plant's medicinal or its physical properties.

I don't know where my lady's mantle came from, but I love it, though I have never used it medicinally. It is an invaluable landscaping plant because it is low growing, has lovely leaves and flowers, and, in my experience, will grow well in sun or partial shade if the soil is moist. When we redesigned my herb and flower garden under the old apple tree, I planted lady's mantle as I had always wanted to, as a low-growing hedge in dappled shade. Here the airy flower sprays spill over the path, leading me gently from the shade to the light at the front of the garden, now that the obstructing elecampane has found another home.

There are other species and cultivars, all variations of *A. vulgaris,* several of them dwarf types that would be effective as a front-of-the-bed edging, in a rock garden, or grown as a low-maintenance, attractive ground cover.

Growing: Lady's mantle is usually grown from roots. These can be planted in the fall or spring, spaced 1 to 1½ feet apart, the closer spacing if you want to create a hedge. Cut back plants after blooming to encourage a fresh growth of leaves and to maintain the plants' vigor; divide as needed. Lady's mantle increases rapidly, but is easily controlled by pulling out unwanted seedlings.

Using: Cut flower sprays for fresh bouquets, or dry them for winter crafts: bouquets and wreaths. Infusions of the leaves are used in compresses for inflamed eyes. Other cosmetic uses as a skin tonic and cream for rough skin are worth exploring. For further information, consult *The Complete Book of Herbs,* by Lesley Bremness (see Bibliography).

LAMB'S-EARS
(Woolly Betony)

Stachys byzantina
Labiatae (Mint Family)
Type: Perennial
Height: 18 inches
Site: Sun
Soil: Well drained
Growing Zones: 4–9

Stachys byzantina

Native to Europe and Asia, the betonys are also commonly known as wound-worts because of their ancient history of healing. Among other attributes, their roots make an acceptable tobacco substitute and yield a yellow dye. Lamb's-ears is distinguished by its low-growing mat of furry, silvery gray foliage, producing wooly flower spikes in early summer that are stuffed with tiny, bright, rose-colored florets

My first attempts to grow this desirable silver-leaved plant came to grief. I planted purchased roots in the wrong place (moist shade), where they quickly succumbed over the winter. Then a gardening friend gave me roots from plants he had from another gardening friend, and thus, through the gardener's network, I obtained a vigorous variant that proved well suited to our climate and soil conditions. No matter where I plant lamb's-ears now, in sun or shade, in moist or dry soil, it lives.

Like the folk or cottage gardener of North America with a limited pool of plant material, I exploit whatever will grow in my difficult conditions. I use lamb's-ears, as I do lungwort, to edge and frame gardens, to draw attention to the planting within, and to keep weeds from intruding. Just as lungwort is best suited to partial shade, lamb's-ears does best in full sun, its wooly leaves protecting it from drought conditions. I let it grow around gardens in exposed sites, often near walkways, where it can insinuate itself among stones as a sort of ground cover, more pleasant to look at than the weeds that sow themselves in such tight spots. When it threatens to take over, it's easy to pull out.

My massed planting on a bank is very effective for keeping the weeds at bay in an area that is hard to mow, providing a splendid, low-growing contrast to the pink and scarlet hues of old and new roses planted above it. And, if I prick my finger on a thorny rose, I can pull a leaf from this "Band-Aid plant" to staunch the wound. Larger leaves also make effective paper towels. Visitors to my garden are always fascinated by lamb's-ears, by the texture of its downy leaves. Seldom is a planting passed by unremarked—leaves must be pulled and stroked and admired.

Two other woundworts have made brief appearances in my garden and now reside in herb heaven with other desirable plants I've killed through either ignorance or neglect, or an affliction of the "move-its." Every serious gardener will know what I mean: that irrepressible urge to move a plant when it is perceived to be in the wrong place. This was my crime with the great-flowered betony *(S. grandiflora)*, a handsome, compact plant with wonderfully showy spikes of rosy purple flowers, growing on stiff stems to 18 inches tall from basal clusters of heart-shaped, scalloped leaves. Margery Fish called it "a good furnishing plant . . . with a regal look when at the height of its beauty" (*Cottage Garden Flowers*, Collingridge, 1961). I thought it needed more exposure in my herb and flower garden, closer to the front so it could be fully admired. I guess it got tired of being moved around like a piece of furniture and simply did not return the following spring.

The other woundwort is the official healing herb, *S. officinalis*, taller and rangier than lamb's-ears, more on the wild side, but very attractive, growing to 3 feet in height with reddish purple flower spikes in whorls, from basal rosettes of heavily veined, scalloped leaves that have a minty aroma.

Someday I'll grow these two beautiful herbs again, and this time I'll treat them with more consideration.

Growing: In the spring, plant roots of lamb's-ears 1 foot apart (or closer for a ground cover) in dry, well-drained soil in full sun (most down-covered plants need these conditions and don't usually survive prolonged dampness on their roots). Lamb's-ears does especially well in exposed, windy sites. Cut back the flower spikes soon after blooming, so the plant's energy can be directed at producing foliage. The other two betonys do well in any well-drained garden soil, in a sunny spot, spaced about 18 inches apart.

Using: Lamb's-ears are beautiful in fresh or dried bouquets, particularly for nosegays—little bunches of hand-held flowers—or tussie-mussies, those charming Victorian flower bunches based on the language of flowers (see chapter 3, Tussie-Mussies). A striking way to enfold these bunches is with a silvery ruff of lamb's-ears (fresh or dried), whose meaning is "surprise." To air-dry lamb's-ears, hang leaves with stem end up, but don't let them get too brittle.

ENGLISH LAVENDER (Hardy Lavender, True Lavender)

Lavandula angustifolia
Labiatae (Mint Family)
Type: Perennial shrub
Height: 1 to 3 feet
Site: Sun
Soil: Well drained
Growing Zones: 4–8

Lavandula angustifolia

English lavender, native to the western Mediterranean, was introduced to Europe centuries ago, perhaps by the Romans. Known as English lavender because of its importance to the development of the English perfume industry and its popularity in English gardens, its numerous straight, square stems grow from a woody base and are clothed with narrow, medium green leaves, soft gray in early growth. These are the bearers of the familiar wandlike flower heads—lavender-colored, two-lipped, and tubular, borne in dense whorls. Both the common and botanical names are derived from the Latin *lavare*, 'to wash', a reference to lavender's widespread use in scenting soaps and bath water. The plant's fragrance, sharply sweet and penetrating, is both soothing and invigorating, and the most sought after among all the lavenders.

One of the goals of my gardening life in Cape Breton has been to successfully grow lavender. My failures have been many, beginning with mail-order plants that have been dead on arrival, continuing with gifts of healthy seedlings that languished before dying over the winter, and ending, finally, with the cultivar 'Lady'.

In 1993, *Harrowsmith* magazine in Canada asked me to grow 'Lady' lavender, an AAS winner, as part of its annual seed trials, reports from which alert readers to new plant introductions. I was skeptical about this experiment considering my track record: It seemed doomed before I sowed a single seed. The results appeared in *Harrowsmith* and in a subsequent article in *The Herb Companion* (February/March 1994) telling the story of 'Lady' and her astonishing ability to mature and produce flowers in a single season even in a cold climate, and even when started in late spring. As it happened, it was a typically cold summer here on Cape Breton, in which temperatures did not warm up until August, so I hadn't moved the potted seedlings outdoors from their greenhouse home until early August. That's where I left readers, with the happy story of 'Lady'. My experience certainly bore out the claim that it was the solution for northern gardeners who have had trouble wintering lavender, for this type can be grown as an annual. I was too wary to put 'Lady' in the ground, so I wintered-over pots indoors.

"The ultimate test," I wrote in *The Herb Companion*, ". . . is reserved for next season. I'll plant one of my prized plants outdoors, while the other, my insurance, will remain in the pot."

I can now report the results of the ultimate test:

✽ 1. 'Lady' did not winter-over indoors in a pot. (I subsequently learned lavenders are hard to grow under these conditions.)

✽ 2. The following season I raised a new crop, and this time I put one plant in the ground and left one in its pot; at the end of the growing season, the potted 'Lady'—an indifferent specimen—was left outside over the winter to fend for itself without protection, just because I couldn't bring myself to toss it on the compost heap. It certainly wasn't worth bringing in.

✽ 3. The following spring the lavender planted in the ground outside was dead, while the small, immature potted plant showed unmistakable signs of life—just a hint of living grayishness emerging from woody stems. (You can bet I did a lot of close inspection on my hands and knees looking for lavender life.) This lavender was promptly planted in the ground.

My scrawny 'Lady' is now a mature plant and has begun to take on a middle-aged spread that is most acceptable, producing an increasing number of flowering wands that I can harvest. I take care to give it full sun in a raised bed by the front door, where I have worked in some peat moss to improve the drainage. I dream of increasing plants and adding them to my new long rose bed. Roses and lavender: I've really arrived.

Sometimes at my lectures, people ask if I ever get discouraged about trying to grow things in this cold, unforgiving climate. The thought has never even entered my mind. I would love to be able to garden elsewhere, but here I am, and I do enjoy the challenge. I've learned, over the years, that if one strategy for growing a particular plant doesn't succeed, you need to try another. But I must admit I don't know why the scrawny, unprotected, potted lavender, violating every rule of sound gardening, lived over the winter, while the one in the ground failed. My experience with growing lavender is one of those enigmas that gardeners learn to live with. In this case, I'm most grateful for modest success in growing one of the loveliest of all herbs.

I widened my knowledge of less hardy lavender types on my trips to Israel, where Spanish lavender (L. stoechas) grows wild. The scent, more camphoraceous than sweet, recommends its use for medicinal purposes, but the plant itself is quite striking, with dark purple flowers growing from the top of each head like a flag. I saw beautiful plantings of Spanish lavender at Neot Kedumim, the Biblical Landscape Reserve, where it is used to edge a wide stone stairway. It's also grown among a small group of aromatic herbs that, the Talmud tells us, are not the true hyssop of the Bible despite their similarity of names.

In areas where Spanish lavender is winter-hardy (Zones 7 through 10), it makes a handsome show in the border or rockery, lining a stairway, or edging a path.

Growing: In my experience, lavender is easy to grow from seed, but the results are variable; named cultivars—except for 'Lady', which comes true from seed—should be grown from roots. Sow seeds close to the surface (it isn't necessary, I've found, to prechill them); germination should occur in 14 to 28 days. As I have written elsewhere, I have seen seeds swelling and beginning to show growth in as little as 48 hours after sowing. Seedlings are slow growing, so start them from seed 12 weeks before the last frost date, then plant them outside in sharply drained soil (a little gritty and on the alkaline, or sweet, side) in full sun, spacing plants 1 foot apart for a hedge, or up to 3 feet for individual specimens. Plants have the best chance of wintering over if they have developed woody stems by the end of the growing season, which is why the relatively fast-growing 'Lady' is a good choice for northern gardeners. Two other reliably hardy cultivars (but slower growing than 'Lady') are 'Hidcote' (18 to 20 inches tall, with deep purple-blue flowers) and the famous dwarf 'Munstead' (12 to 18 inches tall, and a true lavender color). Both of these make fine hedges.

For all lavenders, clip off flowering shoots on young plants to encourage root growth; clip back plants in the spring to stimulate fresh growth; clip back again after flowering to promote more bloom.

Using: Pick lavender flowers in the bud—when they have the strongest fragrance—for potpourri. Spread them on cookie sheets to dry in a just-warm oven; they dry quickly. Cut the flowering spikes all summer long for lavish bouquets, and air-dry stems in bud for use in dried winter bouquets. Try dried lavender—buds, flowers, and leaves—to season meat and vegetables, especially potato dishes. A prepared all-purpose seasoning mix, Herbes de Provence, with fennel and other herbs, is available from Nichols Garden Nursery (see Sources).

LEMON BALM

Melissa officinalis
Labiatae (Mint Family)
Type: Perennial
Height: 2 feet
Site: Sun/Partial shade
Soil: Well drained
Growing Zones: 4–9

Melissa officinalis

Lemon balm, a native of southern Europe, is a neat, bushy plant that bears abundant, scalloped leaves—heart-shaped and light green—growing along square stems. Tiny white flowers, very attractive to bees, appear in the leaf axils as the plant matures. Lemon balm's claim to fame rests on the pleasant lemony scent of its leaves, apparent when lightly brushed. As a medicinal, it has been used mainly to make a soothing tea for headaches and fevers. Like all members of the Mint Family, it is a mild sedative.

I can't recall a garden I've grown in the past 25 years that didn't have at least one healthy stand of this comforting plant: comforting in its aroma, and comforting when sipped as a tea. A symbol of sympathy in the language of flowers, everything about lemon balm seems to soothe, mollify, and calm those who come in contact with it.

Lemon balm is easy to grow, but I have never taken it for granted after it died one very hard winter, leaving a large area of blackened woody stems. Searching the ground the following spring, I found one tiny seedling, so small it could barely be discerned among a fresh crop of weeds. Recognizing the light green, evenly scalloped leaves, I salvaged the lemon balm and replanted it in the garden, where it soon became a healthy little bush.

This early experience taught me a lesson about the importance of being able to identify a cultivated plant in its seedling stage. I have since rescued many desirable plants that seemingly had disappeared, yet in reality left behind new life in the form of a diminutive seedling.

Contrary to some authorities, I don't consider lemon balm homely or coarse. Its bushy form is ornamental enough for the front of a flower border, pretty in a pot for quick harvesting. A golden green variegated form, 'Aurea', is striking, but its leaves tend to revert to all green during the summer.

Recently, I have become acquainted with lemon balm's warm-climate counterpart, lemon verbena *(Aloysia triphylla)*, which is native to Argentina and Chile. While lemon balm thrives in cooler climates, lemon verbena needs heat to produce its narrow, intensely lemon-scented leaves. I was thrilled the first winter I carried it over indoors when by February, just when I had given it up for dead, it sprouted fresh, new growth near the base of the hard, shrubby stems. Lemon verbena's scent is stronger and more long-lasting than lemon balm's, but is not so easily released—a little rubbing of the leaves is necessary. A shrub that can grow 10 feet tall in the favorable climates of California and Zones 8 through 10, lemon verbena lives its life in a pot just outside my front door in the summer for the easy harvesting of its wonderful leaves.

Growing: Lemon balm is easily grown from seed sown indoors near the soil surface at 70 degrees. Space plants outside about 1 foot apart, allowing for spread. Keep them clipped to prevent flowering, which gives plants an untidy appearance and inhibits the production of fresh leaves. Lemon balm dies out when plants become woody, or where winters are wet and drainage is less than perfect. Old plantings can be renewed by dividing and replanting green growth, or by transplanting self-sown seedlings; these are far easier to transplant than are the hardened roots.

Lemon verbena is grown from roots or cuttings taken in late summer. Mature plants drop their leaves when brought indoors, but new growth usually begins by midwinter. Winter-over plants indoors, except in Zones 8 through 10.

Harvesting: Cut back lemon balm plants to the cleanest bottom leaves just before buds have formed. Bunches air-dry fairly quickly. Lemon verbena leaves can be picked all summer long and dried for later use.

Processing: Strip dried leaves from lemon balm bunches and store in a jar away from direct light. Dry lemon verbena leaves on a cookie sheet, let cool, then store in jars away from direct light.

Using: Add fresh sprigs of lemon balm to fruit salads and use them to make lemon butter for fish dishes. Use the dried leaves of lemon balm and the fresh or dried leaves of lemon verbena for tea: Measure 1 to 2 teaspoons dried herb for every cup of boiling water, or 2 to 4 teaspoons fresh leaves. Do not steep more than a minute or two or the brew will become bitter. The dried leaves of both lemon balm and lemon verbena add their aroma to potpourri.

Herbed Tea

This is our mainstay tea, served to guests after lunch and dinner, very relaxing and tasty. Add 2 tablespoons combined dried lemon balm, mixed mints, and catnip leaves to 1 quart black China tea. Briefly steep and serve with honey or sugar.

LOVAGE

Levisticum officinale
Apiaceae (Celery Family)
Type: Perennial
Height: 5 to 6 feet
Site: Sun/Partial shade
Soil: Moist
Growing Zones: 3–9

Levisticum officinale

A tall, striking plant, lovage grows from a long, thick taproot that sends up hollow central stalks with many branches. The leaves are dark green, shiny, and deeply divided, resembling overgrown celery. Its insignificant flowers in tiny yellowish umbels are followed by brown, crescent-shaped seeds. All parts of the plant—roots, stems, leaves, and seeds—are intensely aromatic, often described as yeasty. Lovage tastes like very strong celery with a dash of angelica. A native of southern Europe, it has been used since ancient times as a medicinal to aid digestion and as a flavoring herb, especially for liqueurs.

Jigs first grew lovage from seed in 1963 (plants were not widely available then) when we lived on a hillside farm with four small children, pursuing what is mistakenly called The Simple Life. Our total assets were a cow named Aster, a magnificent view of the valley below, and $300 in savings. The first winter our water line froze from January to April, ditto all the vegetables stored in the cellar, and we ran out of wood. I was not in the mood to learn about herbs.

Over the next 8 years lovage moved with us, grown indoors in Jigs's study in large terra-cotta pots (a handsome, dwarfed houseplant) or outside, tucked away in an herb patch at the edge of the vegetable garden. Wherever it grew, I gave it scant attention until the entire herb operation was turned over to me in 1971.

I first used lovage for landscaping, since, as I soon discovered, its roots can be easily established in most soils, especially damp ones, in sun or shade. I grew it as an all-season green background for cowslips, white bleeding heart, and daylilies in partial shade, and combined with pots of brick red geraniums in full sun.

Gradually, I explored lovage's usefulness in our cuisine. In its very early growth, I learned, the emerging purplish tips are delicious in spring salad (many of my "discoveries," based on need, are uses now abandoned); also, the dried leaves were a good salt substitute. When I began to use it as the main flavoring ingredient in my Herb Salt (see the following recipe), lovage's importance in my life was firmly established.

Growing: Seeds can be sown indoors at 60 degrees to germinate in about 2 weeks, or sown in a coldframe during summer, where they will germinate in spring. Roots should be set 1 foot apart in rich, moist, soil; lovage grows best in partial shade where summers are very hot. Under these conditions, especially in frost-free areas, lovage may have to be grown as an annual, since it requires a period of winter dormancy.

I establish new plantings on sod ground merely by making a deep slit with a sharp spade, shoving in the root (trimmed to fit the space), then closing the gap with my foot. The area around the planted roots is mulched with thick newspaper (to prevent weeds coming through), then covered with a heavy layer of compost. This is my standard no-dig approach for quickly and easily establishing vigorous types of plants on sod ground or where good topsoil is unavailable in quantity. The following season the mulch will have broken down, adding nutrients and tilth to the sod, which will now be soil (see chapter 2). A sharp spade will come in handy to divide old clumps: Jump on the shovel, pry up the roots, chop them apart, and trim them to fit your space. Almost any piece of root will grow if it is kept moist. If the soil is loose, you may be able to just pull up a shoot with enough root on it to transplant.

Harvesting: In early summer, I harvest lovage for drying, my preferred method of preserving, before flowers form on the central stalk, and while the leaves are still dark green and lush. For a small amount, I use kitchen scissors to snip off the whole stalk. Then I snip off the usable leaves with as little of the stem as possible, collecting them in a basket and tossing the stems and large stalks back around the planting as a nutritious mulch.

For harvesting large amounts, I cut the whole plant down about 6 inches from the ground, using a sickle or brush hook, and wearing a protective leather glove on the hand opposite the blade. I run the whole stalks through an old hand-powered hay-chopper with a wooden tray from which I feed plant material into the rotating blades. I try to omit as much of the large stalks as possible because these are difficult to dry. This method reduces bulk and speeds drying without loss of flavor (see chapter 2).

Lovage yellows if hung in bunches. I dry it as quickly as possible to retain its color and flavor. For a small amount, I spread the leaves on cookie sheets and place these in a just-warm oven, under 200 degrees F. For larger amounts I use my homemade dryer—a series of screens that slide in and out of a rack from floor to head height, set up out of direct light in a cool room (see chapter 2). The chopped leaves are stirred daily and finished off to a crispy dryness in the gas- or wood-stove oven set at under 200 degrees F.

Once it's dry, I rub the lovage material through a homemade riddle—a screened hoop (see chapter 2)—placed over a wide wooden bowl. Now broken down into dark green flakes, uniform in size, the lovage is poured onto a folded newspaper shaped into a funnel, then poured into a clean jar, labeled, and stored away in a dark closet or bin until needed. I fill small spice-type jars for daily use, storing them in my old-fashioned "kitchen" or Hoosier cabinet.

Using: I watch eagerly for the purplish tips of young lovage shoots in early May. I cut them and the tender stalks and new leaves into spring salad (see *Dandelion*). I use fresh leaves sparingly in salads and with egg and fish dishes (especially tuna). Their flavor is strong and easier to use when the leaves are dried and flaked. I use dried lovage instead of salt at the table and for seasoning all egg dishes, stewed oysters, stews, and soups. In *Park's Success with Herbs*, Gertrude Foster writes that lovage "probably rates with celery in amount of sodium" (2.3 percent), and for this reason satisfies the desire for saltiness without excessive salt use.

Jo Ann's Kitchen & Garden Herb Salt

I use this in virtually all dishes, cooked or at the table, substituted for regular salt in making mayonnaise and in cooking rice. It is sprinkled on chicken or steak before cooking, added to soups and stews, fresh tomatoes, cottage cheese, salads (especially egg or potato salad), dressings, even buttered popcorn. Customers use it on everything from fish cakes to cocktails (Bloody Marys, for instance). As one ecstatic cook told me, "I use Herb Salt on everything but the bed!" While this mixture contains salt, it is strong, so one-half to two-thirds as much of it will take the place of ordinary salt in any recipe. This mix saves many hours in the kitchen because, just by adding it to any food, the flavor is greatly enhanced.

4 cups table salt
4 cups flaked lovage (part green celery is okay)
2 cups dried, crushed parsley
2 cups dried, cut-up chives
1 handful each of dried chive flowers and calendula petals
1 tablespoon garlic powder
2 tablespoons onion powder
1 tablespoon ground black pepper
¼ cup ground paprika
1 to 2 tablespoons ground dill weed

Mix ingredients in order given. Store in clean, covered jars away from light and excessive heat. The salt will retain its flavor for at least 6 months, but you'll probably use it up before then. To make an **Herb Blend,** omit salt and other seasonings as desired. Add extra lovage for a stronger flavor.

LUNGWORT (Bethlehem-Sage, William-and-Mary)

Pulmonaria officinalis

Pulmonaria officinalis
Boraginaceae (Borage Family)
Type: Perennial
Height: 6 to 18 inches
Site: Sun/Partial shade/Shade
Soil: Moist
Growing Zones: 3–8

Lungwort, an Old World medicinal (officinalis means "from the apothecary"), exemplifies the ancient Doctrine of Signatures, whereby a plant's physical appearance signified its healing virtues: Since lungwort has spotted, lung-shaped leaves, it was used to treat diseased lungs. Contemporary herbalists claim that lungwort is soothing for bronchial complaints, while other authorities caution that preparations from the plant may actually damage lung tissue. What cannot be denied is that lungwort has long been a favorite of cottage gardens because of its ease of culture and early spring bloom. Small funnel-shaped flowers are produced in clusters—pink in bud, turning blue, then violet—on short stems rising from a basal clump of leaves. Insignificant in their early growth, the leaves may grow to 12 inches, becoming quite downy and spotted in maturity. All lungwort species are native to Europe, despite their fanciful, biblical-sounding common names.

When we moved to the farm in Cape Breton in 1971, there was an old planting of lungwort from the 1920s. It had been grown from a neighbor's slips, as were all the still-surviving ornamentals. I was drawn to the plant's charming flowers, so cheerful in early spring when the landscape is dull and bare. For the past 25 years it has unfailingly bloomed by mid-April, even through late snow, gradually expanding its bloom until mid-May, when it is transformed into a 12-inch-wide drift of amethyst, flowering at the same time as tulips and cowslips. Resident honeybees, wild bees, and the first hummingbirds of the season visit each little trumpet flower in search of early nectar.

Lungwort's leaves, spotted with little moons descending in a rush to their tips, also interested me. Like all cottage gardeners with limited resources, I found ways to exploit a thriving, vigorous, attractive plant. I discovered that lungwort makes a fine hedge, providing a frame or low, living wall for the plants within; it is also an impenetrable barrier to weeds. It did not take many years for me to establish lungwort hedges around several plantings of herbs and flowers, in sun and shade. This fast-growing cottage garden favorite was once aptly known as "hundreds-and-thousands."

Over the years, I have given away enough clumps of lungwort to carpet a football field. Though common (at least in older gardens), it is never boring, particularly if it is well used in the landscape. Several species and cultivars of note are the elegant 'Sissinghurst White', with its pearly bells; *P. saccharata* 'Mrs. Moon', named after an actual person and not the plant's almost silvery moon-splashed leaves; *P. angustifolia* 'Azurea', a green-leaved type with blue flowers; and the early-blooming "Christmas cowslip," *P. rubra,* with its coral flowers. However, there's nothing inferior about the old medicinal with its multicolored blooms—still my favorite lungwort. All types make good ground covers, especially under trees to cover up the dying leaves of spring bulbs.

Growing: Lungwort grows, or creeps, by means of its rhizomatous roots. These grow best in cool, moist soil, in sun or shade, spaced 6 to 8 inches apart. Flowers are brighter and last longer in shaded conditions. Lungwort does not do well in exposed, windy sites, especially in thin, light soil on the dry side; nor does it like very hot summers. I renew lungwort each season by cutting the whole plant down to the ground after its month-long flowering. Fresh leaves usually grow back in a week without extra watering. The hedge—18 inches wide—is maintained by mowing around the outside of the planting and by chopping out extra growth every 2 years, or as needed.

COMMON MALLOW
(Blue Mallow, Cheese Mallow, High Mallow, Wild Mallow)

Malva sylvestris
Malvaceae (Mallow Family)
Type: Perennial or self-seeding annual
Height: 3 feet
Site: Sun/Partial shade
Soil: Well drained
Growing Zones: 4–9

Malva sylvestris

The common mallow, widely distributed throughout Europe and Asia and naturalized in North America, is a stout branchy plant with large-lobed and dark crinkled green leaves growing on thick stems to 3 feet from a deep, fleshy taproot. The trumpetlike flowers, nearly hidden under a multitude of leaves, are typical of the Mallow Family: five smooth, mauve-pink petals, slightly overlapping and wavy-edged, with dark purple stripes and a prominent bushy central column of stamens. Its fruits, developing quickly after the flowers fall, resemble little round cheeses, hence, the common name of "cheese mallow." Both the leaves and seeds have been used as a food for people and grazing animals for millennia. All parts of the plant, from root to seeds, contain a mucilaginous substance and have a long history of medicinal use in poultices for wounds and in infusions to treat coughs. "Whosoever takes a spoonful of Mallows," according to the first-century naturalist Pliny the Elder, "will from that day be cured of all diseases that come to him." The genus name, *Malva,* meaning "softening," suggests the common mallow's (and other mallows') healing, soothing powers.

Thomas Jefferson and I have one thing in common: our fascination with members of the Mallow Family. He grew hollyhocks, the marsh mallow *(Alcea officinalis),* and lavatera as well as the common mallow—all of them, apparently, for their beautiful flowers rather than for food or medicine.

I first grew the common mallow out of curiosity. I knew from my experiences in Israel that the leaves could be used as a cooked green; mallow pie is an elegant quiche made with cheese and yogurt. I was also enchanted by the plant's beautiful dark pink, striped flowers that bloom all summer long. One season, our resident rooster showed a preference for the sweet nutlike cheeses or fruits, actually hopping up to pick them off the plant. (We don't usually allow roosters to roam free, but this one was in danger of collapsing from overeating, so we turned him out of the barn for exercise.)

My adventure with annual mallows, however, might have ended here, because I found them awkward and weedy, with the beautiful flowers hidden under large leaves. But I was soon introduced to the 'Zebrina' mallow, a variant of unknown origin, with the same 2½-inch flowers I admired in the common mallow, but a little different: creamy white and satiny smooth, crisp to the touch, with dark purple stripes, growing in showy clusters on more upright stems. There was nothing hidden about these flowers. A more compact, slender plant, 'Zebrina' was easier than the common form to fit into the landscape: against a fence in the sun; at the shady end of a flower garden, to fill in after bleeding heart; or featured in a dooryard garden with the black hollyhock. Like all mallows, its raison d'être is to bloom and bloom and produce seeds. 'Zebrina' is astonishing in this regard, flowering early in the season when less than a foot high and throughout the summer, through drought, through freezing temperatures, even through late-fall and early-winter snow. As the plant matures, the flowers turn from cream to pastel pink, still with vivid, dark purple stripes, giving them a bright glow.

'Zebrina' was followed in my garden by another variant of the common mallow, *M. sylvestris mauritiana,* or tree mallow—a taller, blowsy, bushy type with extravagantly beautiful ruffled flowers of a rich rose color that are veined, rather than striped, with purple, resembling an old-fashioned rose. But like the common mallow, this variant was too overblown to fit into my landscape. I admired a cultivar, 'Bibor Felho', in a friend's garden, and so it joined my gallery of lovely mallows. 'Bibor' has the old rose look in its 3-inch-wide flowers. These, as in 'Zebrina', are borne on a more upright stalk—to 6 feet tall—in clusters. Each gorgeous flower is heavily ruffled with a showy, glistening central column of stamens—a handsome accent or background plant.

More recently, I have grown mallow-wort *(Malope trifida grandiflora),* an improved form of a Spanish wildflower that has been largely ignored by North American gardeners. It has the largest flowers of all the annual mallows (3½ inches wide); it is a warm, glowing reddish pink, and streaked like lavatera; its lime green calyx shows in the flower's center like cat's eyes; its outer lime green bracts enfold all in their fluted heart-shaped embrace—in short, it's a real show-stopper. Mallow-wort makes a wonderful flowering hedge: Each plant is about 3 feet tall, spreading 3 feet wide on strong stems that need no staking, and every inch is covered with large, hibiscus-like flowers. It elicits gasps of admiration and I have yet to discover any faults with this marvelous mallow.

Growing: The common mallow and its variants will persist as perennials in warm, frost-free areas. Elsewhere, they self-seed once established in almost any garden soil, from rich to lean as long as it drains well; they grow equally well in sun or partial shade. Start seeds of all annual types indoors 6 to 8 weeks before the last frost to get a head start. Fresh seed, just covered, should germinate in 2 days (expected germination time is 5 to 21 days). Mallows prefer heat to get started, so the seedlings should be planted out after the last expected frost. They will grow slowly until warm temperatures prevail, but they will begin blooming almost the moment they are set in the ground. Annual mallows, favorites with Elizabeth Lawrence in North Carolina as well as Thomas Jefferson in Virginia, do well in southern as well as northern gardens. In rich soil and on windy sites, the mallows may need staking. Cut down stalks at the end of the season. You'll have enough seeds to share with all your gardening friends. Before sowing the following spring, be sure to separate the seeds in the cheeselike fruits.

Using: Mallow flowers can be used fresh or candied to decorate cakes and desserts, or pressed for craft projects: glued onto stationery or pressed between glass and framed. The flowers dry to a mauve color and are often added to lavender potpourri. *Malope* (mallow-wort) makes a fine cut flower.

MUSK MALLOW

Malva moschata
Malvaceae (Mallow Family)
Type: Perennial
Height: 2½ feet
Site: Sun/Partial shade
Soil: Well drained
Growing Zones 3–10

*Malva
moschata*

The European musk mallow, naturalized as a field weed in North America, possesses similar properties to the common mallow, and has been used medicinally when other mallows were not available. Altogether a more refined and compact plant than the common mallow, its flowers, pure white or light pink, have narrow, notched, transluscent petals, blooming in such profusion that the whole plant glistens. The musk mallow gets its common name and Latin epithet, *moschata,* from its finely divided, musk-scented leaves. A soft green, these are attractive all summer long—never flagging, always providing delicate foliage.

This mallow's presence in our fields many years ago told a story of neglected farmland. As we plowed and planted, it disappeared, surviving only at the edges of cultivation. But by this time, I had dug it up and planted it in my first herb and flower garden where it continues to thrive, producing two crops of flowers a season—in early and midsummer—so it is never really out of bloom. It is so eager to blossom that it is already forming new buds at its base before the old flowers on its stalks are quite spent. The white-flowered form has recently been rediscovered as an elegant perennial. It goes with everything, combining well with hot reds like Jerusalem-cross *(Lychnis chalcedonica)* and orange lilies, as well as pastels, purples—virtually any color, in any garden situation, in full sun or light shade. It blooms its heart out (not completely, though) with the scarlet bee balm, reviving by late summer to bloom again with the purple heads of anise hyssop *(Agastache foeniculum),* forming a lower mound of bloom the second time around. The light pink musk mallow also combines well with virtually anything, even the brightest, most outrageous orange-red Oriental poppy.

The hollyhock mallow *(M. alcea fastigiata)* is a close relative, with medium pink glistening flowers borne in profusion all summer. It is a taller, more robust plant than musk mallow, 3 feet tall and wide. Take care where you plant it, since it needs room to spread.

Growing: Both these mallows grow readily from seed and may bloom the first season. Seeds sown in a coldframe in summer will germinate the following spring. Cut back spent flower stalks to allow a second blooming for the musk mallow. The hollyhock mallow, which blooms a little later in midsummer, has only one bloom period, flowering for the rest of the summer and through several light frosts.

Using: These mallows make fine cut flowers. The dried flowers are used for potpourri; they fold up and fall off the plant in great numbers (hollyhock mallow) and are very easy to harvest. A tincture from the fresh leaves of musk mallow, steeped in rubbing alchohol for 2 to 3 weeks, then strained, helps relieve bee stings; dab on as needed. I've never needed to use this remedy, but it comes from a reliable source: *Plants for Beekeeping in Canada,* by Jane Ramsay, published in 1987 by the International Bee Research Association.

SIGNET MARIGOLD

Tagetes tenuifolia
Asteraceae (Aster Family)
Type: Annual
Height: 6 to 12 inches
Site: Sun
Soil: Well drained

Tagetes tenuifolia

This little citrus-scented marigold from Mexico and Central America was introduced to North American gardeners by 1850. The dwarf varieties today are identical to those grown decades ago to produce the colorful outdoor "carpets" so popular in the Victorian era. Small bright yellow or bright orange flowers the size of a dime, some blotched with brown, bloom in masses, their stiff stems well covered with ferny, fragrant foliage. One need merely brush the plant to release the aroma of lemon verbena combined with something more assertive and pungent—that peculiar odor associated with ordinary African and French marigolds—from its flowers and lacy leaves.

I had been growing signet marigolds for years when I discovered, through the Richter catalog, that they are regarded nowadays as an herb, brought to our attention because of their edible flowers and powerful perfume. Their scent alone would qualify the signets as herbs, so that was no surprise, but I was delighted to learn that the flowers and leaves can be used for flavoring wines and other foods. I imagine that they also yield a yellow dye, as do other marigolds.

Grown in wooden barrels, tubs of all kinds, even in an old wheelbarrow with the bright scarlet Texas sage *(Salvia coccinea)*, signet marigolds lend panache to the landscape, spreading in a great, bright, 2-foot mound by late summer, still compact, never sloppy, always brilliant. Visitors invariably want to know their name; when we stop to admire the multitude of blooms, I gently brush the plants so their exotic perfume will fill the air. The signets possess both visual impact and an unusual scent, a combination I can't resist.

Fragrant plants are very important in my landscape. I plant them by doorways, stairs, any place I frequently pass. Why not? Pleasant scents are refreshing and invigorating to the spirit. One of my favorite cultivars (perhaps for its name alone) is the golden yellow 8-inch 'Lulu'. The only other cultivars are the 12-inch-tall, lemon-scented, bright yellow 'Lemon Gem' and the splotched orange, tangerine-scented 'Tangerine Gem', both named for their scent as well as their color. The signet marigolds can be grown to great effect in rock gardens as well as containers. It's a shame that the decline in popularity of the carpet bedding style has so obscured the virtues of these bright flowers. They deserve to be more widely grown.

Another fragrant marigold used for flavoring is Mexican tarragon or Mexican mint marigold *(T. lucida)*, which does not grow readily in a cool climate, so I have so far resisted the urge to try it.

Growing: I raise signet marigolds from seeds sown indoors 8 to 10 weeks before the last expected frost; these are slower growing than ordinary marigolds and need a head start in cooler growing zones. Seeds, just covered, should germinate in 5 to 14 days or sooner at 70 to 85 degrees. Outdoors, space seedlings 6 to 8 inches apart after the last frost, keeping in mind that one or two plants will form a wide mound of bloom. Spent flowers are easily removed by running your hands gently through the clusters. The signets seem to be hardier than other marigolds, surviving several frosts before succumbing.

Using: I pick flower clusters and leaves to dry for potpourri. Whole flowers make striking cake decorations, candied or fresh, just lightly pressed into frosting. Individual flowers can be easily pressed to decorate (and scent) stationery. Toss flower petals into fruit cups and fruit salads. Flowers and leaves release their scent more generously when steeped in hot liquid, for example, in wines, sauces, and puddings. The bouquetlike flowers are charming in fresh nosegays, appealing and fragrant.

MARJORAM
(Sweet Marjoram,
Knotted Marjoram)

Origanum majorana
Labiatae (Mint Family)
Type: Tender perennial
Height: 12 inches
Site: Sun
Soil: Well drained

Origanum majorana

Marjoram, one of the most popular cooking herbs, is native to the Mediterranean region, where it grows as a perennial. However, in most areas of North America, except in Zone 10, it is grown as an annual. An attractive little plant with plenty of small, oval, pointed leaves that exude a sweet, spicy aroma, marjoram produces tiny white flowers in knots along the stem, hence the origin of one of its common names, knotted marjoram.

We have always grown this aromatic herb, indispensable for flavoring all tomato dishes. Its taste is both sharp and sweet, hard to describe. "To know it you have to grow it," wrote Gertrude Foster in her classic *Park's Success with Herbs.* In Vermont, growing marjoram was straightforward: Just sow the seeds in the ground at the same time as beans and you will have a fine crop of flavoring herb to harvest all summer and into the fall. (Marjoram is remarkably hardy, able to survive hard frosts until deep winter.)

In Cape Breton, it's a different story, and the same strategies worked out for basil are applied to marjoram, though not as zealously. In other words, I raise plants from seeds indoors and plant them out in protected areas, but not necessarily a coldframe or hotbed (though I have done this too), as I usually do with basil. With some luck in the form of a sunny, warm summer, marjoram can be grown here in the great outdoors, right in my harvest bed. It's a pretty plant, though, and deserves more attention for edible landscaping as an up-front edging plant, among rocks (where sun collects the heat marjoram loves), and in containers of all kinds. I plant it in a wooden half-barrel by the kitchen door with other herbs I need for quick picking: salad burnet, parsley, basil, and fernleaf dill.

Marjoram is one of the few herbs I can winter-over indoors with little difficulty. It is particularly well suited to a hanging basket, where its indoor habit, more sprawling than upright, is shown off to advantage. By spring its stems are woody, but by then there's a new crop of tender seedlings getting their start upstairs under grow lights.

Growing: I start marjoram indoors 4 to 6 weeks before the last frost date. Seeds lightly pressed on the surface of moist soil germinate in 8 to 14 days at 70 degrees. I used to soak seeks overnight in warm water to speed germination, but that's not necessary. Where soil is early-warming, seeds can be sown outdoors. Thin seedlings to 6 to 8 inches. Cut back and divide wintered-over plants, or make stem cuttings, to get a head start on the new growing season. Cut sprigs all summer to keep plants bushy.

Harvesting: Cut back plants to the cleanest bottom leaves before flower buds open; lay stems on cookie sheets in a just-warm oven (below 150 degrees F) and, when they are crispy dry, run your hands down the stems to remove the leaves. Store in labeled jars in a darkened cupboard.

Using: Use marjoram alone or combined with basil, fresh or dried, in all tomato dishes; in pastas, pizza sauce, omelets, and beef dishes (especially stews); and in salads, dressings, cottage cheese, and bean soups. Substitute it for sage in any recipe if you prefer its flavor.

Herbed Lamb Chops

This recipe is adapted from Irma Goodrich Mazza's pioneering
Herbs for the Kitchen *(Little Brown, 1939).*

Combine two pinches of the following dried herbs for each lamb chop: marjoram, parsley, basil; add enough olive oil to make the mixture spreadable. Add salt and pepper to taste and a bay leaf if desired. Let stand at least 1 hour before using so the flavors blend. After chops are broiled, paint each with the herb-oil mixture and serve at once.

WILD MARJORAM (Common Marjoram, Common Oregano, Oregano)

Origanum vulgare subsp. *vulgare*
Labiatae (Mint Family)
Type: Perennial
Height: 3 feet
Site: Sun
Soil: Well drained
Growing Zones: 4–9

Origanum vulgare
subsp. *vulgare*

Wild marjoram belongs to a group of plants from the Mediterranean area loosely known as oregano, but differing from one another in habit, flower color, and—most importantly—flavor. The one we call wild marjoram is a hardy, vigorous plant with tiny pink flowers tucked into purplish bracts on tall reddish stems growing from a mat of green, somewhat rounded, downy leaves containing thymol. This chemical substance gives the leaves the peppery flavor of a mild thyme, but little scent. Where conditions are warm and dry, as in its native Greece on rocky, sunny slopes, the plant is reputed to develop the sharp, spicy flavor we associate with the name "oregano," and is used accordingly. Wild marjoram also has a history as a medicinal due to its antiseptic properties.

One of the first plants to go into my new herb and flower garden under the old apple tree was wild marjoram: not just one plant, but probably a dozen, to line a path leading into the middle of the circular planting. As I recall, it was interplanted with English daisies, and as I set out the seed-grown plants I fondly imagined a dainty edging of soft green, aromatic mats of foliage interspersed with little gay, pink and white, daisylike flowers.

How often do our garden dreams come to grief because we are not well acquainted with the material in hand, because it is inappropriate for the occasion, for the vision in our heads? Of course, in time the downy green mats became overbearing, taking over the English daisies and everything else, smothering other, less vigorous plants—eventually obscuring even the path itself.

But I like wild marjoram, despite its rampant nature, despite its lack of flavor for cooking. It's a handsome plant, both in its early mat-forming stage and later, when the pink and purple flower clusters bloom on and on in late summer and into the fall, attracting our resident bees. I have seen striking combinations of wild marjoram and rudbeckias grown as accents near a driveway or building, but in my own landscape I deal with wild marjoram as a wild plant, naturalizing it in sunny, open situations with wild bergamot *(Monarda fistulosa)* by one of our beehives.

I am still looking for a hardy oregano with true oregano flavor. I learned years ago that "oregano" is not a specific plant but a flavor, but the oregano I'm looking for is a true *Origanum* species. Jigs tells me he has been through all this before, that he has grown all the oreganos worth growing in a search for oregano flavor, but since I remember very little about his early efforts, I have been conducting my own growing experiments.

For the past several years, I've grown Greek oregano, as it was called in the seed catalog, wintering it over indoors in case it was not hardy, but recently I put it in the ground when the potted plants began to look shabby. It perked up at once, spread out in a lovely mat and produced flowers identical to those of wild marjoram—plentiful and showy pink blossoms tucked into purplish bracts on stems not more than 6 inches high. The flavor seems to be stronger than that of the tall type, but it is not Greek oregano, the kind reputed to have such excellent flavor. True Greek oregano is *O. vulgare* subsp. *hirtum* (also known as *O. heracleoticum*), which bears white flowers and is probably not hardy in colder climates. There is so much confusion about oreganos in the trade and in reference books that it's hard to tell anything for certain about them, their growing zones included. If my dwarf oregano winters over, I shall be overjoyed (*Origanum,* incidentally, is derived from the Greek meaning "joy-of-the-mountain"), not because it has true oregano flavor but because it is a handsome plant, useful for landscaping in sunny, exposed sites.

I suppose Jigs is right. There are no hardy oreganos worth the name that will grow in the North as a perennial. I was once complaining to a friend about this situation, and she noted with pride that she grew a hardy cooking oregano and would gladly give me a piece. I hadn't the heart to tell her that the vigorous green mats she delivered to me were those of wild marjoram.

Growing: Wild marjoram grows readily from seed sown indoors near or on the soil surface at 70 degrees; germination should occur within 10 days. It will grow in partial shade as well as sun and in most soils except very moist ones. It is attractive in a garden setting, but will have to be carefully watched to avoid its spreading where it is not wanted. In this situation, cut back plants after flowering. Otherwise, let wild marjoram grow as it loves best, on its own in an open, sunny site. Mow grass around it to discourage its spread and to show it off.

Using: Wild marjoram is highly prized for crafts. Cut it when the flowers and bracts are most colorful; air-dry the flowering stems and use them in dried bouquets and wreaths.

Spearmint
Peppermint
Curly mint
Apple mint
Mentha spp.

MINT

Mentha spp.
Labiatae (Mint Family)
Type: Perennial
Height: Creeping ground cover to 3 feet
Site: Sun/Partial shade/Shade
Soil: Moist
Growing Zones: 3–9

Most garden mints, selected for cultivation from among hundreds of species and varieties for their superior aromas or attractive forms, originated in Europe and Asia. They can be recognized by their square-sided stems and tiny two-lipped flowers usually growing in terminal spikes; their scents vary from species to species (even within species), and from cultivar to cultivar, from sweet to sharp, from fruity to spicy. Because they are so variable, identification is often difficult, determined in the end by the chemistry of their essential oils. Mint leaves of all types are plentiful and toothed, sometimes beautifully marked or mottled with gold. Mints have a long history of use for flavoring and for medicinal purposes—especially peppermint, whose leaves have the highest concentration of menthol; they have been used effectively to treat common complaints ranging from indigestion to insomnia.

Our first mint was peppermint *(M.* x *piperita),* obtained from a friend's garden in Vermont. We carried it with us to Cape Breton, as an inseparable part of the household, indispensable for hot and cold tea and for general flavoring. There are mints and there are mints, but there is only one peppermint (and its many named variations). This is the one with an intensely minty aroma packed into smooth, lance-shaped dark green leaves; its extracted oil is said to contain 50 to 78 percent menthol. Peppermint has distinctive dark reddish stems and lilac-colored flowers borne on terminal spikes, the whole spike eventually turning dark purple, bringing the plant to 3 feet in height; variations include types with crisped, lined, and even variegated leaves.

When we moved to Cape Breton, I lovingly planted our "Vermont mint" in my new mixed herb and flower garden, a former rock pile beneath an old apple tree. It loved the damp, deep earth there and its roots spread and spread. I tried a barrier of rocks (plenty of them around), but of course the rhizomes just crept under them, invading other plants. This was my first lesson in growing mints: Control them before they rule your gardens.

Peppermint found a home in a series of plastic-lined mint beds, each type separated by large logs, controlled at the edges by mowing. Because I need a lot of peppermint for home use and for my Jo Ann's Kitchen & Garden products, I also naturalized it in various damp habitats, where it is allowed to form great stands, quite striking in bloom. An old, rusty, leaky oil barrel—cut in half, turned on its side, and set at the shady end of a flower garden—makes a surprisingly handsome planter, the dark green mint leaves poking through holes and over the sides of the container's rim. Only a few steps from the back kitchen door, it's a handy place for quick picking during iced-tea- and mint-jelly-making season.

I made the mistake early in my gardening career of raising mint from seed, with the inevitable result: an inferior mint lacking in flavor. Because mints are so variable and some of them, like peppermint, are sterile hybrids, it's best to grow mint from roots to be sure of what you'll get. For years I thought that my seed-raised mint was spearmint *(M. spicata,* one of the parents of *M.* x *piperita),* but it lacks the flavor of spearmint I grew from a purchased plant. Spearmint is a nice mint, not as strong as peppermint and, therefore, more useful for culinary purposes where a subtle flavor is wanted (for seasoning peas, carrots, or beets, for instance). It, too, has lance-shaped leaves and purplish red stems, but is shorter, growing only to 2 feet. Its leaves are variable, some quite hairy, crisped and wrinkled and lighter in color on stems of lighter or darker purple.

Apple mint *(M. suaveolens)* is not only intensely sweet (nothing like apples, as far as I can tell), but also beautiful, with large, soft, light green downy and rounded leaves. One little piece from a gardening friend soon turned into a monster, colonizing a complete flower bed. I spent many hours (and years) undoing my own stupidity, for I actually *planted* it in this garden after my experience with peppermint—but it was so beautiful. Eventually, it was relegated to the plastic-lined beds for harvesting. I plan to invite it back to a less utilitarian setting, but this time on my terms, in a container of some sort.

Like other types, ginger mint *(M. x gentilis)* came to me uninvited, a bit of its root intertwined with something else, and thus went into the garden. It took several years of pulling out the insinuating roots, but finally I had it where I wanted it, in a deep plastic fish tub (from a local fisherman) at the back of the house. I think it is one of the most beautiful foliage plants, streaked with gold under optimum conditions: cool, moist, rich soil and partial shade. It fairly lights up a no-man's-land on the north side of the house, formerly reserved for tethered calves in the summer because I thought nothing would grow there. Ginger mint, like many of the mint varieties, is fancifully named, but it does have a sharp, almost hot flavor. I use it sparingly.

Other mints have come and gone in my garden, not because I wanted them to leave, but because I could not give them a proper home. A friend gave me chunks of the delightful Corsican mint *(M. requienii),* an exquisite, bright green, ground-hugging mat of round, nicely flavored leaves, requiring uninterrupted moisture; the dark-stemmed orange or bergamot mint *(M. x piperita* 'Citrata'), its large leaves thinly lined with red at their edges, and with a citrusy or sharp flavor; English pennyroyal *(M. pulegium),* a lax plant with a very strong camphor-mint scent and purplish flowers in whorls. It's reputed to be hardy to Zone 5 or 6, but Jigs wintered it over in Vermont where temperatures dipped to 35 degrees below zero, and it did survive several consecutive years in my Zone 4 garden.

The mint story hasn't ended, as far as I'm concerned. There's pineapple mint; the variegated apple mint *(M. suaveolens* 'Variegata'), its wooly leaves edged with cream; and chocolate mint, a selection from white peppermint, with, I gather, no detectable chocolate flavor but red-veined leaves. And I'd like to find the right place to grow the little Corsican mint, one of the tiniest of flowering plants. I love mints—in their place. I would like to establish a container garden full of mints out of bright sun, where watering would be minimal and they could blend their cool leaves, varied forms, and refreshing aromas.

Growing: Grow mints from pieces of root; even small pieces should take hold if kept moist. Most mints except for variegated types grow well in sun if the soil is deep, rich, and moist, but they will also grow well in partial shade or full shade if such soil conditions are provided. Apple mint, with its downy leaves, is drought resistant and does well in exposed, sunny sites. Space plants 12 to 18 inches apart, advice that is really academic since their creeping rhizomes will soon spread in a mass beneath the soil's surface, sending up many stems.

To keep ginger mint variegated, plant out of direct sun and provide plenty of compost to keep the roots cool; cut back before flowering to encourage fresh foliage. Ginger mint makes a beautiful ground cover under trees and shrubs or in any other shady area.

Harvesting: Cut back mints to the lowest set of clean leaves before flowers have formed, when the leaves are most plentiful and in prime condition. Most types of mint can be hung in small bunches to air-dry in a short time; the exception is apple mint, whose downy leaves take longer to dry. I spread these, with their stems, on screens in my drying rack until fairly dry, finishing them off to a crispy dryness in a just-warm oven. The leaves can be stripped from the stems before or after crisping. Store leaves in labeled jars in a dark cupboard. They should be crumbled only before using, thereby retaining their flavor until it is needed.

Using: An entire book could probably be written about the various ways to use mints. They are extraordinarily useful, soothing (mints are natural sedatives), and delicious. Be sure, when harvesting mints from the wild, that you taste them first; many are rank or without much flavor.

Jo Ann's Kitchen & Garden Mint Blend Tea

This is one of the most popular of my herb teas, with a strong, yet pleasant, mint flavor. It's very relaxing and soothing, effective for colds, nervous tension, insomnia, digestion, or just to enjoy. For best results, take after meals and before bed. The same blend can be used to make Lemon-Mint Tea (use equal parts lemon balm and mint), or for general seasoning purposes, as on cooked carrots, new potatoes, or peas.

1 part each dried peppermint and apple mint leaves
½ part dried spearmint leaves
¼ part dried ginger mint leaves

Combine dried mints in the proportions specified. To make 1 or 2 cups of tea, put 1 to 2 teaspoons of the mint mixture in a tea ball and pour boiling water over it; cover the cup with a saucer and let the herbs steep for no more than a minute or two, reserving the tea ball for another cup, if desired. Prolonged steeping of the dried herbs makes a bitter tea.

Iced Herb Tea

1 good handful fresh peppermint and apple mint
1 good handful fresh lemon balm

Stuff herbs, with their stems, into your favorite quart teapot; cover the herbs with boiling water and let them steep 10 to 15 minutes to make a strong infusion (ice cubes will dilute it). Strain, bottle, and chill. Serve in glasses filled with ice cubes; add a sprig of mint to each glass and sugar to taste. A long-handled teaspoon facilitates stirring.

Iced Tea Deluxe

⅓ part chilled lemon-mint infusion
⅓ part chilled rhubarb juice (an infusion of stalks with lemons and
    oranges with sugar added to taste; easy to make, or see directions in
    my book *The Old-Fashioned Fruit Garden*)
⅓ part chilled China tea (leftover hot tea is okay)

Mix all ingredients together. Serve in glasses filled with ice cubes; add a sprig of mint and a slice of lemon to each glass. This tea is sweet enough without additional sugar.

Cold Beet Salad

This dish—discovered by Jigs in my cookbook collection—was regularly featured years ago when our water supply and all our stored vegetables froze during our first winter in Vermont. The root crops—beets, carrots, potatoes—froze, thawed, froze, and so on, but remained usable. It was a very limited diet that winter (and the next), and learning to make do was elevated to a high art. Now, with a much more varied homegrown food supply, I still make Cold Beet Salad because it's a great way to use leftover cooked beets.

Cooked beets cut up in slices or bite-sized pieces

Onion slices

½ cup oil: vegetable and olive mixed

¼ cup dill vinegar

Freshly ground black pepper to taste

1 to 2 pinches dried mint blend (see recipe for Mint Blend Tea in this portrait)

Put the beets in a bowl and arrange the onion slices on top of them. Pour the mixed oil over the vegetables (as much as is needed to almost cover them). Gently stir the beets and onions so they are mixed, grind pepper over them (to suit your taste), and add a pinch or two of mint (or more, if you like). Let this dish sit for at least 30 minutes before serving so the flavors will blend. Mop up any leftover oil with thick slices of homemade Italian bread.

Mint Jelly

There's more than one way to make Mint Jelly. I've tried them all, with and without commercial pectin (using apples for jelling), and have concluded that the following recipe produces the best flavored jelly. Apple jelly flavored with mint is nice, too, but not the same thing.

1½ cups mint (peppermint, spearmint, apple mint), cut up with stems

2 cups water

2 tablespoons white or cider vinegar

3½ cups sugar

Green vegetable coloring if desired

1 pouch or ½ bottle liquid pectin

Bruise mint with a wooden pestle or the bottom of a glass jelly jar. Add water, bring just to a boil, and let steep, covered, for 20 minutes. Strain the hot liquid and mint into a 1-quart glass measuring cup; let the liquid stand until impurities sink to the bottom, then carefully measure out 1¾ cups of the liquid. Add the vinegar, sugar, and food coloring, and bring the mixture to a boil that cannot be stirred down. Stir in the pectin and continue to stir for 1 minute (use a watch with a second hand), counting from the time the mixture again returns to a boil that cannot be stirred down. Let the hot mixture settle and skim off any impurities (foam); then pour the hot liquid into the glass measuring cup and from there into scalded jelly jars, leaving ¼ inch of headroom. Seal the jars at once with sterilized lids and rings. For gifts, use new jelly jars with a pretty label; the small 4-ounce jars are best for this purpose.

MUGWORT

Artemisia vulgaris
Asteraceae (Aster Family)
Type: Perennial
Height: 4 to 5 feet
Site: Sun
Soil: Well drained
Growing Zones: 3–10

Artemisia vulgaris

Mugwort, a familiar weed of waste places, originates in Europe and Asia but is naturalized throughout the temperate regions of North and South America. Its stiff purplish stems bear deeply cut green leaves, silver on the undersides, and tiny yellowish flowers in long spikes. This humble herb of myth and lore—it was a talisman against evil spirits—has a long history of practical application, having been used to flavor beer (a use preserved in its common name), treat digestive disorders, and palliate rheumatism, tired feet, and "female complaints" (menstruation and menopause). In some cultures, the young shoots and leaves are eaten as potherbs and made into a condiment eaten with fatty poultry.

One day while walking in the city down toward the railroad tracks, I amused myself by picking samples of all the flowers I found along the way, in between sidewalk cracks and in back alleys. I meant just to show them to my friend, but she mistook it for a bouquet and thanked me for my gift. In fact, it wasn't bad: bright yellow toadflax, wild chamomile, pineapple weed, and mugwort. Later that fall, when I had to make a dried bouquet to order and didn't have sufficient flowers on hand, I noticed the healthy stands of mugwort that had made themselves at home along the edges of our cultivated ground (I can't recall ever having planted it). I looked at the plants with a more appreciative eye, their spikes now reddish brown, their foliage silvery gray, altogether resembling very bushy, overgrown heather.

This ancient herb is so taken for granted that it is not always mentioned in the literature. After all, there are other artemisias, so why bother with this one? Adelma Simmons gave it one of the finest tributes I've ever seen in print, praising it as a landscape plant of note, and describing how it was effectively used as a shrub in a planting she admired:

> Common mugwort is one of the most spectacular herbs in the garden at the old Captain Paul House . . . There they stand on either side of a planting of other artemisias that leads into a brick terrace surrounded by beds of old roses. These mugworts grow to 6 feet, and they are the wonder of many vistors who know herbs but do not recognize this most common member of an aristocratic family.
>
> —Adelma Simmons, *Herb Gardening in Five Seasons*

I've also grown mugwort as a shrub by our cellar door, where it's held at bay by variegated goutweed. (Or is it the other way around, with the mugwort halting the spread of the rampant ground cover?) I like to have it at hand to trim off side branches for drying, to harvest for my Kitchen & Garden Herbal Foot Soak (see *Comfrey*), and to make tussie-mussies for departing guests. In the language of flowers, mugwort brings good luck to travelers, the symbolism arising from its actual use in soothing tired feet.

Growing: Since mugwort grows so readily, plant only one root; you'll soon have more. To grow it as a shrub, chop out extra growth every year and cut back the plant to the ground in the fall to discourage self-seeding. You can dwarf plants and keep them green longer by cutting them back about a month before they flower; new growth will be bushier and flowering will be delayed.

Using: The bitterish flower stalks can be substituted for hops in any beer recipe. Mugwort is highly regarded by wreathmakers for its silvery foliage. For this purpose, it is crucial to cut branches just before they flower. The buds and leaves all dry to a lovely soft silver. After the yellow flowers open they turn a reddish brown and can still be dried on the stalks, but the effect will be different. Use fresh or dried sprays for tussie-mussies (see chapter 3).

In 1981 I made a tussie-mussie for our departing friend, Bob. We took him in our horse and buggy down to the railroad tracks, a mile from the farm, to catch the train. As it rounded the bend, we waved as usual, but it failed to stop at the crossing. Thrusting my little present at our friend, he jammed it into his shirt pocket and chased the train up the tracks, where it finally came to a halt. I like to think it was the inclusion of mugwort—friend of the traveler—in the tussie-mussie that helped him catch his train. Its stem wrapped in damp moss inside a plastic bag covered with a foil cone, the little nosegay arrived home in fresh condition, despite its trip of at least a thousand miles. The accompanying card read:

> The pansy carries our sad thoughts at your departure, the rose and forget-me-not send our love, horehound and marjoram will bring you both health and happiness, yarrow is to cure your heartache at leaving, and mugwort is sent to protect you in all your travels.

WHITE MUGWORT
(Ghost Plant, Sweet Mugwort, White Wormwood)

Artemisia lactiflora
Type: Perennial
Height: 5 to 6 feet
Site: Sun/Partial shade
Soil: Most soils
Growing Zones: 3–10

Artemisia lactiflora

Also called ghost plant in reference to its quantity of feathery white blooming stems, and sweet mugwort because of its hawthorn-vanilla, lightly camphora-ceous scent, white mugwort is one of the plants that Ernest Wilson brought back from China in 1901. Taller and more shrublike than common mugwort, its leaves are midgreen and deeply divided (no silver on the reverse), its tiny creamy white flowers borne in loose panicled 2-foot plumes in late summer. In

China, where it is known as Junn Jui Choi, white mugwort is a culinary herb for flavoring soup and other dishes. In North America its uses are confined to wreathmaking and associated crafts.

A gift to me from renowned herb authority Gertrude Foster, my own white mugwort is treasured for that association, as well as for its ease of culture and scented flower sprays that appear in late summer, just when fresh flowers are most appreciated. The only artemisia grown for its flowers rather than its foliage, it is a vigorous plant without being overbearing, spreading slowly unlike its close cousin, common mugwort. I am favorably disposed toward anything that grows well in my damp, northern soil. Yet when it also bears fragrant blooms late in the season, I'm positively charmed. Among discerning gardeners the plant is highly regarded for these virtues, but it remains, nevertheless, largely and undeservedly unknown. Everyone to whom I have introduced white mugwort admires it.

The late Helen Fox, who grew and studied herbs before they became popular, was well acquainted with white mugwort, which she described as "hardy and handsome at the back of the herb border" (*The Years in My Herb Garden,* Macmillan, 1953). I grow white mugwort wherever I can fit its large proportions into my small plantings—not always an easy task. I grow it against the house in a small dooryard planting, and as a green background all season long for more delicate plants such as annual poppies, pinks, golden thyme, and violas. In my herb and flower garden it looks wonderful in full bloom in late summer, the foaming, feathery plumes rising up like an apparition, one that lives up to its reputation as the ghost plant. Scarlet bee balm complements white mugwort in form and color, and as it fades by late summer, anise hyssop's purple-flowered cones then take up the slack. Since I like to harvest the flowering stems at their peak of creamy, fragrant bloom for potpourri, I also plant white mugwort in my harvest bed.

Growing: White mugwort is adaptable to moist or dry soil conditions. It grows well in sun or partial shade, attaining its maximum growth (to 6 feet) in rich, moist soil, where it may need staking in windy conditions. To keep growth to a more manageable height, cut the plant back by a third to a half in midsummer, or plant it in dry soil in full sun. Since it does not set seed, it is always planted by roots, spaced 3 feet apart, or 18 to 24 inches for a hedge effect. White mugwort is not invasive; clumps can be easily reduced by chopping out excess growth in the spring.

Using: I harvest white mugwort stems at their peak of bloom to use in quantity for making potpourri; they can be laid out on screens or hung up in bunches to air-dry. Then the dried flowers are stripped from the stems. The scent of white mugwort when dried is a pleasant floral-fruit aroma. The flowering stems, especially in their creamy white stage, are striking in either fresh or dried bouquets.

Tropaeolum majus;
T. minor

NASTURTIUM

Tropaeolum majus; T. minor
Tropaeolaceae (Nasturtium Family)
Type: Annual
Height: 6 inches to 6 feet
Site: Sun
Soil: Well drained; light

Garden nasturtiums are mostly hybrid forms resulting from crossing two wild-flowers from South America: the low-growing *T. minor* with the tall, scrambling vine *T. majus*. This has produced a variety of dwarf, semitrailing, trailing, and climbing types with succulent stems; round, shield-shaped leaves; and bright, spurred flowers in shades of red, orange, and yellow, some streaked and loosely doubled. Nasturtiums have long been admired as a decorative flower and as a food plant. All parts possess a warm, spicy flavor similar to that of watercress, whose Latin name is actually *Nasturtium*.

I've been growing nasturtiums for a long time, ever since I realized how much pleasure a single sprouted seed could bring: a spreading mound of attractive foliage and a profusion of cheerful, bright flowers attractive to hummingbirds. I began to explore the range of plants, becoming familiar with the upright, bushy nontrailing kinds; with the lax, semitrailing sorts; and with the modern spurless flower form, 'Whirlybird'. While the latter's pastel shades—salmons and creams—as well as its gold, tangerine, and rose colors, are lovely, and the flowers are held well above the foliage, I must admit that I'm partial to the classic, spurred nasturtium. When I saw the large-flowered climbing nasturtium draped over a friend's white arbor, of course I had to add this to my collection, too. Among my favorites are 'Empress of India'—a striking, nontrailing, turn-of-the-century introduction, its large, brilliant vermilion flowers nearly obscuring a mound of beautiful gray-green leaves on purplish stems—and the 'Gleam' group, with their very fragrant, double trumpet flowers and a semitrailing habit.

All of these nasturtiums find a welcome place in my landscape, as a low edging for a sunny annual bed ('Dwarf Double Jewels'), in hanging baskets ('Gleam' types), and in containers and tubs close to the kitchen door for quick picking. I grow the tall scramblers up a trellis and in an old barrel, where they are paired with white sweet-alyssum *(Lobularia maritima)*. Here, the sweet-alyssum foams over the side of the barrel, while the nasturtium stems clamber up to the roof of our old garden shed (formerly the coal shed), the stems supporting themselves by working their way between the weathered boards—an archetypal cottage garden scene.

When a British friend gave me her recipe for Nasturtium Sauce, I made sure I had a variety of flower-producing plants to make the peppery, soy-based sauce for winter stews and rice and meat dishes. With so many tubs of nasturtiums planted by the kitchen door, I could not miss their delicious scent, so warm and sweetly spicy. I began to pick flowers to eat in salads and use fresh in other summer dishes. For me, summer begins when I can pick a handful of bright flowers to garnish our Summer Salad Extravaganza (see the recipe on next page).

Growing: Sow seeds outdoors by twos and threes when soil temperatures have reached at least 60 degrees, covering seeds with 1 inch of soil (they need darkness to germinate). The tall climbers need a longer growing season, so they can be started indoors in peat pots or 2½- to 3-inch plant cells 6 weeks before the last frost. Outdoors, space nasturtiums 6 to 12 inches apart, depending on the variety. Provide some sort of support for the climbers; a straight-sided trellis or arbor works well. Where summers are very hot, a little shade will prolong flowering; otherwise plants may stop producing blossoms until cooler weather prevails. Seeds are easy to save and in my experience come true to type.

Using: Nasturtiums are edible flowers par excellence, delicious in salads either whole or broken (it's okay to include the peppery stems). For special occasions and for workshop lunches I press whole flowers onto an herbed cottage cheese–yogurt spread and serve on thinly sliced and trimmed whole wheat bread. Or I stuff large, single-petaled flowers like 'Empress of India' with the same spread and place them on a platter ringed by sprigs of dark green parsley. Before using nasturtiums for culinary purposes, though, check for bugs deep within the flowers.

Nasturtium Sauce

This recipe from my British friend first appeared in Gertrude Foster's book, Park's Success with Herbs. *It is indispensable for flavoring pork chops. Brown them on both sides in a little fat, douse with Nasturtium Sauce, and add a little water to keep the meat from sticking to the pan; cover and simmer until the meat is tender.*
Use Nasturtium Sauce as a general seasoning, as you would Worcestershire sauce.

4 large onions
3 cloves garlic
1 pint malt vinegar
½ teaspoon salt
6 whole cloves
½ teaspoon cayenne pepper
1 cup fresh nasturtium flowers, loosely packed
1 cup soy sauce, or to taste

Mince the onions and garlic and bring to a boil with the vinegar, salt, and spices; continue to boil for 10 minutes. Pour this mixture over the nasturtium flowers. When cool, pour the flower-vinegar mix into a crock or jar; cover and let sit for 2 months to blend. Strain the mixture, add soy sauce to taste (about 1 cup), and bottle for later use. It's most convenient to use small, narrow jars, like the ones used for vinegars. Nasturtium Sauce will keep indefinitely in a dark cupboard.

Summer Salad Extravaganza

We take our salads seriously, making a meal of them with homemade bread and butter on hot summer days. We plant a great variety of lettuces—sometimes as many as 27 kinds, both looseleafs and butterheads. We also sow an early and a late crop

*so we are sure to have large salads into the fall. Summer salads are an aesthetic
as well as a culinary experience, combining a variety of leaf forms, textures,
and colors with the delicious flavors of fresh herbs.*

Wash and prepare a mixture of looseleaf and butterhead lettuces such as these looseleaf varieties—'Black-Seeded Simpson', 'Oak Leaf', 'Prize Head', 'Red Salad Bowl', and 'Red Sails'—and these butterheads—'Four Seasons', 'Juliet', 'Red Boston,' and 'Bella'. Fill a wooden bowl with the unbroken leaves—crisp and tender, ruffled crimson and creamy greens—to which add a handful of washed, dark green, wavy-edged arugula leaves. Now mince a small handful of salad burnet, fernleaf dill, and basil, and mix them throughout the salad. Place nasturtium flowers (in mixed colors) on the lettuce bed and serve with the following dressing: ½ cup olive oil, ¼ cup vinegar (basil or dill or your choice), a pressed clove of garlic, a small handful of minced herbs (basil, dill, burnet), lots of fresh-ground pepper, and salt if desired. Stir this mixture and pour it into a salad-dressing jar to blend for at least an hour before using. If the dressing is served at the table, any leftover lettuce can be stored in a bag in the refrigerator and used the following day.

NIGELLA
(Love-in-a-Mist)

Nigella damascena
Ranunculaceae (Buttercup Family)
Type: Annual
Height: 18 inches
Site: Sun
Soil: Well drained

*Nigella
damascena*

This pretty plant from the Mediterranean region earned its common name, love-in-a-mist, by virtue of its fascinating flower construction: Spidery green bracts first surround the bud, then the opened flower with its sky-blue petals and extended anthers; thus, at all stages the flowering parts appear through the airy bracts, as in a mist. As the petals fall, the pod swells like a striped balloon, dispersing its small black seeds through openings that eventually form at the top of the pod. The seeds have a peppery taste and are used as a seasoning, although the preferred culinary type is *N. sativa,* fennel flower or black cumin. The dried pod of love-in-a-mist is used in the West for crafts, as in wreaths and dried bouquets.

For a flower from the warm Mediterranean countries, love-in-a-mist has made itself right at home in my cold northern soil. I seeded it years ago in the harvest bed and have done nothing to encourage it, yet every spring it produces a large number of self-sown seedlings that I thin out to a small stand of plants. I enjoy watching the progress of this dainty flower, so appealing in all of its stages, from the puffy bud to the flower-in-a-mist to the inflated balloon.

I have also grown a close relative, *N. hispanica,* with larger purple flowers and striking horned seedpods, similar to those of black cumin. Its seeds have the same fiery taste and can be used for seasoning. I first tasted the seeds of black cumin when I was in Israel, where they are baked into bread and bagel crusts. This nigella, mentioned in the Bible (Isaiah 28:27), is the only one of the 14 species cultivated since ancient times.

Although I grow nigella primarily to harvest its plentiful seeds for my Kitchen & Garden seed line, I also like it as an ornamental, a filler plant for the front of flower borders. For this purpose, I seek out choice cultivars such as 'Miss Jekyll', with its semidouble blue flowers on tall wiry stems, and 'Miss Jekyll Alba', an all-white variant. 'Persian Jewels', slightly shorter, introduces rose into the mix, creating a pretty haze when in bloom.

Growing: I always seed love-in-a-mist and its relatives directly in the ground early in the season; thin plants at least 3 to 4 inches apart for strong growth.

Harvesting: I was thrilled with my first crop of love-in-a-mist—so many dried pods for winter bouquets. However, when I went to use them after they were dried and stored, they were a tangled mass, the wiry stems intertwined, impossible to separate without shattering the pods. The next time I cut the stems when the pods were striped purple, and I carefully trimmed them to one pod per stem, making them much more manageable. The dried stems should be laid in a box on a layer of tissue paper until ready to use, or placed upright in an ice cream tub. You can also cut love-in-a-mist to dry when it's in the fresh-flower stage. It dries to a powder blue with its airy bracts intact.

Using: Bunches of dried pods or dried flowers are very attractive in posies, or small dried flower bunches. The flowers are an airy filler for brighter dried blooms. I once tried to use the seeds for seasoning, but they had a hallucinatory effect on Jigs, so my culinary experiments came quickly to an end.

PARSLEY

Curly Parsley
Petroselinum crispum
Italian Parsley
P. crispum var. *neopolitanum*
Hamburg Parsley
P. crispum var. *tuberosum*
Apiaceae (Celery Family)
Type: Biennial grown as an annual
Height: 1½ feet
Site: Sun/Partial shade
Soil: Well drained

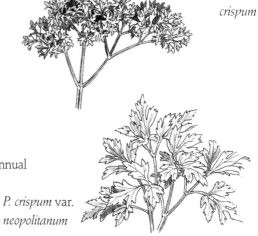

Petroselinum crispum

P. crispum var. *neopolitanum*

Parsley, a native of southern Europe and western Asia, is indispensable in many cuisines. Used to flavor virtually any dish but dessert, it is valued for its extraordinary ability to blend with a variety of foods, yet contribute its own distinctive fresh taste. The three types are curly parsley, bright green with tightly curled, frilly leaves, instantly recognizable as a restaurant garnish; Italian or flat-leaved parsley, generally taller and more vigorous than curly parsley, with flat, glossy green, celery-flavored leaves; and Hamburg parsley, better known in Europe than in America, which is grown mainly for its peppery, parsniplike root. All three parsley types are high in vitamins A and C.

We grew all three parsleys in our large Vermont vegetable garden. The only problem was what to do with it all. I was not very imaginative about herbs in those days. I must have used parsley in cooking, but not significantly. Then we discovered a recipe for Savory Tomato Juice in my cookbook bible of the day, the ninth edition of the *Fannie Farmer Boston Cooking-School Cook Book* (1951), and our parsley problem was solved.

As I read the list of ingredients from its now spattered and well-thumbed pages, I recall the bushels of parsley (all three kinds), the heaps of tomatoes, celery, and carrots that we picked and dug from the dark, rich Vermont loam in early fall. No blenders or food processors back then, just the simple instructions, "Cut all vegetables in pieces . . ." The finished product—a hearty juice, one that is thicker and stronger in flavor than V-8—filled many quart jars that were stored on shelves in our copious root cellar alongside jars of Golden Bantam corn, string beans, and gallons of tomato juice; the floor of the cellar was lined with huge crocks of sauerkraut, heads and heads of cabbage, and much more. Never again would we raise and store so much food. Savory Tomato Juice, in its gigantic proportions, is a symbol of that time when we successfully fed our growing family, as well as our students (we always had at least six teenage boys on board as part of our tutoring school operation), and many guests from our large harvests. It was, in this sense, a time of plenty.

Then came the move to the lonely hinterlands of Cape Breton and the struggle to grow anything from the impoverished, heavy soil. Making Savory Tomato Juice was not high on our list of priorities, although we still grew parsley. Ironically, now that conditions were so difficult, I developed a keen interest in herbs, especially parsley. I began to appreciate its importance as an all-around flavoring herb, handy to sprinkle as dried flakes on our morning eggs even in the dead of winter, and indispensable to Jigs's fall feast—a breakfast of garden tomatoes, a good handful of cut-up fresh curly parsley, and homemade "curds" (cottage cheese), embellished with our own mayonnaise. Perhaps adversity helped me to see the material world with fresh eyes. Nothing could be taken for granted. Everything that grew for us deserved special attention.

So the parsleys, both the curly and the Italian, assumed economic importance when I incorporated them into my Herb Salt and Herb Blend products for Jo Ann's Kitchen & Garden. I value them for the same reasons all cooks do: They go with just about everything, and they combine well with other flavors. Consequently, a lot of thought and care go into choosing cultivars, growing them, harvesting the plants at the proper time, and processing the leaves so they retain their bright green color and fresh flavor—not an easy job.

I read somewhere that "parsley is strictly for the herb garden," which must mean that it's strictly utilitarian. Whoever wrote that has never seen the beautiful emerald mounds of 'Bravour'—our favorite curly type for its vigor and strong regrowth after cutting—edging a flower garden, a cool frill among hot pinks, bright orange, and red tones. We plant it in rows in the vegetable garden, but it certainly has a place as an ornamental (one you can eat, too). I like to plant it in a half-barrel by the kitchen door, with herbs like salad burnet and fernleaf dill, for quick picking. A single plant among these of the golden yellow signet marigold, 'Lulu', creates an all-season herb garden with aesthetic appeal.

Growing: Parsley must be raised every year as an annual, since it quickly goes to seed its second season with little in the way of leaves to harvest. An old saying aptly describes its slow germination: "Parsley goes to the Devil and back again nine times before it comes up."

Jigs used to raise seedlings indoors, where they may take a month to germinate. Now, however, he sows the seed directly in the ground at the same time the other vegetables are planted, sowing radishes with the parsley to mark the rows. By the time the first radishes are ready to pull, the small parsley plants have filled out the rows. No time is saved by raising seedlings indoors since they are usually set back after being planted. Direct seeding produces more vigorous plants. However you raise plants, be sure to use fresh seed. Thin curly and Italian parsleys to 6 to 8 inches apart, and give Hamburg parsley 8 to 10 inches of room between plants so it can develop large roots. Soil should be enriched (high in nitrogen) for good leaf production. Italian parsley is reputed to tolerate dry growing conditons better than the curly kind.

For winter houseplants, start parsley in midsummer, in pots, and gradually introduce the plants to indoor conditions in the fall. Indoors, keep soil moist and give plants at least 5 hours of sun a day. Mature plants, dug and potted in the fall from the garden, will go to seed by midwinter indoors, so it's best to winter-over young plants.

Harvesting and Drying: You'll want to use your parsley all winter long if it is harvested and dried to maintain its flavor. (I prefer drying herbs to freezing them.) Cut parsley to the cleanest stems above the growing crown, wash if necessary, then cut in small pieces (it's okay to include some stems), and lay them on clean screens—elevated for air circulation—to dry away from direct light. Finish off the parsley to a crispy dryness in a just-warm oven (set no higher than 150 degrees F). Gently rub the dried parsley until it's the texture of flakes, not powder; you can put it through a strainer, then pulverize the stems if you wish, and add them to the mix. You can mix the two types (curly and

Italian) or keep them separate. Store the parsley in labeled jars out of direct light. Never try to air-dry parsley in suspended bunches; it will quickly turn yellow and won't be worth using.

Using: Cut leaves all summer to use fresh, as soon as plants are growing vigorously. It hardly seems necessary to spell out parsley's versatility: Use it in everything, alone with carrots, potatoes, egg and cheese dishes, or in combination with other herbs, as in the traditional French mix, *fines herbes*. The term is used to describe various combinations of finely chopped fresh herbs used for general flavoring purposes. Although you can make up your own *fines herbes* mix, the traditional combinations are parsley, chervil, and chives; parsley, basil, and chives; and parsley, thyme, and burnet. Use these mixtures freely in cream sauces, omelets, herb butters, and just about anything else.

The flat-leaved Italian parsley can be used in place of celery, especially in soups and stews. Hamburg parsley is grown like turnips or parsnips and used the same way. Young leafy tops and young roots are eaten raw; the roots are sweeter if left in the ground until exposed to frost.

PEARLY EVERLASTING
(Ladies' Tobacco,
Rabbit Tobacco)

Anaphalis margaritacea
Asteraceae (Aster Family)
Type: Perennial
Height: 1 to 3 feet
Site: Sun/Partial shade
Soil: Well drained, dry
Growing Zones: 3–6

*Anaphalis
margaritacea*

Pearly everlasting is a native plant appearing in poor, dry ground at the edge of woodlands, and in cutover land around tree stumps across Canada and the United States to the Dakotas. Plants grow pointed silvery leaves on hard, dry stems, topped by button- or pearl-like clusters of little white pompons whose centers turn tannish yellow as the flowers mature. Pearly everlasting was used as a medicinal among various Native American tribes to treat bronchial ailments; the early settlers stuffed the dried flower heads into sleep pillows thought to alleviate asthma, using it also as a plant dye and a tobacco substitute. As its common name suggests, pearly everlasting is a dry plant in all of its parts, recommending its widespread use in dried bouquets and related crafts.

It's one thing to read about how people used plants in the past—the uses seem quaint to us today—but it's quite another to live in a society where such uses are still within living memory, as they are on our remote island. I've met men in their 80s who recognize pearly everlasting as the plant used to stuff pillows, who know it as the tobacco substitute, "rabbit tobacco," and who remember when it was harvested to yield a yellow dye.

I first noticed pearly everlasting growing in our upland pastures and at the wood's edge. Walking the old woods roads to a neighbor's house to make a phone call, we would pass cutover land grown up to spruce trees, the old stumps now garlanded with circles of the dainty wildflower. I used them to great effect in dried nosegays to sell at the fall craft sales, the heads like little roses, so pretty with the pinks and blues of annual clary *(Salvia viridis)*. Everyone wanted to know what I did to produce such pure white, fluffy flowers with no hint of a muddy center. The answer is quite simple—I just pick them before the buds open.

This is easier said than done, though, since the plants are ready to pick in early August, and some years we are still busy haying. No time to pick flowers when there's hay to make, when all of our energies are devoted to this single cause. Just as soon as the last load rumbles into the barn, however, Jigs and I head for the woods right behind the house, up the old logging roads to the spots here and there where the flowers grow. Each of us carries a basket, going our separate ways as we spot good picking, a stand of plants still in bud. Sometimes, depending on conditions, the flowers may have already bloomed, but usually there are still some immature plants around. Back in the kitchen, I strip the stems of leaves and hang the white-headed bunches upside down to dry. Just as harvesting the first mauve chive flowers signals the beginning of haying, pearly everlasting marks the end of our great summer labor.

Pearly everlasting is also a garden flower, highly regarded for its button-like flowers and silvery foliage. The leaves provide a striking contrast among darker foliage, attractive throughout the growing season, and, unlike other silver-leaved plants, it is tolerant of both moist and dry soils. There are some choice cultivars available of the closely related *A. triplinervis,* like the dwarf 'Summer Snow', used effectively to edge borders.

Growing: If you want to grow pearly everlasting, set plants 12 to 15 inches apart in whatever soil you have, even a poor and dry one. If you can find seeds, sow them in summer and the plants will bloom the following season.

Using: Pearly everlasting makes a fine cut flower for fresh bouquets or a dried flower for bouquets, wreaths, and other dried flower crafts. Pick the stems before the flowers have opened, strip off the leaves by running your hand along the hard stems, secure them with an elastic band, and hang bunches to dry out of bright light.

ROSES
Apothecary Rose (French Rose, Red Rose of Lancaster)
Rosa gallica 'Officinalis'
Rugosa Rose (Japanese Rose)
R. rugosa 'Rubra Plena'
Virginia Rose (Common Rose, Shining Rose)
R. virginiana
Rosaceae (Rose Family)
Type: Perennial shrubs
Height: 3 to 6 feet
Site: Sun
Soil: Well drained
Growing Zones: 3–10

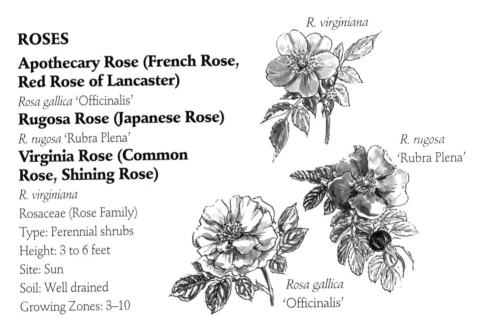

R. virginiana

R. rugosa 'Rubra Plena'

Rosa gallica 'Officinalis'

Roses have always been with us, admired for thousands of years for their beauty, scent, and medicinal properties. Rose petals have been used to impart their astringency, color, and flavor to tonics, syrups, and washes; their scent to essential oils and potpourri; their hips or fruits, high in vitamin C, to tea and jam. *Rosa gallica* 'Officinalis', probably the oldest form of this rose in cultivation, may have been introduced westward from Damascus to France in the 13th century. The New England settlers brought it to the New World for its general medicinal and flavoring uses. Tons of petals were once exported from Provence (from which it earned the name of French rose) to be used in medicines and perfumes; the petals gain in fragrance when they are dried. A low, spreading bush to 3 feet in height, with crisp, loosely doubled, rich crimson petals surrounding glistening yellow stamens, the apothecary rose has a remarkably modern look and habit, its stems nearly thornless, its fruits small, round, and rosy red.

The rugosa rose was introduced to America from Japan in the mid-19th century because it could be grown near salt water. 'Rubra Plena' is a semi-double variant with strongly clove-scented dark pink petals and dark green wrinkled leaves—*rugosa* means "wrinkled"—followed by large, round, orange-red hips. In favorable conditions (good soil) the thorny shrubs reach 6 feet in height.

The Virginia rose, native to North America and found growing from Newfoundland to Missouri and south to Georgia, has the classic wild form: five translucent, fragrant pink petals—from light to dark in color—loosely clustered around numerous golden stamens, with dark green, glossy leaves on thorny canes that grow to 6 feet. Its dark red hips are small and borne in numerous clusters, giving the bush the appearance of blooming again.

My romance with roses began when we dug up several plants of the Virginia rose that grows wild along our back roads and planted them as a hedge by our front porch. It was accidentally successful, for although we knew nothing about growing roses, we had chosen well: a low-maintenance, disease- and bug-resistant rose that prefers heavy, damp soil. Although seldom cultivated, it is marvelous for landscaping. Planted 25 years ago, it has remained right where we put it, kept in place simply by mowing the grass in front of it. It gives us little trouble and much pleasure, producing its pretty, scented, variably pink flowers in season (mid-July here), and its hips by the fall when its foliage turns bronzy red.

For many years thereafter, this was the sum total of my experience with roses, except for the old double-pink shrub rose (the 'Banshee' or Loyalist rose, of unknown origin) that we inherited with the property. Called "Grandmother's shrub rose" locally, it bears intensely perfumed, double, light pink blossoms (it is thought to be a natural hybrid of the highly scented old alba rose), but they often fail to open because of a fungus disease. I had no desire to add possible problems to our life by acquiring more roses. I was content to harvest the petals from these two roses to use in my Kitchen & Garden potpourri.

Then, I discovered the rugosas, the toughest group of roses in the world, able to withstand salt spray and poor growing conditions. We had admired the semidouble variant 'Rubra Plena' growing all over the end of our peninsula in the little village of Iona, where it was introduced by the 1920s. There it is buffeted by strong winds blowing off the Bras d'Or Lake (actually an arm of the North Atlantic Ocean). After a first flush of bloom in July, the tall bushes bloom again in the fall, giving the appearance of rose-bearing trees. Such a vigorous, tough rose, with a deliciously intense clovelike scent to boot, seemed a likely candidate for our difficult backlands terrain, and friends on the peninsula gladly gave us a few chunks of roots. I planted them at the top of our half-mile lane on clay sod ground with virtually no topsoil. Even with good feeding they have reached only 3 feet in height, dwarfed by their growing conditions.

These experiences with roses piqued my curiosity and soon I expanded my repertoire to include a number of hardy types: species or wild roses; hybrid rugosas; classic old garden roses; indestructible climbers such as 'Dorothy Perkins'; and the apothecary rose, an old garden rose in a class by itself in my landscape because of its history as the herbal rose "from the apothecary." All of these have proved hardy without winter protection in my Zone 4 gardens. They are disease- and insect-resistant, requiring little maintenance except annual pruning. Most of them are scented, have landscape value, and are pressed into service for the production of various Kitchen & Garden products. Picking their blossoms and silky petals on a fine summer day is hardly labor; it's a time to savor each rose type with its unique coloring, scent, and form.

Our favorite is the ancient apothecary rose, shoots of which I obtained from our eccentric gardening neighbor, Henry. He walked down the row of plants and pulled up canes here and there, with no digging at all. I planted these as a hedge behind our coldframe on a south-facing bank with good air circulation. Like our first hedge of wild roses, it too has thrived (not difficult when you're dealing with naturally vigorous types). It blooms the whole month of July, a spectacular sight in full flower with its bright, richly colored blossoms in profusion, immediately striking to the eye when one drives up to the top of our lane.

It was the apothecary rose that really inspired me to make rose petal products; its petals—strongly colored and scented—are especially suited. I pick the blossoms to make rose petal syrup, jelly, skin freshener, and vinegar, and gallons of petals go into potpourri. It's hard to pluck the flower heads of any rose—for years I only harvested petals from the ground, not wanting to rob the plants of their glory—but now, with a moderate collection, I can allow myself the double pleasure of admiring roses as they grow and using them, too.

Growing: All roses thrive in full sun, in open conditions with good air circulation; this discourages fungus diseases. All need well-drained soil (moist and heavy is okay) enriched with organic matter. Dig the planting hole as deep and wide as you need to accommodate the roots. If you can't dig a deep enough hole (authorities never consider the possibility), trim the roots to fit. Enrich the planting-hole soil with rotted manure or compost, and mix in a few good handfuls of bonemeal. Try to drape the roots over a mound of soil to ensure a good start in life by providing super drainage. Tamp down the soil, water well, and continue to water (unless the season is wet) until you see signs of growth. Mulching will keep weeds at bay and reduce the need for watering in dry spells; roses really thrive with a steady supply of moisture. None of these roses requires special pruning. Just clip out the dead, crossed, or old canes in the spring. (Clip back the Virginia rose to 4 feet to maintain it as a bushy hedge.) Also in spring, make sure the soil bed is rich in rotted manure or compost.

If your rose is grafted (indicated by a thickness or swelling at or near the soil line on the main stem), bury the graft 2 to 4 inches below the soil if you live where winters are severe. Frost damage to the graft will result in the death of the top of the rose (the desired part) and the plant, if it survives, will take on the characteristics of the rootstock (usually the dog or multiflora rose, both rampant spreaders). The apothecary, rugosa, and Virginia roses are easily propagated by replanting suckers or by making stem cuttings from flexible young canes just after blooming.

Using: Pick lots of bouquets. Aside from enjoying them indoors, you can have the satisfaction of knowing that picking will encourage the production of more blooms. If roses are picked just as they begin to open, they will last longer. Sprays of *Cynoglossom amabile* (Chinese forget-me-not) or curled tansy complement a variety of rose forms. When the bouquet has passed its prime, all the flowers can be recycled for making potpourri. Pick fresh petals for potpourri on a sunny day after the dew has dried; spread them to dry on screens or on cookie sheets in a just-warm oven, where they will probably dry overnight. They should be crispy dry; otherwise they will mold when stored in covered containers. The following are some of my favorite ways to use fresh and dried petals.

Rose Petal Jelly

2 quarts dark, fragrant rose petals (apothecary and/or rugosa), loosely
    packed
3 cups water
1 package fruit pectin crystals
2 tablespoons lemon juice
4 cups sugar

Heat the petals to boiling in the water. Bruise with the bottom of a jelly jar, cover, and let steep for 20 minutes, mashing occasionally with the jar. Strain out the petals, reserving the liquid; add water, if necessary, to make 3 cups. Stir in the pectin crystals and lemon juice and return to the heat. When this mixture comes to a rolling boil that cannot be stirred down, add the sugar and again bring the mixture to a rolling boil. Stir and boil for exactly 1 minute. Remove the pot from the heat and let the mixture subside, skimming off froth if necessary. Pour into scalded jelly jars and seal at once. The jelly will be a rich rose color and will taste the way roses smell. This is delicious on buttered bran muffins.

Rose Petal Sandwiches

I serve these sandwiches at herb and rose workshops in the month of July when the roses are at their peak of bloom. Gather petals from any fragrant rose (these have the most rose flavor; an assortment is pretty) after the dew has dried on a sunny day. Press the petals into cream cheese spread on thinly sliced whole wheat bread. Trim the crusts, lightly sprinkle a little cinnamon-sugar mix on top of the petals, then serve on a platter embellished with small whole roses (I use the small double-flowered, scented cinnamon rose, R. cinnamomea.) It's generally advised to cut out the white part at the base of the petals because of its bitter taste; I have neither the time nor the inclination to do this, and I really don't think it's necessary.

Rose Petal Vinegar

Steep apothecary and rugosa petals in a jar full of white vinegar that has been brought just to the boiling point. Place the jar in sunlight until the petals have infused the liquid with their color and scent, perhaps a week. Do not leave the jar in the sunlight too long or the mixture will lose both its color and its scent. Strain out the petals. **To use as a skin freshener,** dilute mixture half-and-half with water. Add 1 cup to bath water or 2 tablespoons to a basin of wash water (do not get the mixture in your eyes); or dab the solution on your forehead, behind your ears, and on your wrists, using a piece of cotton batting. This is both soothing and invigorating, much like my Herbal Skin Freshener (see *Costmary*). Rose Petal Vinegar is also soothing for headaches. Wring out a washcloth in the diluted solution and place on your forehead. Add a dash of undiluted Rose Petal Vinegar to fresh fruit cup desserts.

Rose Petal Potpourri

This is simple to make if you have lots of rose petals. Add 1 teaspoon essential rose oil to 3 tablespoons of fixative (orrisroot, cellulose, or your choice) in a small jar. Shake the jar every now and then for 3 days, after which the mixture can be added to 1 quart of dried rose petals and stored in a tightly closed container for 3 to 6 weeks; turn the container upside down every other day so the oil-fixative mixture is well dispersed. The dried petals can be supplemented with any pretty flowers or herbs whose scent you like. Lemon balm and/or broken, dried orange peel add a citrusy note to the mixture, for instance, as well as visual interest. You can also add a few drops of lemon or sweet orange essential oil to the rose essence to make your own blend. My favorite rose variation is **Rose-Spice Potpourri:** Add dried bayberry leaves (these grow wild in poor ground at the woodland's edge), dried carnation heads, and dried, broken orange peel to the rose petals. Then add a few drops of cinnamon and/or clove oil to the rose oil–fixative mixture.

ROSEMARY

Rosmarinus officinalis
Labiatae (Mint Family)
Type: Tender perennial/Shrub
Height: 2 to 8 feet
Site: Sun
Soil: Well drained
Growing Zones: 8–10

Rosmarinus officinalis

Rosemary is a tall, wide Mediterranean shrub that northern gardeners know as a potted plant of more modest proportions. The narrow, needlelike leaves bear the unmistakable aroma—sweet and piney—that makes this one of the most beloved of all herbs. Where it grows as a shrub it is often in flower; these are small, two-lipped, and light blue, growing in leaf axils from stems that turn woody, often twisted, in maturity. Rosemary has an ancient history of use—comparable to that of lavender—for scenting, for strewing, and for alleviating stomach disorders and headaches. It is traditionally used with pork and lamb, because, like sage, it is supposed to aid in the digestion of rich meats. Rosemary is associated with enduring values—remembrance and fidelity—because its leaves retain their penetrating aroma long after they are picked.

Like many northern gardeners, I've broken my heart over rosemary, raised it from seed, carefully potted the seedlings, summered potted plants outdoors, wintered potted plants indoors, only to have them all expire every few years, initiating another round of life and death.

On my first trip to Israel I had the chance to observe rosemary in a quite different setting: a sea of blue lining the streets of Jerusalem, in full bloom in midwinter and early spring (apparently it is seldom out of bloom there), growing everywhere like a weed. This is the trailing type (*R. officinalis* 'Prostratus') that the late American herb authority Helen Fox had admired on a trip to Israel in the 1950s. For those living in California and other frost-free areas with a Mediterranean-like climate, the sight of everblooming rosemary draped over low walls or growing as enormous, spreading shrubs is taken for granted. But for the northern gardener, it's a continual source of wonder. "So that's rosemary!" I found myself exclaiming more than once.

Although there is only one species, it is variable, giving rise to many named cultivars. 'Prostratus' is one of the hardier types, grown outdoors year-round in Zone 7. 'Miss Jessup' an upright variety with pink flowers, and 'Tuscan Blue', an extraordinarily vigorous upright plant, to 10 feet with blue flowers, are both hardy to Zone 7; 'Hardy Hill', with blue flowers, is hardy to Zone 6. 'Arp', discovered by the author Madalene Hill in Arp, Texas, is hardy to Zone 6 and may prove hardy in some areas of Zone 5 with protection. Basically, rosemary is supposed to be able to survive where winter temperatures do not dip below 10 degrees, but a lot also depends on the site, whether it is protected or exposed.

Meanwhile, if we have to raise or buy new plants every few years, this opens up the opportunity to try different cultivars. Fortunately, rosemary looks great outdoors in tubs, especially when it attains some size. I "plant" it in my sunny, so-called Mediterranean garden—a southern-exposed raised bed filled with lavender, thymes, and basils. By judiciously placing the pots behind other plants, the rosemary appears to be growing from the ground. Its distinctive narrow, slightly textured leaves, and graceful, twisting stems add distinction to any grouping of plants.

Growing: I have not found rosemary seeds difficult to germinate in a week at 70 degrees, although it may take up to three weeks. The seedlings should be raised like lavender, in somewhat gritty soil that allows water to drain quickly from the roots. Don't be disappointed if your rosemary seldom blooms or blooms sporadically. That will depend on the plant type, the amount of light and heat it receives, as well as the quantity of leaves that have been cut for use, since flower buds form on old growth. Indoors, most plants need cool, sunny, and moist conditions, yet rosemary should be kept on the dry side; waterlogged soil is the main cause of early death.

It's not difficult to propagate rosemary by stem cuttings; even with my rude technology, I've created dozens of healthy little plants from 4-inch stem tips cut from healthy plants in midsummer when outdoor temperatures are in the 70s. I raise these cuttings in a vacant hotbed until they can be potted and placed in a sheltered site protected from wind near the back door (where I'm reminded to water them).

Using: Leaves can be dried year-round to use in potpourri or "sweet bags"—sachets for scenting linens, clothes, even bath or rinse water. For this purpose, wrap a good handful of dried leaves in a piece of cheesecloth, steep the bag in 2 cups of very hot water for 10 minutes, then add to your bath or other water as desired. Rosemary scent, like lavender, is soothing and invigorating. I use the leaves sparingly on roasted potatoes and pork dishes. For herb workshops, I add a teaspoon of fresh chopped rosemary to biscuit or sugar cookie dough.

RUE
(Herb-of-Grace)

Ruta graveolens
Rutaceae (Rue Family)
Type: Perennial
Height: 3 feet
Site: Sun
Soil: Well-drained
Growing Zones: 4–9

Ruta graveolens

Rue is a perfectly mounded miniature shrub, woody at its base, with striking blue-green scalloped leaves, and, late in the season, ½-inch-wide yellow flowers borne in loose clusters. Originating in southern Europe, rue earned a reputation throughout Europe as a protector (hence its other common name, herb-of-grace), guarding against everything from snakebite to evil spells, probably based on the pungent-acrid scent of its leaves and the fact that its brushy stems were used by priests to sprinkle holy water.

I first became acquainted with rue from Jigs's plant, which we toted from Vermont to Cape Breton. Here it was one of the plant pioneers in my new herb and flower garden, handsome at the front of the circular bed among the purple-flowered hyssop and the yellow, daisylike flowers of dyer's chamomile *(Anthemis tinctoria)*. It was a successful planting from every point of view, an interweaving of complementary leaf forms and flower colors. Looking back, I wonder how I knew enough to combine these particular plants. Was it instinct?

I especially learned to appreciate rue's late and long flowering, enduring several hard frosts. Even after the flowers are gone, the desiccated flower and seed heads remain attractive, stiffly waving in brisk winds. Rue's flowers have been undervalued, in deference to its outstanding foliage.

But the "move-its," an affliction known to most gardeners, kept nagging at me to dig up this perfectly happy plant and put it somewhere else. Rue had its revenge—it died. I felt its absence in this garden of mainly ornamental herbs, where the herb-of-grace so obviously belonged, and several years later I bought the plant from an herb nursery. It's as handsome as I recall, a perfectly shaped mound of blue-green lace and late-blooming clustered flowers.

I saw rue from an entirely different perspective on a trip to Israel, where the Middle Eastern species *R. chalapensis,* fringed rue, is in full showy bloom by late winter. A taller plant than European rue, with more significant flowers, I saw it growing wild in many areas, often crowned by flocks of swallowtail butterflies. I met a fisherman by the Sea of Galilee with 10 children, who, their father told me, had all been raised on herbal remedies for their various ailments. He used rue leaves in his olive cure (homemade olives are highly prized in Israel, as are the various recipes), to which he attributed its fine taste. I also saw rue growing in the garden of a woman who was originally from Libya. "Why do you grow it?" I asked, thinking she, too, had a use for its oddly flavored leaves. "Because our parents grew it," she said, "because it brings good luck." Rue's reputation as the protector plant seems to have universal application.

When I returned home after this trip, I was surprised to learn that the very same rue I had admired in Israel is offered for sale to discerning herb gardeners. Well-Sweep Herb Farm in New Jersey offers it as Egyptian or fringed rue. Of course, it must be grown in the Northeast as a tender perennial, but, like rosemary, it is very handsome in a tub. The most popular cultivar of the European rue, *R. graveolens,* is 'Jackman's Blue', a dwarf, hardy form with deeper blue foliage.

Growing: Start rue from seed 12 weeks before the last frost date, when it should germinate in 10 to 14 days at 70 degrees. Although it will tolerate partial shade, for best results plant it in full sun, in sharply drained, not overly rich soil, spacing 1 foot apart if you are growing more than one plant. Clip it back in the spring to new growth; plants may die back almost to the ground, but they should recover as the season warms. Propagate by division in spring or by making stem cuttings during summer.

Take note that, under certain conditions, handling rue can cause skin irritation. This may occur through the action of the hot sun on the oils in the plants' leaves and is more likely to occur when one is handling mature plants. I have never had a reaction, probably because those conditions do not obtain in our climate.

Using: The dried flower or seed heads are attractive in dried bouquets.

SAGE (Cooking Sage, Common Sage)

Salvia officinalis
Labiatae (Mint Family)
Type: Perennial
Height: 1 to 2½ feet
Site: Sun
Soil: Well drained
Growing Zones 4–10

Salvia officinalis

When one says "sage," one usually means cooking sage, a popular culinary herb most widely associated with seasoning poultry and pork dishes (it's supposed to aid in their digestion). Sage has also been highly regarded as a medicinal plant from ancient times to the present. Preparations from its leaves have been used to induce sweating and to treat fevers, sore throats, mouth sores, and rheumatism. It is not surprising that its genus name, *Salvia,* means "to save." Native to the Mediterranean region, sage grows on wiry stems that turn woody by their second year, when the plant sends up a flowering stalk packed with small, two-lipped, purplish or white flowers in whorls. Sage leaves are very attractive—pebbly textured, slightly puckered, a soft apple green when young and a silvery gray-green in maturity. Their flavor, strongly camphoraceous and pungent, is enhanced by drying.

We have always grown sage, an indispensable seasoning for the pork sausage we have been making every year for over three decades. I didn't find it as easy to grow in our new home in Canada, where soil conditions are cold, heavy, and moist (not at all Mediterranean-like), but since I didn't have to try to winter it over in unfavorable conditions—cooking sage is usually grown as an annual for its tender leaves—I always managed to have enough for our modest needs.

Then one fall I left some plants in the ground instead of discarding them. The next season, I was surprised to see that they had wintered over, and even more surprised when they bloomed. How pretty they were in early summer, the striking purplish spires above silvery green leaves. From that time on, I regarded my "just cooking sage" quite differently, as a handsome perennial shrub and a reliable, long-lasting flower. I now grow first-year plants in the harvest bed and older plants wherever their attractive leaves and flowers can be shown to advantage, near yellow daylilies and orange lilies. Cooking sage is tougher than I thought. It's a shame that its fame as an annual culinary herb has so obscured its virtue as a beautiful perennial.

There are several cultivars of *S. officinalis* that I would like to grow: the white-flowered 'Albiflora'; the short and small-leaved 'Dwarf' or 'Nana' form (it would be great in a rockery, if I had one); and the magnificent 'Berggarten', a low, wide, mounding plant with enormous, soft, silvery green leaves, introduced from Germany. I first saw it at the Herb Society of America's Western Reserve Herb Garden at the Cleveland Botanical Garden (where I was giving a lecture on heirloom herbs and flowers). I shall always associate it with with the beautiful plantings there and the warm, gentle Ohio fall. I hope it can be induced to grow on our rough backlands farm.

Growing: Since sage seeds quickly lose their viability, use new seed every year; older seed will germinate, but poorly. You can sow seeds directly in the ground, or, to get a head start, sow them indoors 6 to 8 weeks before the last frost, just pressing the seeds into moist soil; germination usually takes 4 to 12 days at 70 to 85 degrees. Plant seedlings outdoors after the last expected frost, spacing plants 18 to 24 inches apart. Clip back mature plants to growing points to encourage fresh growth from the woody base. Plants also can be divided. Sage is a short-lived perennial, so plan on raising new seedlings every few years or making stem cuttings during the summer.

Using: Over the years I've found other ways to use sage beyond sausage. It is used fresh in jelly, fresh or dried in Jigs's Barbecued Chicken and in Herbed

Cottage Cheese Spread. Sage is always nice in fresh bouquets. I've also dried leaves on their stems—they curl attractively and turn gray-green—to use in dried bouquets and tussie-mussies (it signifies good health in the language of flowers). A friend of mine uses dried sage to great effect in little herb wreaths.

Jigs's Barbecued Chicken

ABOUT 1 HOUR COOKING TIME FOR A SPLIT, 6-POUND CHICKEN

This is a specialty of the house, popular in the summer (especially with me, since I don't have to cook the chicken) and in the fall, when Jigs roasts ears of 'Golden Bantam' corn in the coals after the chicken is cooked.

Mix the following sauce an hour before cooking the chicken:

½ cup cooking oil (vegetable and olive)

½ cup vinegar

¼ cup water

2 teaspoons salt

¼ teaspoon pepper

1 tablespoon sugar (optional)

1 teaspoon paprika

1 pressed clove garlic (or ½ teaspoon powder)

1 teaspoon fresh sage (or ½ teaspoon dried)

1 teaspoon fresh marjoram (or ½ teaspoon dried)

Split the chicken, put it in a deep roasting pan, and give it to the barbecue pit-master, along with a long fork and pot holders. Carry out the sauce in a little jug as well as a container of extra water. This is how Jigs cooks the chicken outdoors: A fire is started in a small, open pit (the same one used for our smoke-house). He uses hardwood so it will make a bed of coals. When the fire is going well, the split chicken is seared through the flames. Then it is put into the roasting pan, the herb sauce is poured over the chicken, extra water is added to the pan (about 1½ cups), and the pan is tightly covered and set on a rack above the bed of coals. This procedure, cooking in a covered roasting pan, ensures a moist chicken with herb gravy. We usually serve this with rice and our Summer Salad Extravaganza (see *Nasturtium*). The sauce is put in a gravy bowl and guests are encouraged to cut their chicken in pieces, lay them over the rice, and pour on some of the herb sauce.

Alternatively, you can roast the split chicken in the oven, browning it first at 400 degrees F for 15 to 20 minutes, then lowering the heat to 350, adding the herb sauce and extra water, and proceeding as above.

Herbed Cottage Cheese Spread

(ADAPTED FROM IRMA GOODRICH MAZZA'S *HERBS FOR THE KITCHEN;* LITTLE, BROWN, 1947)

1 pound cottage cheese
1 teaspoon minced chives
½ teaspoon each of poppy seeds and caraway seeds
2 tablespoons cream
1 teaspoon olive oil
1 full teaspoon each of fresh, minced marjoram, basil, thyme, sage
Salt and pepper to taste
Paprika as desired

Mix all the ingredients together, adding more olive oil if necessary to make a spread. Put the mixture into a covered crock or bowl to blend for at least an hour before using; then refrigerate. This is delicious on thinly sliced homemade rye bread.

TENDER SAGES

Mealycup Sage (Blue Sage)

Salvia farinacea

Texas Sage (Scarlet Sage)

S. coccinea

Type: Tender perennials
Height: 1 to 3 feet
Site: Sun
Soil: Well drained
Growing Zones: 7–10 for *farinacea;*
8–10 for *coccinea*

Salvia farinacea

Both these frost-tender sages are native to North America. Mealycup sage grows wild from New Mexico to Texas, reaching 2 to 3 feet in height. A slender plant, it bears bright blue-flowered spikes of closely packed, tiny flowers on stems that rise from a base of medium green, small, heart-shaped leaves. The flowers, very attractive to bees, look as if they were dusted with flour at their base, perhaps explaining the origin of the plant's common name. Texas sage has a wider natural range, growing from South Carolina to Florida, west to Texas and Mexico, and throughout the tropics (it is sometimes referred to as tropical sage). A rangier plant, it grows to 2 feet or more with spikes of bright red, 1-inch tubular flowers in loose whorls on dark stems. These grow above sharp-scented, pointed green leaves. Mealycup and Texas sage are grown as annuals in most of North America (north of Zones 7 or 8).

Years ago, I got some seed of Texas sage through a seed exchange. I grew it in a tub during the summer, wintered it over indoors (where it continued to flower for a long time), then planted it outside in early summer the following season. It soon expired. I know now that I should have waited until the soil was warmer since this is a tropical plant, but in those days I was not a very conscious gardener. I dismissed this failure with the comforting thought that flashy salvias weren't for me, that they were too much trouble. I should add that, at that time, there was virtually no information on how to grow frost-tender salvias in the Northeast.

Several years later, a friend from Texas sent me seeds of Texas sage, and, remembering the vivid flowering stalks, I planted the seeds once more. This time I kept the planted container (an old sap bucket) in the greenhouse until the weather had warmed in late June, then placed it on our front porch, where I could just see the flowers through the kitchen window. What fun it was to watch hummingbirds feeding on the flowers' nectar as I ate my own breakfast. This was such an enjoyable experience that I reconsidered my attitude toward growing frost-tender salvias, and when I saw the seeds of the dwarf cultivar 'Lady in Red' advertised in a seed catalog, I decided to try it.

Winner of several awards (All-America Selection, 1992; Fleuroselect Gold), 'Lady in Red' is a great improvement over the rangy wildflower. A compact plant from 12 to 15 inches tall, it is also early blooming. The wildflower I grew from seed blossomed in late summer here, just in time to catch the hummingbirds before they moved south for the winter. The improved cultivar, on the other hand, bloomed by early July from seeds sown indoors in early April.

Taller forms of Texas sage—from 2 to 3 feet, in white, peach, and bicolors (pink and cream)—are well worth hunting for; I've seen them growing in fancy herb gardens down-country (available from specialty plant and herb companies; see Sources). Thompson & Morgan offers seeds of 'Starry-Eyed Mix', which I intend to try.

Mealycup sage, like Texas sage, is better known as an annual, especially in the dwarf form 'Victoria', which grows to 20 inches, producing masses of spectacular deep blue flowers, each one set off by a pure white calyx. It, too, is an award winner (Fleuroselect, 1978) and a boon to gardeners in the Northeast who want to grow showy salvias that bloom reliably the first season from seed. Dwarf forms are always earlier-blooming, definitely a virtue where the growing season is short. I'd heard so much about mealycup sage as a prized dried flower that I decided to try 'Victoria', the hardiest *farinacea* cultivar. In my experience, it takes a little more coddling than 'Lady in Red' and doesn't respond as well to pot culture unless the soil is kept moist. I've seen 'Victoria' growing in the ground in other gardens, and I think it does better under these conditions. Seeds sown at the same time as 'Lady in Red' started to bloom at the same time in early July, attracting bees and butterflies.

An increasing number of tropical and Mediterranean species and their cultivars are being introduced to the trade these days. Some of them are stunning, but little is known about their hardiness and most of them are not widely available. You should probably know, by the way, that non-herby types (or those whose uses are not known) are listed in nursery catalogs under *Salvia*—the code word for ornamental sages—rather than under Sage, which connotes culinary use.

Growing: Sow seeds indoors 12 weeks before the last frost on the soil surface, as you would other *Salvia* species (see *Sage*). Do not plant out seedlings until outdoor temperatures are consistently warm. Plants thrive in rich, moist soil in full sun. *S. coccinea* (and its cultivars), as well as 'Victoria', withstands frosts to about 28 degrees before succumbing. Both types can be wintered-over indoors; *S. coccinea* is especially free-flowering. Stem cuttings can be made anytime you have 70-degree conditions, either outdoors in summer or indoors in winter and early spring. Mature plants can be cut back and put outdoors again, in the ground or in containers. (It's easier to move container-grown plants indoors than to dig up and pot plants growing in the ground.) All frost-tender salvias can be grown this way.

Using: Cut spikes of *S. farinacea* when about four-fifths of the flowers have just opened. Small, rather than large, bunches air-dry fairly quickly, with the spikes retaining their deep blue color.

Satureja hortensis

SUMMER SAVORY

Satureja hortensis
Labiatae (Mint Family)
Type: Annual
Height: 12 to 18 inches
Site: Sun
Soil: Well drained

WINTER SAVORY

S. montana
Type: Perennial
Height: 6 to 12 inches
Site: Sun
Soil: Well drained
Growing Zones: 5–10

S. montana

Summer savory, an annual from Eurasia, and the perennial winter savory, from the Mediterranean region, are both used for seasoning. They differ, however, in flavor and growth habit. Summer savory is an upright, slender plant with narrow, lance-shaped leaves set at intervals along weak, branching stems. Tiny lavender-pink flowers appear in leaf axils by midsummer. The sweet, tangy-tasting leaves are traditionally used with beans (the German name for summer savory is *bohnenkraut* or "bean herb"), strong-flavored vegetables like cabbage, and poultry dishes.

Winter savory, actually a small shrub with a woody base, is a low, wide plant with smaller, pointed, and glossy leaves that have a sharper flavor than those of summer savory. A mass of tiny white flowers blooms in late summer, giving the plant the appearance of being covered with snow.

Summer savory is a staple herb we have always grown, either in the vegetable garden with dill, parsley, and basil, or in a separate planting of herbs. It took to the cold, northern soil of Cape Breton, which must explain why it's the only herb regularly used for seasoning in the Canadian Maritimes.

One year, when I failed to harvest summer savory until late in the season, I was surprised to note that the flowering tops had turned deep purple, most attractive. My daughter, Nellie Call, who runs a cut-flower business in upstate New York, grows this and several other herbs—mints, sage, tarragon—for bouquets. One of these years, I may just grow summer savory as an ornamental.

I was quite surprised to learn that the local Acadian population, of French stock, does not share in the general enthusiasm for using summer savory as a culinary herb, but prefers the harder-to-grow, more strongly flavored winter savory. One summer when my friend Monique and I went out to inspect my harvest bed, she shook her head over what I thought was a fine stand of summer savory.

"That's not what we use," she said emphatically, as she rubbed the leaves and smelled their scent. I thought she must be thinking of a special variety of summer savory and I was eager for her to bring me a sample. When she came again she handed me a little packet of dried winter savory leaves, their scent quite sharp, even pungent. Once you get used to it, it's nice to use for a change in place of summer savory.

Some authorities advise picking the leaves only from second-year winter savory plants (not until, I assume, they have become well established), but on our island winter savory has been grown as an annual for generations, the small leaves harvested every season, and the seeds carefully saved to start new plants the following spring. Monique told me that she couldn't give her mother a more welcome gift than seeds of this treasured herb.

Where it can be grown as a perennial, winter savory makes a fine low hedge or edging, with its shiny, pointed evergreen leaves and dainty white bloom. A rare creeping savory that can be grown from seed, *S. repandra,* has the same flavor as winter savory, and is recommended for rock gardens.

Growing: Seeds of summer savory can be sown directly in the soil in the spring. Because of our cold soil, I prefer to start plants indoors 4 to 6 weeks before the last frost at 70 degrees; seeds germinate in 10 to 20 days and should be just covered with soil. After the last expected frost, space seedlings outdoors 9 inches apart in lean, rather than enriched, soil for best results. If you let plants flower, summer savory may reseed itself.

Seeds of winter savory, slower to germinate than those of summer savory, should be sown 12 weeks before the last frost. Outdoors, space seedlings 12 inches apart in sharply drained soil on the light side. Plants winter-over best where the soil is not heavy and where moisture quickly drains away from the roots. Pinch back growing tops to encourage bushy growth.

Once plants have wintered-over and become woody, clip back to new growth in the spring. Propagation is by division every few years, by stem cuttings in the spring, or by layering leafy stems. Potted plants do well indoors on a sunny windowsill; these can be replanted outdoors in the spring. This is a good way to grow winter savory in areas where it is not winter-hardy.

Harvesting: Leafy stalks of summer savory should be cut before the flowers have formed in the leaf axils. Cut stems to the cleanest set of bottom leaves and place on screens to dry; finish them off in a just-warm oven (set below 150 degrees F) if necessary. When crispy dry, strip leaves and store them in labeled jars away from light. You can place chicken wire over the seedlings when they are planted out; stalks will grow up through the mesh, allowing you to cut the green leafy tops several times during the season. This eliminates a lot of sorting out of hard stems and dirt-splashed bottom leaves. I discovered this method after we placed chicken wire over the catnip to protect it from feline ravages. Of necessity, I could only cut the top, leafy stems, but this proved to be more convenient and productive than the traditional method of cutting whole stalks almost to the ground.

The leaves of winter savory are smaller and harder to harvest, yielding smaller amounts (less is needed, though, because of their stronger flavor). Cut tip growth before flowers have formed and spread the leaves on a cookie sheet to dry in a just-warm oven. Let plants flower and collect seeds to start plants the following season if you want to grow it as an annual.

Using: Aside from using either savory with beans, vegetables, and meat dishes, I make a soup seasoning with fresh herbs.

Soup Seasoning

*This recipe was handed down to a friend from her French grandmother in Québec.
Preserving herbs in a brine is a very old method, more popular in Europe than in the New
World. My friend adapted the recipe to suit her needs and I find it very handy.*

Chop the following ingredients to fill a 10-ounce coffee jar: onions, onion greens,
½ cup parsley, ½ cup celery leaves, ½ teaspoon oregano, 2 to 3 teaspoons
savory (either one), a little grated carrot, and about 1 cup of table salt. Mix the
ingredients together, and keep this mixture in the refrigerator, letting it ripen for
about a week. To season soups, take out 1 or 2 tablespoons of the herbs at a
time and rinse them in cold water to freshen and remove excess salt before
adding them to the pot. Their texture and flavor will be almost like fresh herbs.

SOAPWORT
(Bouncing Bet)

Saponaria officinalis
Caryophyllaceae (Pink Family)
Type: Perennial
Height: 2 to 3 feet
Site: Sun/Partial shade
Soil: Moist
Growing Zones: 3–8

*Saponaria
officinalis*

The Eurasian soapwort, a well-known wildflower along roadsides and in
ditches and wet wastelands, forms wide colonies by means of its creeping rhizomatous roots. The clove-scented flowers are five-petaled, usually light pink,
and carried at the end of an inflated or tubed calyx, an arrangement that pro-
claims the plant's membership in the Pink Family. Its leaves, pointed and shiny,
growing along thick-jointed stems, are a source of saponin, a lather-producing
substance once used like a detergent, for which purpose it was introduced to
America in the 18th century. The double-flowered form, a cottage garden
favorite, has been grown as an ornamental in North America at least since the
19th century.

I discovered soapwort when I was collecting old-fashioned flowers from local gardens and abandoned plantings. It had always been there—blooming profusely in roadside ditches in midsummer—but I had not recognized its importance, nor even its identity, until I became involved in researching and growing once popular herbs and flowers. Hearing of my interest, people would arrive at the farm with freshly dug specimens, either because they were genuinely interested in saving or sharing them or because they saw the opportunity to unload a vigorous nuisance. Soapwort fell into the latter category. "It just grows all over the place, no matter what I do . . . I can't kill it," was the unflattering introduction to what is considered a desirable antique flower in some circles.

Introduced to me as "London pride" (the common name generally given to Gertrude Jekyll's favorite, *Saxifraga umbrosa*), it caused a little controversy in our household, with Jigs maintaining that the small clump with a few basal leaves did not at all resemble what he remembered as the common midwestern wildflower, bouncing bet. I settled the matter definitively when, on a hunch, I rubbed the leaves vigorously and produced a green, soapy lather. What I planted on the knoll in front of the house was the double-flowered variant of the ancient soap plant "from the apothecary" *(officinalis)*. Very popular in local gardens from the late 19th century through the 1920s and '30s, it had been abandoned (the real meaning of the euphemism "garden escape") to fend for itself as a roadside weed, often growing in damp ditches just below the edges of cultivation.

As I got to know this plant, I loved it, not for its double, pale pink, shaggy flowers, and certainly not for its agressive ways (bouncing bet aptly describes the movement of its roots), but for the intensity of its spicy-sweet fragrance carried on the warm evening air. This is my aromatherapy in the garden—scented plants strategically placed for my pleasure. In this case, I let it grow as a corner accent—easily controlled by mowing—outside a raised dooryard garden, so that as I pass in and out of the house by the back kitchen door, I will always catch its wonderful perfume. As with most scented double forms, the double-flowered version pours out more fragrance per bloom than the single type. It's not surprising that the varieties 'Rosea Plena' and 'Rubra Plena' (a darker pink) were once popular in North American gardens all over the country. I consider myself very lucky to be the recipient of this unwanted weed.

I use soapwort as a teaching plant at workshops to graphically illustrate herbal properties. The saponin in its leaves is speedily released by rubbing a minimum of 10 leaves together. As everyone stands around me in anticipation,

I, like a magician, pluck the leaves, vigorously rub them together, and, to audible gasps of surprise, drop the leaves to show them my soapy hands. Still used by museums to clean tapestries and other delicate materials, soapwort's cleansing action is gentler than that of modern detergents.

Growing: The double-flowered soapwort is offered as plants from specialty and herb nurseries. Plant roots outside in the spring, spacing them 2 feet apart (academic advice, since the roots will spread fast). Although the double garden forms are reputed to be less vigorous than the wildflower, they are vigorous enough and should not be planted in a small garden unless you are willing to reduce it every year. This is difficult to do, since it rapidly regains its spread by underground runners; better to naturalize soapwort in a damp area, or contain it by mowing around it in an open situation.

The self-seeding wildflower can be grown from seeds sown in the spring. Hints on the propagation of both types are superfluous.

Using: Cut soapwort for fresh bouquets, to which it will add its scent. The lather from rubbing 10 leaves together will wash your hands—very convenient when you're in the garden grubbing in the dirt and someone arrives who insists on shaking your hand. I have never made the soap solution, but all parts can be used (roots have the highest concentration of saponin). See Rita Buchanan's *A Weaver's Garden* (Interweave Press, 1987) for reliable directions; she's actually done it.

SORREL
(Garden Sorrel)

Rumex acetosa
Polygonaceae (Buckwheat Family)
Type: Perennial
Height: 18 inches to 3 feet
Site: Sun
Soil: Moist
Growing Zones: 4–9

Rumex acetosa

Garden sorrel, native to Eurasia, should not be confused with common or sheep sorrel *(R. acetosela)*, a weed in cultivated and acid soils, or French sorrel, an extremely acid type seldom grown. To confuse matters, "French sorrel" has become synonymous with "garden sorrel." The leaves of garden sorrel are popular in Europe to flavor soups and sauces. As they push through the spring soil, they are small and curled, tinged with red at their tips. In maturity, they are oval in shape, to 5 inches, spreading out to form a thick basal clump. Their sour taste—sorrel's main claim to fame—is due to the presence of oxalic acid, also present in rhubarb, to which it is closely related. By midsummer or earlier, plants develop flowering stalks, up to 3 feet tall, of small-flowered green panicles that slowly turn reddish, then brown as the seeds develop.

Sorrel seems to have been always with us, moving with our household from farm to farm, deeper into the countryside. Now, in Cape Breton, it has found a permanent home, flourishing in the cold, moist soil. Its use is limited to early spring salad and dried bouquet material (from the flower stalks). There is always too much sorrel to use.

I recently asked Jigs why he decided to grow sorrel in the first place, and he told me that, many years ago when he began to grow herbs, he felt it was his mission to grow unusual, even bizarre plants that he thought were unjustly neglected. Sorrel, it seems, has changed his mind on the subject. He now says that plants like sorrel are neglected for good reason—because people find little use for them. Now that he's more concerned with other matters like running the farm, he no longer has an interest in growing odd herbs. But he is still a keen and curious gardener, always trying out new varieties in the vegetable line.

I agree with Jigs that if obscure plants are not generally grown, it is probably for a good reason. However, just as he once did, I like to satisfy my curiosity, to find out for myself if such types have something to contribute to my life.

Now, sorrel is wickedly sour. It makes your mouth pucker when you taste it—more so than spinach—so you can't eat too much of it at one time. You either love it or hate it. If you love it, the sourer the better (there are cultivars and species that deliver even more acid flavor than the species). Then you can make the fabled sorrel soup or purées (supposed to be good with fish). Frankly, though, we've never found sorrel palatable as a potherb.

Picking the young sorrel leaves for early spring salads is a ritual, however, and for that reason alone I would not want to be without them. That's why I tolerate the mature inedible sorrel: indomitable, always spreading, always in need of containment. I anticipate that raw spring day, sometime in April, when we're hungering for something fresh and green. Then the sorrel tips are a welcome sight pushing through our northern soil. I dig my cold fingers into the cold soil and pull out a small handful of the emerging red-tipped leaves, tossing them into a colander with the dandelion greens, lovage, chives, and perennial Egyptian onions *(Allium cepa,* var. *proliferum).* Nothing tastes quite like these tangy greens, and nothing could replace them. They are a sign that life from the soil has returned to our backlands farm. I am grateful, then, that Jigs grew sorrel first, for although it has marginal use, it is an important element in our lives. Perhaps one has to live as we do, dependent on the land, exposed to the harshness of the natural world in ways most people today in North America cannot even imagine, to appreciate how precious spring greens can be. Where winters are long and harsh, the ritual is an old one, rooted in a spiritual as well as a material need for renewal.

As the season progresses and I leave sorrel to its own devices, I watch for its flowering stalks so I can harvest them for dried bouquets. I think sorrel, like rhubarb, has its ornamental value, and I like to leave the stalks in place as long as I can before cutting them to the ground.

In case your curiosity is piqued too, consider your options: 'Belleville' is a small French cultivar with paler leaves than the common strain and is very productive; 'Blonde de Lyon' has huge leaves, also paler than the species form, is somewhat milder in flavor, and is resistant to bolting; and one cultivar with the prosaic name 'Low Oxalic Acid' is described as "only slightly sour" (then why grow sorrel at all?). If sourness is what you crave, there's an extemely acid type, French sorrel *(R. scutatus),* highly prized among sorrel aficionados for its zesty flavor in soups and sauces.

Growing: Sow seeds outside in early spring, in rich, moist soil, burying them about 1 inch deep. Thin seedlings to 1 foot apart, but keep in mind that you'll need only a few plants (one, really). Plants will multiply from new shoots and these will supply fresh plants; chop out old plants every few years or as needed. Cut back plants by midsummer (or when they begin to form a seed stalk) to stimulate a fresh growth of tender leaves for the fall, and to prevent the spread of seedlings. Leaves are attractive to slugs, so keep the planting cleaned up; otherwise the slugs will raise families under old leaves.

Using: Pick young leaves for salad in spring and fall. For dried flowers, cut the flowering stalk when it is just turning red, or the dried flowers will shatter.

SOUTHERNWOOD
(Lad's Love, Old Man)

Artemisia abrotanum
Asteraceae (Aster Family)
Type: Perennial subshrub
Height: 4 feet
Site: Sun
Soil: Well drained
Growing Zones: 4–8

Artemisia
abrotanum

Southernwood, named for its southern European origins, is a hardy plant with numerous upright, woody stems covered with feathery foliage—gray-green with a camphoraceous-lemon scent—and panicles of small yellow flowers, which rarely form in most areas. In its long history of human association, southernwood has been invested with magical powers to ward off disease, induce male passion (as in the name lad's love), and cure baldness in old men (as in another common name, old man). Southernwood's traditional uses—to expel worms in humans and repel moths in woolens—are closely related to those of wormwood (see *Wormwood*), and are based on the plant's strong essential oil, absinthol.

Locally, southernwood goes by the name old man. It's a true heirloom plant found in older gardens and at gravesites, probably favored for its hardiness and scent (it was never used as an herb). Mine was acquired as a 6-inch piece of stem from a plant that had been passed on through several generations, from mother to daughter, for almost a hundred years.

That little piece of southernwood has given birth to countless offspring, planted here and there in my gardens. It's a wonderful landscaping plant for difficult conditions—dry and exposed—easy to train as a low hedge or accent, or allowed to grow as a medium-tall shrub. It combines well with roses, and provides a soothing accent for bright calendulas, a foil for rosy yarrow, and an accent for almost anywhere in a garden of herbs and flowers. I like to have it nearby so I can run my fingers along its leaves to release their invigorating scent. I use the plant at workshops to teach stem propagation to beginning gardeners. Sure success with it inspires confidence to try more difficult plants. I can't think of a single fault except for southernwood's vigor, which is really not hard to control.

The taller, citrus-scented southernwood, sometimes offered as tangerine southernwood, is a striking, columnar plant that grows to 6 feet (it's also called tree southernwood). I've seen it grown to great effect in demonstration herb gardens, and it's well worth looking for from specialty herb nurseries.

Growing: Plant roots 2 feet apart in sun and well-drained soil on the light, even dry side (it will grow in almost any soil, though). In partial sun, southernwood assumes a wide, sprawling shape that I find most attractive. To confine its height to a 1-foot mound, clip back stems to 6 inches in the spring and again in early summer.

The easiest way to make new plants is from 6-inch stem cuttings because they root so fast (transplanted divisions are woody and not as satisfactory). Remove bottom leaves, insert them in fine soil, and firm the soil around them (this can be done almost any time during the growing season); they will be well rooted by the following spring or earlier. To produce many no-fail plants for a no-fail hedge, insert stems in bunches (I use my coldframe for the purpose) and proceed as already described.

Using: Pick sprigs for bouquets, or cut and dry branches to scent closets and protect clothes from moths. The scent lasts around 6 months, from one growing season to another. I combine several aromatic herbs with repellent properties in a mixture I sell under the name Herb Guard. According to Mrs. Grieve (*A Modern Herbal*), the French name for southernwood is *garderobe*.

Jo Ann's Kitchen & Garden Herb Guard

This mixture gives drawers, storage chests, and even musty areas a refreshing scent, and protects clothes from moths if they are stored in clean conditions that discourage insects from making themselves at home. The tea bags are handy to use either dry, like sachets, or simmered in boiling water (2 cups per tea bag). See chapter 3, Potpourri, for information on the bags and corn cellulose mentioned below.

Mix 1 part each of the dried leaves of southernwood, tansy, and wormwood. For every large tea bag (4 inches by 4½ inches), use 2 tablespoons of the herb mix and 1 teaspoon of corn cellulose prescented with clove oil. Seal the open end of the tea bag with a hot iron set on or below the cotton setting. Scatter tea bags in drawers and chests or in rooms that need to be refreshed.

SWEET CICELY

Myrrhis odorata
Apiaceae (Celery Family)
Type: Perennial
Height: 3 feet
Site: Partial shade/Shade
Soil: Moist
Growing Zones: 4–9

Myrrhis odorata

Sweet cicely is native to continental Europe and widely naturalized in the British Isles wherever it finds moist ground and shady conditions. Growing from a deep taproot, it first produces a low, soft green mound of anise- or licorice-scented foliage, then tiny, sweet-scented flowers in wide saucerlike umbels on rising stems. Although their period of bloom is short (only 2 weeks), they are quickly followed by great numbers of seeds—almost an inch long, dark brown, and shiny—in showy, upright clusters, giving sweet cicely the appearance of a second flowering. All parts of the plant are edible and share the characteristic candylike flavor. Oil from its seeds was once used for polishing furniture.

Seldom has a cultivated plant found such a compatible home in our landscape as sweet cicely. It loves the cool, moist, humusy soil beneath the old apple tree, the site of my first attempt to make a garden for pleasure. It was a gift from an elderly and knowledgeable gardener who must have known from experience what would thrive in our soil and climate. It blooms in early June when the air is sweet from lilacs, late narcissus, and dame's rocket, and when butterflies come in flocks to feed on the nectar of these and dozens of other nearby herbs and flowers, as well as sweet cicely itself.

I treasure sweet cicely, always beautiful, always content, blooming with the blue comfrey and bright yellow leopard's-bane, at the most delightful season of the year, early summer. And, when its flowers are spent, and I've gathered the resolve to cut back the stems (I'm always mesmerized by the appealing seed clusters and hate to disturb them), those wonderful ferny leaves grow back again to form a lovely mound of distinctive foliage. Such a plant is in a class by itself, a perfect wildflower that needs no improvement; there are no varieties, no cultivars, not even another species in its genus.

I don't share the enthusiasm of those who regard sweet cicely as food, although a few leaves chopped up with rhubarb or gooseberries do add a nice touch and may even, as claimed, reduce the amount of sugar one would ordinarily use. The fact that John Evelyn, the 17th-century writer, found them "delicious in salad" does not move me at all, for many greens were once consumed when little else was available. I do enjoy eating the seeds like candy when I'm working outside, but a little goes a long way, and one soon tires of their sweet licorice taste. I once got carried away and harvested a whole bagful of seeds, which eventually found its way onto the compost heap. As Jigs observed about licorice flavor in plants, he'd rather have the real candy. I'm especially intrigued by the old use—if one can believe herbal gossip—of eating the roots (cooked, I assume) with oil or vinegar. Have you ever tried to dig up a well-rooted plant, though?

I prefer to enjoy sweet cicely for its beauty and outdoor aromatherapy: to rub a leaf and breathe in its sweet aroma, to be in its vicinity and enjoy its fragrance.

Growing: Sweet cicely is usually grown from roots because the seeds, like those of angelica, must be fresh to germinate. Plant sweet cicely in shade, partial shade, or even sun if the soil is sufficiently moist and deep and enriched with organic matter. Seeds from mature plants will fall to the ground and germinate the following spring to supply an army of seedlings if you want them. If you happen to acquire seeds and want to try your luck with them, copy nature: Freeze the seeds for 1 to 3 months, then sow them outside in early spring. Established plants can be left alone unless they lose their vigor, in which case chop out old growth to reduce the girth of the plant.

Using: I use the dried flowers for potpourri (they retain their scent) and the fresh seeds as candy, as described. Chop a few leaves into stewed rhubarb or other sour fruit and see how you like it; increase the amount of leaves as desired. After cooking, sweeten with sugar to taste.

SWEET ROCKET
(Dame's Rocket)

Hesperis matronalis
Brassicaceae (Mustard Family)
Type: Perennial
Height: 2 to 3 feet
Site: Sun/Partial shade
Soil: Moist
Growing Zones: 4–9

Hesperis matronalis

Sweet rocket, a wildflower from Eurasia, is found naturalized in wet meadows and at the edges of woodland from Newfoundland to Georgia. Sometimes called wild phlox, it does bear a resemblance to garden phlox, but it is rangier, has four petals rather than five, and its seedpods are decidedly mustardlike, in long pods almost identical to those of arugula. The toothed leaves form a basal clump, then become sparse along the stem. The flowers—light and dark pink, purple, or white—exude a strong clove scent in the evening, attracting butterflies by day and moths at night.

I don't know where my sweet rocket came from. It has been in my herb and flower garden, and now naturalized in the landscape, for many years. By now you must know I favor scented plants, among which sweet rocket rates very high. It's a pretty, if invasive, flower, and one must be firm about allowing it to self-seed with abandon (fortunately, it's not hard to control). It often manages to create brilliant combinations that I did not plan, but which, once in place, I make an effort to maintain: with the elegant white bleeding heart in dappled shade, with the hot red Oriental poppies in full sun (sweet rocket's pastel colors cool the fire), and with bistort and mountain bluet *(Centaurea montana)*. By early June, I stand in the garden in their midst, admiring the great activity of bumble-bees, butterflies, and a host of other flying insects whose names I don't know, watching them move around each flower and methodically work it over, seemingly oblivious to one other.

It's not hard to imagine that this member of the Mustard Family was once used for food, valued for preventing scurvy. In its early growth, the leaves have a pleasant, tangy taste. Sometimes confused with its more edible cousin, arugula or garden rocket, it is now grown primarily for its scent, but more often it is not grown at all, just allowed to plant itself where it may. Except for double forms (of fabled sweetness), which are no longer widely available, there are no cultivars except 'Alba', the white variety.

Growing: Seeds sown on the soil surface in early spring may bloom the first year. Plants will thrive wherever conditions are moist, in sun or partial shade. If the elongated seedpods are cut back, flowering will continue into the fall (although not as full as the early-summer bloom). Daughter plants form at the base of mother plants; these can be separated in the fall or spring and replanted. They may wilt at first, but will recover if kept well watered. Sweet rocket is actually a short-lived perennial, but it ensures its continuation by prolific self-seeding.

Using: Sweet rocket is a nice cut flower, though not as fragrant when brought inside as it is in the garden. The podded stalks, when dried, add interest to dried bouquets.

SWEET WHITE CLOVER

Melilotus alba
Fabaceae (Bean Family)
Type: Biennial
Height: 3 to 10 feet
Site: Sun/Partial shade
Soil: Most
Growing Zones: 3–8

Melilotus alba

An Old World wildflower once grown as a forage crop, sweet white clover is widely naturalized in North America along roadsides and in waste places. It's a tall, airy plant with many side branches clothed in three-part, cloverlike leaves and five-petaled, small white flowers typical of the Bean Family—the two lower petals form a keel, the two side petals form the wings, and the upper one forms a flag; these bloom in tight, spiky clusters. The wonderful sweet scent, like new-mown hay, of the dried leaves and flowers comes from the chemical coumarin. Sweet white clover is valued as a bee plant as its genus name, *Melilotus,* from the Greek word for honey, suggests.

For many years our floral world was divided. Jigs preferred wildflowers (an interest he developed as a graduate student when we lived in Wisconsin), while my province was the cultivated ones. This may seem strange for one who has lived so long in a clearing in the woods, wholly surrounded by nature (with a capital N) 24 hours a day. In fact, that's probably why I was indifferent, if not hostile, to natural flora. We devote a good part of our waking hours to coping with nature in one form or another: keeping it at bay in the hayfield, battling vigorous weeds in the gardens, and struggling to grow food for ourselves and our animals.

But on our daily mile-long walks to and from the mailbox, I couldn't help noticing the wildflowers that grow along the lane in dappled shade at the woodland's edge, among the soft grays and greens of mosses and lichens. I admired the low sweeps of glistening white bunchberry and the dainty drifts of the diminutive, light pink twinflower. Deeper in the woods there are great colonies of tall, handsome cinnamon fern and—always a wonderful surprise—the moccasin flowers (lady's-slipper orchids) in splendid isolation, with their heavily veined, rich pink pouches.

Gradually, virtually every growing thing came under my scrutiny, even the most humble pasture weed. I trod on creeping self-heal *(Prunella vulgaris)* for many summers when I walked back and forth with the cows to the ridge pasture, before I stooped, one day, to examine its purple-velvet–flowered, upright hoods. I learned that this was once a famous healing herb, one of those invaluable astringents for both internal and external application for treating diarrhea and healing wounds. Today, hybrid forms are grown as elegant garden flowers.

As my interest in wildflowers developed, my need for using plants expanded with the establishment of my little herb business. I was on the lookout for scented plants that could be harvested in quantity to use in herb and flower potpourris. Sweet white clover was certainly available, growing so thickly along the edges of the main road that the highway department cuts it to the ground in midsummer, because it obstructs the view for those driving there.

After I cut it, I was astonished by the sweet vanilla-like scent that floated throughout the whole house from its drying branches, spread out upstairs on every available surface (this was before Jigs built the great drying racks). Although it contains the same substance found in drying hay, the aroma is more powerful; it is also long lasting. After a year in storage, the same scent wafts out of a container when I lift the lid. Just as hay must be cut at the right time to preserve its sweetness (before the plants are overripe), so sweet white clover should be in full, fresh bloom for drying. The advantage of using sweet white clover in potpourri is that, besides being scented itself, it blends other scents together and functions as a fixative, preserving them.

Gathering sufficient quantities of sweet white clover from along the highway is not easily arranged since we don't have a vehicle. One summer during a drought we were hard pressed to find a source; woodland plants behind the farm were stunted and sparse. So one day, when our neighbor was at the farm on business, we persuaded him to take his old pickup and cruise the back roads with us, hunting for the sweet wildflower.

Lauchie, our neighbor, is a rough-and-ready sort, though very kind, who cuts wood pulp, milks a few cows, and lives as we do, in the backlands. Hunting for sweet flowers is not one of his usual pastimes. In fact, he pays no heed to them. We had already questioned him closely about sweet white clover, trying to find out if it was in bloom along the highway (we seldom travel, so we wouldn't know). He claimed he'd never seen such a plant as we described.

Off we went, rattling and bumping down the lane, onto the network of back roads in Lauchie's old green Chevy, its body rusted, its doors broken, the floor of the cab practically nonexistent. Lauchie loves it, though, and doesn't see its deficiencies, and all who ride in it must swear it beats anything new: "They don't make them like this anymore . . ." Jigs was in the back of the pickup, looking for the thickest stands along the road. When he spotted one, he banged on the hood of the cab and Lauchie stopped abruptly, Jigs and I hastened to the spot, cut back the plants, then jumped back in the truck.

As we proceeded, Lauchie became very sharp eyed, identifying every stand, large or small, in the backlands area, determined that we should not miss any. Many times we stopped, climbed down, hastily cut a bunch of stems, then, with increasing weariness, returned to the truck. As we pointed out to Lauchie other wild plants and told him their uses, he was thrilled, insisting that we harvest some of them, too; so we cut some Queen Anne's lace for their showy pods, a few handfuls of pearly everlasting still in bud, and some green glossy leaves of the nutmeg-scented shrub, northern bayberry *(Myrica pensylvanica)*. At last Lauchie was satisfied, and we returned to the farm with our treasures.

Harvesting: Cut stems when the flower heads are open, but still fresh (no need to cut the whole plant down, just some stems from each plant). Lay them out away from light to dry; they are thin, so they dry quickly. When the leaves and flowers feel crispy dry, strip them from the stem—this will considerably reduce the quantity of material—and store them as you would any dried herb, in labeled jars or containers stored in a cool, dark place.

Using: I use dried sweet white clover in my Rose Potpourri (regular and spiced), and in Orange Blossom Potpourri (see *Costmary*). I also use it in simmering potpourri tea bags for a room freshener.

Simmering Sweet White Clover Room Freshener
Put 2 tablespoons of dried sweet white clover in each large tea bag (4 inches by 4¾ inches), add a teaspoon of prescented cellulose, and seal the bags by ironing, with the setting at COTTON or lower. Any scent can be used, but a sweet, vanilla-like scent, close to the natural one of the sweet white clover, works best.

To use: Bring 2 cups of water to a boil in a saucepan, and drop in a sealed tea bag. You should soon be aware of the aroma throughout the area; its intensity will depend on the size of the room. You can also use dried sweet white clover in sachets by itself to scent linens. Crush the bags occasionally to release their fragrance.

SWEET WOODRUFF

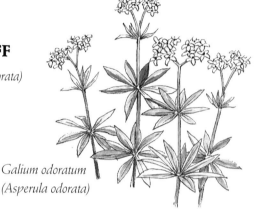

Galium odoratum (Asperula odorata)
Rubiaceae (Madder Family)
Type: Perennial
Height: 6 inches
Site: Shade/Partial shade
Soil: Moist
Growing Zones: 3–9

*Galium odoratum
(Asperula odorata)*

Sweet woodruff is a woodland plant native to Europe, North Africa, and Asia. Lying close to the ground, it creates a mound of dark green, shiny, pointed leaves in whorls, topped in late spring or early summer by a mass of small, white, starry flowers. The sweet scent, mainly in the leaves, is intensified when they are dried. Like sweet white clover, the plant contains coumarin, still used in perfumes. Sweet woodruff's classic use is in flavoring May wine, a custom originating in Germany and associated with the arrival of spring.

I don't recall how I acquired sweet woodruff, but I know it grew for several years in my herb and flower garden, finding it a nourishing home beneath the old apple tree in deep, moist, humusy soil—conditions similar to those in its native habitats. So, quite naturally, it spread, and spread, and spread. A relatively inexperienced gardener at the time, I didn't yet understand or appreciate the many uses of ground covers, literally, plants that cover the ground. This, I now know, is an invaluable characteristic if wisely exploited, but I was not then a wise gardener and I ripped out the plants because they were crowding out other plants, replanting clumps beneath an old lilac in very difficult, weedy conditions.

Not surprisingly, the sweet woodruff disappeared. I missed it, and just when I had decided to purchase new plants, I found a few that still survived my abuse. I carefully replanted them in a more favorable site near the house beneath the wild rose hedge, where I could keep an eye on their progress. I carefully weeded them, and in a few seasons sweet woodruff had returned to its glory, spreading out in a glossy carpet once more. This time, it had room to spread; in fact, I encouraged it to do so to bar the entry of weeds beneath the roses. Thus, I had learned a very important lesson about using ground covers. In the wrong location, they can cause misery to the gardener—spreading faster than they can be controlled; but in the right place, they bring pleasure and satisfaction, doing the work for which they are most suited, covering the ground in difficult situations as a general barrier to weeds.

Sweet woodruff is among several herby ground covers that I've learned to use in my landscape, among them bugleweed (*Ajuga* sp.), dead white nettle (*Lamium* sp.)—far more attractive than its common name—the little creeping speedwell *(Veronica* sp.), and creeping Jenny *(Lysimachia nummularia).* And these are just the low carpeters; there are other, taller types like the variegated goutweed (*Aegopodium podagraria* 'Variegatum') that perform the same function admirably. All of these, once nuisances in the garden proper, now serve me well—aesthetically pleasing in the landscape, soothing to the eye. Basically, any vigorous plant, from low-to-the-ground to taller types, can be used to cover the ground in a variety of conditions.

Growing: Sweet woodruff is usually grown from plants (seeds are slow and difficult to germinate). Set them out in early spring, 1 foot apart (they will quickly fill in), in moist, enriched soil on the acid side, planting the roots close to the soil surface. Propagate in the spring by digging up clumps and replanting them; clip out dead stems of established plantings to encourage fresh growth. Rotted manure or compost will ensure a high nitrogen level, needed to produce a healthy leaf cover. Sweet woodruff grows best in shaded conditions, where the leaves are a glossy, dark green.

Using: To make the classic May wine, simply fill a wide-mouthed jar with fresh leaves and flowers and cover to the top with white wine; let the herbs steep until the desired flavor is achieved (usually 2 weeks in a sunny window). Dry the leaves and flowers for potpourri, or try something a little different, May Jelly, adapted from a recipe developed by a local herbalist, Wendy Macomber.

Wendy's May Jelly

YIELDS FIVE 8-OUNCE JELLY JARS (ABOUT 5 CUPS)

⅓ cup fresh sweet woodruff, leaves and flowers
2 cups white grape juice
3 cups sugar
Rind of 1 orange
2 teaspoons lemon juice
½ bottle liquid pectin

Steep the sweet woodruff for 3 hours in the grape juice, in a jar set on a sunny windowsill. Strain the juice into a saucepan, and stir in the sugar, orange rind, and lemon juice; bring this mixture to a boil and let simmer for 5 minutes. Stir in the pectin and bring the mixture to a rolling boil. Stir for 1 minute, then remove the pot from the heat, skim off any foam, and pour the jelly into sterilized jars, sealing at once.

TANSY

Tanacetum vulgare
Asteraceae (Aster Family)
Type: Perennial
Height: 3 to 4 feet
Site: Sun/Partial shade
Soil: Well drained
Growing Zones: 4–9

Tanacetum vulgare

Tansy, grown in North America since the 1600s for its herbal properties, is native to Europe, but now widely naturalized throughout our continent. The garden historian Ann Leighton observed, "Considering the New England countryside today, it is wonderful to think of a time when anyone would need to buy tansy seed for twopence" from England, as did the early settlers. Its uses included flavoring egg and custard dishes, treating worms in children, repelling moths and ants, and making a green or yellow dye. Plants increase rapidly, creating large colonies from their creeping rootstocks; these send up many tough stems with ferny, aromatic leaves—almost tropical in their lushness—their scent rather medicinal, but not unpleasant. Tansy's yellow button flowers are ½ inch across, bright and rayless, and borne in profusion by late summer. The belief in tansy's ability to arrest decay (it was often packed into coffins) originates from the longevity of its scent and color. This trait is preserved in its common and Latin name, which derives from the Greek word for immortality, *athanasia*.

I still recall that early spring morning so many years ago when, in sublime ignorance, I so joyfully planted three little tansy seedlings that I had carefully raised from seed in one of our first coldframes: three of them set out in the classic planting triangle, for "the natural look." Oh, what pretty little plants, what attractive leaves. I envisioned this modest planting as a filler for one corner of my new herb and flower garden, a sort of ferny canopy.

It didn't take long for me to see my mistake—only one short growing season, by which time that modest planting was threatening to take over everything. Fortunately, it was still possible to dig out every trace of root. Theoretically, tansy looks nice in an herb garden with its aromatic, finely cut leaves and bright flowers, but it would take a staff of gardeners to monitor its spread. I hope those folks who interplanted it with potatoes and other garden vegetables (following the precepts of "companion planting"), in the hope of scaring off the potato beetles, have since managed to reclaim their land.

My plan, evolved over many years, is not to banish such aggressive plants from the landscape—they have too much to offer—but to find them more suitable quarters than the garden proper. This means naturalizing them, letting them grow to their heart's content in their favored habitat with a minimum of interference: simply mowing around them, removing unwanted competition. The most beautiful and healthy tansy I ever saw was a magnificent, untended stand by an old barn foundation, where, in late August, it was a mass of bright yellow bloom. Tansy did so well there because the ground had been enriched by decades of manure, and with no competition it flourished, taking command of the area. Tansy is one of the few herbs the Scottish settlers on Cape Breton used, so it grows wild all over the island near abandoned farms and homesteads.

I first saw the variant fernleaf tansy (*T. vulgare* 'Crispum') at the home of Henry, my eccentric neighbor down the road with the exceptional collection of heirloom flowers and herbs. Henry is the only person I ever met who actually minces tansy leaves (a small amount) into egg dishes, as described in the old herbals; its taste, he says, is peppery. Fernleaf tansy, a root of which I quickly acquired, is a most attractive plant. Not as tall as regular tansy (to 2½ feet), its finely cut foliage is emerald green, lush and arching, reminding me of the plumes in Victorian ladies' hats. Reputed to be less invasive than regular tansy, it still needs to be tightly controlled in close quarters, so for this reason I grow it alone, a specimen planting by one of our hotbeds that is easily controlled by mowing. I have never seen it bloom. I have also grown it in a tub where it is somewhat dwarfed. The advantage of growing it alone is that its lovely leaves can be fully appreciated.

The 3-foot silver tansy *(T. ninevum)* is a new plant for me, with silvery, deeply cut leaves that will grow in a 3-foot-wide mound. It's supposed to bear many daisylike flowers with yellow centers, but so far I haven't seen them. It, like all the tansies, is vigorous and needs to be controlled, but it is still worth growing for its beauty.

Growing: Sow seeds of tansy outside in the fall (a coldframe works well) to germinate the following spring, or grow from roots (I should say "root," since one will soon supply all your needs). Tansy grows best in full sun and enriched, well-drained soil, although it will survive under far less congenial conditions. Fernleaf and silver tansy are grown from roots, available at herb plant nurseries.

Using: I dry tansy leaves to use in my Herb Guard moth repellent–freshener (see *Southernwood*). Cut the flowers for dried bouquets when they are just becoming slightly rounded or convex. This is very important, since they will not retain their bright yellow color if picked too late (they turn brownish). Hang small bunches upside down to air-dry. Fernleaf tansy's foliage is great for fresh bouquets. Nothing quite offsets a double, blush pink old garden rose like a ruff of the emerald green plumes.

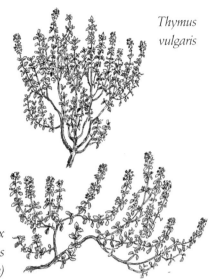

Thymus vulgaris

Thymus praecox subsp. arcticus (T. serpyllum)

THYMES

Cooking Thyme (Common Thyme, Upright Thyme)

Thymus vulgaris

Creeping Thyme

Thymus praecox
subsp. *arcticus (T. serpyllum)*
Labiatae (Mint Family)
Type: Perennial
Height: 3 to 15 inches
Site: Sun
Soil: Well drained
Growing Zones: 3–9

The thymes belong to a large genus of over 400 species distributed throughout Europe and Asia. Because of confusions over nomenclature, though, the number could be smaller, since the same plant may be offered under different names. Basically, there are two main groups: the upright, shrubby types like cooking thyme, and the ground-hugging varieties like creeping thyme. Within these two groups are a number of natural variants, cultivars, and hybrids, their forms often falling between the two, semi-upright or semi-sprawling—very confusing for the novice.

Cooking thyme, in all its variations, is definitely upright and shrubby, with twiggy stems growing from a woody base. Its evergreen leaves are sharply pointed, differing in shape and flavor according to the variety: French, or summer, thyme has very narrow leaves, is grayer and sweeter in flavor than English thyme, and less hardy; English (also called winter, or German) thyme is the hardiest, most popular cooking thyme. Small, pink, tubular flowers bloom profusely in the leaf axils of both types by early or midsummer, at which time the thymol concentration is said to be the highest.

Creeping thymes are ground covers, forming tight mats of foliage—green, variegated, or wooly—used to grow between pavings and from rock walls. The classic creeping thyme, *T. praecox* subsp. *arcticus,* is sometimes found naturalized on banks and hillsides; it bears numerous rose-purple flowers close to its leaves, creating a colorful mass of bloom. Creeping thyme is scented, but not generally used for cooking. The famous honey from Mount Hymettus in Greece is probably derived from this species.

Thymes have an ancient history of use for their culinary and medicinal properties. In cooking, thyme contributes a sharp, tangy flavor considered indispensable in bouquet garni (with parsley and bay leaf) to season soups and sauces, and in slow-cooking meat dishes (especially when combined with wine). Like sage, thyme is supposed to help in the digestion of fatty foods. Medicinally, thyme has been used to treat a range of complaints often associated with colds and coughs. Its essential oil, thymol—a proven antibacterial agent—is used in a number of manufactured products, including cough medicines, mouthwashes, even toothpastes.

Before I fully understood what I had to do to grow thymes, I just planted them in the ground with minimum preparation. I'd read the words and phrases describing ideal soil conditions so often repeated in gardening texts—"well-drained," "sharply-drained," "deep," "friable"—but in my soul I didn't know the effort I'd have to expend to create these favorable conditions, nor how crucial they were for the successful growth of certain plants, like thymes.

In my innocence, I thought it would be nice to have creeping thyme insinuate itself among the paving stones as I'd seen so often in glossy photographs of perfect gardens. It died more times than I care to remember from seed-grown plants. (I eventually grew creeping Jenny—*Lysimachia nummularia*—there instead, a plant that is a lot more tolerant of heavy, damp soil.) Sometimes called mother-of-thyme (meaning the original species), or wild thyme, creeping thyme is very hardy. Jigs still recalls finding a large patch on a remote, barren hillside in northern Vermont when he went looking for mushrooms. It was beautiful and fragrant, thriving in seemingly inhospitable conditions.

I have often observed that plants I find difficult to grow will prosper on their own when their most important requirements are met. In the case of creeping thyme, this means lean, sharply drained soil—where moisture quickly drains from the roots—and an open, sunny situation, as on that remote hillside. A cold climate is obviously not a deterrent to its survival. Taking more care, I have managed to establish it in a raised bed of roses, where it fills in a corner and, to my delight, is beginning to cascade over the edge. There are wonderful cultivars I would like to try: 'Coccineus' with crimson flowers; 'Pink Chintz' with light pink flowers and somewhat wooly leaves; and 'Annie Hall', bright pink.

The hardiest thyme I've grown so far is golden creeping thyme (*T. praecox* 'Aureus'), no more than 4 inches tall, forming a wide, spreading, golden mat in the early spring and summer that gradually turns greener by fall. Its flavor is pleasant, not as sharp and clovelike as cooking thyme, but it's still unmistakably thyme, and I use it for flavoring. It is also beautiful, sprawling over a low stone wall (one is not happy until thymes embrace stones), enjoying the company of the spreading maiden pink—a bright rosy mass of bloom—and 'Black Crystal' violas, the blackest flowers I have ever seen. This sunny, sheltered site has also proved successful with lavender, so I have hopes of inducing more thymes to winter-over there.

My greatest disappointment has been with cooking thyme, even the hardiest English or German type. I have managed to winter it over several years in succession, however, so I know it can be done. A cover of spruce or pine boughs would probably help (winter protection is advisable even in Zone 5 for the upright thymes).

Growing: I have not found thymes difficult to raise from seed; it germinates in 21 to 28 days at 70 degrees or cooler. In the Northeast, however, I think it's better to start with plants because they have a better chance of reaching maturity by the fall, and therefore will be more likely to survive the winter. Be sure to order plants from a reputable nursery, though, since you want to be confident that what you are growing is what you ordered. (This can be a problem with thymes.) Space cooking thyme 9 to 15 inches apart; space creeping thyme 6 inches apart. Light, lean, gritty soil (from the addition of sharp gravel, not sand) is best. In colder climates, thymes need full sun, but where summers are very hot and humid, partial shade is recommended. In early spring, clip back stems to growing points to encourage fresh growth; this is most important to maintain fragrance and vigor. Scratch a tablespoon of bonemeal around each plant.

Propagate cooking thyme in the spring by division or by stem cuttings when there is sufficient growth. Creeping thyme is easily propagated by layering: Peg down a low-lying stem, then cover it with soil, leaving its growing tip exposed. Separate it from the mother plant when roots form on the pegged stem. Mulch thyme in exposed sites or where winters are harsh.

Harvesting: Leaves of either type of thyme can be picked anytime to use fresh, but by late summer, harvest no more than a third of the stem so plants are not encouraged to make tender growth that will winter-kill. To dry a quantity of cooking thyme, cut the stems to the cleanest bottom leaves and lay them out on a cookie sheet to dry in a just-warm oven (at a setting below 150 degrees F). When the leaves feel crispy dry, rub the stems together in small bunches and the leaves will fall off. Store them in labeled jars away from light.

Using: The flavor of thyme is sharply pungent, so I use it sparingly in beef and chicken dishes, stews, vegetable-rice casseroles, and herb rolls (see below). Thyme jelly made with purple grape juice is delicious (substitute the juice for water in the Basic Herb Jelly directions in chapter 3). Add dried sprigs of creeping thyme to potpourri.

Herb Rolls

MAKES 24 ROLLS

1/2 cup warm water
1 teaspoon sugar
1/4 teaspoon powdered ginger
2 tablespoons traditional dry yeast (2 packets)
2 tablespoons sugar
1 teaspoon salt
8 cups unbleached white flour (use part whole wheat flour, if desired)
2 cups warm water
3 teaspoons chicken broth powder, dissolved in 1/2 cup warm water
1 teaspoon each: dried thyme, dried summer savory, dried rosemary
1/2 cup shortening, margarine, or butter

Combine the first four ingredients in a large bowl and let them stand, covered, until bubbling. Stir this mixture to make sure it is all dissolved, then stir in the rest of the sugar, 3 cups of the flour, and 2 cups of the warm water, along with the dissolved chicken broth powder and the salt. Beat well with a wooden spoon, add the herbs, shortening, and 4 cups of flour. Stir dough, adding some of the remaining flour as needed to make a dough that pulls away from the sides of the bowl and is smooth and elastic after kneading. Rub a small amount of oil over the dough to prevent it from forming a crust, cover it with a clean towel, and let it rise until doubled in bulk—about 45 minutes. Punch down the dough, shape into two dozen rolls, and let them rise again until light (almost doubled in bulk). Bake the rolls for 25 minutes at 350 degrees F.

VALERIAN
(Garden Heliotrope)

Valeriana officinalis
Valerianaceae (Valerian Family)
Type: Perennial
Height: 3½ to 5 feet
Site: Sun/Partial shade
Soil: Moist
Growing Zones: 4–9

Valeriana officinalis

Valerian, an Old World medicinal "from the apothecary," is famous for its sedative power, derived from the active ingredient in its roots. These are fibrous rhizomes that send out runners and offshoots, from which grow hollow, wandlike stems. Valerian's leaves are long and ladderlike in form, arranged on opposite sides of the stems. In early summer, pale pink, 4-inch-wide flower clusters waft aloft their heavy musk aroma. Today, preparations from valerian are still widely used in Europe to treat nervous disorders. The root extract is used to flavor a variety of foods, including ice cream, baked goods, and soft drinks. It is sometimes confused with heliotrope or cherry-pie *(Heliotropium arborescens)*, a frost-tender, fragrant perennial grown as an annual north of Zone 9.

I'd read about valerian long before I ever grew it. Its reputation as a strange-smelling plant did not attract me. Then one day, when I was visting my friend's city garden, I asked her what was responsible for the heady aroma that pervaded the air. "Oh, that's valerian," she said, and on the spot I became an enthusiast. Any plant so free with its perfume earned my attention.

Descriptions of valerian's aroma vary, but most agree it is the dried roots that are fetid smelling, "like old socks." The fresh roots smell sweet and when disturbed—when the plant is dug up or propagated—attract cats. Valerian is an old cottage garden favorite, admired for its ease of culture and prolific, scented flowers—precisely why I like it, too. The pale pink flower clusters, atop swaying stems at the back of the border, bloom at the same time as purple foxglove, orange and yellow Asiatic lilies, white bellflower, and blue borage. It complements them all in form and color and, at the same time, envelops them (and me) in its heady, musky perfume.

All around the farm, everywhere I go in early July, scented blooms sweeten the air. It's a time of prolific bloom in fields and gardens. By the guest log cabin it is the old mock orange; as I walk to the swimming hole, it is the bank of elderflowers; in the field, I brush past sweet red clover. But all around the house and its general vicinity it is valerian—freer, more powerful than all the rest—whose scent is unforgettable, whose aroma I most associate with the season. Its soothing powers are free to anyone who grows this old-fashioned herb. Variations in color have been mentioned in the literature (white and lavender), but I've never seen them offered for sale.

Growing: Valerian is usually grown from roots, planted 2 feet apart. It grows best in rich, moist (not wet), humusy soil. It is said to do well in partial shade, but I have only grown it in the sun. Propagate by division in spring or fall; chop out unwanted spread every year, and every 2 or 3 years renew the whole planting with young growth.

VIOLA (Heartsease, Johnny-Jump-Up, Wild Pansy)
Viola tricolor

Sweet Violet
Viola odorata
Violaceae (Violet Family)
Type: Perennial
Height: 4 to 12 inches
Site: Sun/Partial shade/Shade
Soil: Well drained, moist
Growing Zones: 4–10

Viola tricolor

Viola odorata

Violas, forerunners of today's pansies, originated in Europe but are now naturalized almost everywhere throughout the world's temperate zones. In their early growth they might be confused with garden pansies, but there is no mistaking the viola's small, bewhiskered face: four ¼-inch overlapping petals, and a fifth petal forming an elongated spur; their colors vary, usually purple toward the petal edges, white and yellow toward the center, from which radiate pencil-thin lines or whiskers. Violas have been used medicinally for centuries, especially in compresses to treat skin problems; they were once regarded as a heart stimulant, hence their common name, heartsease.

Sweet violets, native to Europe, Asia, and North Africa, are also widely naturalized throughout the temperate zone. They, too, have five overlapping petals (twice as large as those of *V. tricolor*), with the fifth one spur shaped; flowers are usually purple-violet or white. These grow on stems from clumps of deep green, nearly heart-shaped, glossy leaves. Sweet violets form large colonies in favorable conditions (moist soil), by aboveground creeping runners or stolons that root every 3 to 5 inches, creating tight mats of mounded foliage. Often recommended to alleviate headaches and insomnia, they do, in fact, contain the glycoside of salicylic acid, an ingredient in aspirin.

Both violas and sweet violets have been with me a long time. I couldn't banish them even if I wanted to (I don't), because their will to live and multiply is irrepressible.

My youngest daughter, Curdie, first raised violas, choosing a dark purple cultivar from a seed catalog. Growing 5 to 6 inches high, its faces are a deep velvety purple, shading to a bit of violet, then orange-yellow toward the center, its black whiskers just visible. According to my records going back to the early 1970s, it was 'King Henry', but the colors of that hard-to-find cultivar are described as "violet, sky blue, and gold." Perhaps the writers of these catalog texts have never really seen it, or perhaps I have the name wrong. If you ever see a viola you like growing in someone's garden, the best way to make sure you get it is to ask for a little clump (seeds can be variable).

Violas, once planted, will self-seed with abandon, coming up where you least expect them (the common name Johnny-jump-up is apt, indeed), and growing with no encouragement whatsoever, always delightful to find. In my travels around the farm, I see them in the most unlikely places: under the wooden stairway leading down from the knoll to the swimming hole; in the crevices of wooden timbers by the compost heap; and, of course, in the garden proper, where I encourage them to grow along the pathway through the middle of the bed. The most enduring of all flowers, they continue to bloom until the snow flies, and even beyond. Their faces change over the years, some with more yellow or violet, but every one is welcome.

Sweet violets grow readily, too, but not in the same way because their growth requirements are more specific: They need moist, rich soil. They turned up uninvited in my herb and flower garden, inadvertently tangled in the roots of something else. I was forever pulling up the glossy-leaved clumps to make room for other plants, for, unless inhibited, they would take over the whole planting. With only a vague idea of naturalizing them (a concept I really knew nothing about at the time), I tossed them into a pile outside the garden, spreading them out, then stepping on them to push them into a spot of damp, weedy ground. That's the end of them, I thought. I hadn't really discarded them (heaven forbid!), and I'd given them a fighting chance, so my conscience was clear.

I needn't have fretted at all, since the sweet violets wholly won over the area: completely shading out and killing weeds; moving with astonishing speed to consolidate their position; spreading out to form a low, attractive canopy of heart-shaped leaves; then, in early June, creating a specactular display of white flowers, blooming at the same time as other sweet white flowers—sweet cicely in the garden and the wild hawthorn tree—attracting early butterflies in search of nectar. The scent of sweet violets is wonderful but light and elusive, fading almost as soon as it is detected.

Growing: Refrigerate viola seeds for 1 day, then sow them indoors in late winter at 70 degrees; germination should take 8 to 12 days if seeds are just covered (they need darkness to germinate). Or sow seeds outdoors in a coldframe anytime during the summer or early fall; seedlings will be ready to plant out the following spring. Space plants 6 inches apart in ordinary garden soil (they'll grow almost anywhere except in bogs). Bloom will be prolific in cool weather, but plants flag as the summer progresses. Cut them back so they'll be ready to bloom again as temperatures fall. Even if they are planted in shady conditions (where blooming will be extended), you will need to trim them to encourage fresh flowers. Save seeds of favorite colors or isolate clumps in different areas. Although violas are short-lived perennials, they ensure their survival by self-seeding.

In early spring, space sweet violet plants 12 inches apart in moist, enriched ground. Plant them for accents outside the garden proper, or wherever you want to smother weeds. Maintain the planting to desired size by mowing around it when you cut the grass.

Using: Violas and sweet violets can be candied using the method described for calendulas. I prefer to use sweet violets fresh; their texture is crisp, their flavor lightly sweet. Since they are a mild laxative, I use them sparingly, but to great visual effect, to decorate chocolate cake frosting.

WORMWOODS
Wormwood (Old Woman)
Artemisia absinthium

Roman Wormwood (Old Warrior)
Artemisia pontica

Sweet Wormwood (Sweet Annie, Sweet Mugwort)
Artemisia annua
Asteraceae (Aster Family)
Type: Annual, Perennial
Height: 1½ to 6 feet
Site: Sun/Partial shade
Soil: Well drained
Growing Zones: 3–10

Artemisia absinthium

The perennial wormwood (sometimes referred to as true wormwood) is native to Europe. Famed as a vermifuge (for expelling worms) as its common name suggests, it is an important ingredient in the now banned liqueur, absinthe, whose name is based on the Latin epithet *absinthium,* meaning "without sweetness" (an understatement, since the taste of wormwood is one of the most bitter). The active principal, thujone, is so powerful that preparations made with it, including the drink, can be fatal. In small quantities it can be beneficial in treating stomach complaints and relieving the pains of rheumatism and arthritis. It is used today in antiseptic lotions and liniments.

Wormwood is a shrublike plant that grows from a woody base to 4 feet, its stems covered with aromatic, deeply divided leaves, silver-gray in color. Insignificant yellow flowers occur in small clusters, nearly hidden by the long leaves.

Roman wormwood, so-called because of its origins in southern Europe, is a much smaller plant with more silvery, very finely cut, lacey foliage that grows in a soft, low mound little more than a foot tall, spreading apart as it matures. Roman wormwood is bitter, too, but not as strongly aromatic as wormwood. Like wormwood, it is used to flavor vermouth.

Sweet wormwood, native to China, is an annual species that grows to 6 feet in one season: treelike in shape, wider at the bottom than perennial wormwood (to 3 feet), and tapering to a point at its top. Its soft branches bear filmy, green, much-divided foliage and, later, small, bright yellow flowers. As the plant matures and the flowers turn reddish brown, the supple branches become hard and brittle. Its aroma is warmly citrus with a camphoraceous note. In China, sweet wormwood is a medicinal herb used to treat malaria. In North America it is used for crafts, especially wreathmaking.

Over the years, without any plan, I have been steadily acquiring artemisias, whose intricate silvery foliage (with the exception of the flowering white mugwort) is recommendation enough. The first one was the true wormwood, which we have been growing for over 30 years for its household use (to repel moths) and its medicinal application (to treat stomach complaints). It was Jigs who many years ago read of its uses for indigestion in the English classic *Herbs and the Fragrant Garden,* by Margaret Brownlow (1957). I grow wormwood in the harvest bed so I can cut its branches for our pharmacopoeia. So far, I have not used it for landscaping, but I like Margaret Brownlow's suggestion of growing it as a striking background for the bright bergamots and blue chicory, all of which are always in my gardens. The silver-leaved wormwood cultivar 'Lambrook Silver' would be the one to grow in this situation.

Roman wormword first came to my attention when I was researching old-fashioned herbs and flowers. A woman in her 80s brought me a little piece from which many silvery mounds have grown. Like southernwood, it was popular in older gardens solely for its ornamental qualities. I grow it in difficult sites, since it withstands wind and poor soil. It grows beneath the wild rugosa rose hedge at the top of the lane, a silvery marker that stands out at all seasons, when the deep scarlet roses are in bloom, and, later, when their foliage turns bronzy red. It also marks the path leading into the herb and flower garden, a silver foil for the dark purple spikes of the the dwarf salvia 'East Friesland'.

I have recently grown another artemisia, the well-known 'Silver Mound'

(*A. schmidtiana*), which is exactly as described in its name: a low, perfect ball of silvery foliage that glistens in the sun. Adelma Simmons describes it aptly: "So elegant and extravagant looking that it seems too much to expect the plant to be hardy, easily divided, and generally well behaved" (*Herb Gardening in Five Seasons,* Plume reprint, 1990). The only thing it does not like is a bit of extra moisture in the soil, which could cause it to die over the winter. I grow it solely for its fantastic looks (it has no herbal use) at the front of the border with bright annual pinks (*Dianthus* sp.).

As you must know by now, I'm a sucker for anything with the name "sweet" attached to it. So it was inevitable that I should one day add sweet wormwood to my repertoire of sweet herbs: sweet cicely, sweet Mary (costmary), sweet rocket, sweet violet, sweet woodruff, and the wild sweet white clover. I was aware that sweet wormwood is highly regarded by wreathmakers, but there is not much about the herb in the literature. An exception is Gertrude Foster in *Park's Success with Herbs* (1980). She and her husband offered the seeds in the 1940s under the name "Chinese Fragrant Fern," but, as she pointed out, it did not become popular until the Herb Renaissance more than 20 years later. Nothing prepared me for its astonishing growth in a single season, from a slender seedling to a magnificent 6-foot tree against a slab fence in the harvest bed. I didn't notice sweet wormwood's progress until late summer, when scarlet runner beans had entwined themselves in its stems, a purely chance and effective combination worth repeating.

Sweet wormwood's warm, citrusy fragrance, released by running your hands along the branches, is different from any I've ever experienced. I now understand what pleasure it must be to work with this plant, cutting and tying little sprigs together to make a wreath. Sweet wormwood is also an outstanding landscaping plant for any garden, a dramatic point of interest in the fall.

Growing: Sow wormwood seeds outside in the fall to germinate the following spring, or grow from purchased plants, spacing them 2 feet apart. Wormwood will grow in most soils and in sun or partial shade, but sun is better. After a few years, established plants become quite woody; they can be rejuvenated by clipping back plants in spring, or by taking stem cuttings in summer. Plants also propagate themselves by self-sowing.

Roman wormwood is usually grown from plants spaced 1 foot apart in the spring. It needs some warmth for established plants to push through the soil, so be patient. Its form is improved by chopping out extra growth (it wants to spread) and cutting it back anytime during the growing season that it gets out of hand. If kept neat, it makes an effective low hedge.

Sow seeds of sweet wormwood indoors 10 to 12 weeks before the last frost at 70 degrees; germination is rapid (by 7 days). After all danger of frost is past, space seedlings outdoors 2 feet apart. Their growth is slow, but sure. If not cut back after flowering, seedlings will appear in the ground the following season.

Harvesting and Using: Cut stems of wormwood for use as a moth repellent by midsummer, or after flowers have formed. Hang up the stems to air-dry, or, if they are long, they can be laid out on screens. Later, the intact dried stems can be hung up in closets, or placed in storage areas with woolens, or stripped for their leaves and flowers to use in sachets for the same purpose (see *Southern-wood—Herb Guard*). Working with wormwood releases its scent; this can cause some discomfort (it does to me), including a bitter taste in the mouth and a slight headache, just from the vapors. For this reason, I advise harvesting it in small quantities only. A few dried stems lend a refreshing scent and silvery contrast to dried posies or small bouquets.

Cut the stem tips and side shoots (not the hard main stem) of sweet wormwood for wreaths and other crafts when the flowers are bright yellow. Or dry them for use in potpourri.

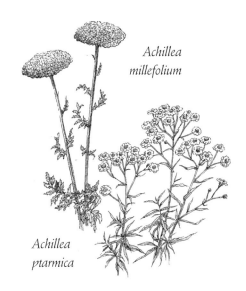

Achillea
millefolium

Achillea
ptarmica

YARROW (Milfoil)

Achillea millefolium

SNEEZEWORT
(Bride's Bouquet)

Achillea ptarmica
Asteraceae (Aster Family)
Type: Perennial
Height: 2½ feet
Site: Sun
Soil: Well drained
Growing Zones: 3–10

Both these Old World herbs of the *Achillea* genus are naturalized across North America. Yarrow is found along roadsides and in old fields on dry ground. It grows on very straight, fern-leaved stems from creeping roots. Its flowers, usually white, sometimes light pink, bloom in midsummer in flat umbels 2 to 3 inches across. The whole plant exudes a fresh, pungent scent. Yarrow has an ancient history of use especially associated with healing wounds, as preserved in the genus name, *Achillea,* after Achilles, who is supposed to have used it to stanch the wounds of his soldiers; the epithet *millefolium,* 'a thousand leaves,' refers to the plant's much divided leaves.

Sneezewort, a shorter, sprawling plant that prefers damp ground near streams and meadows, also grows by creeping roots that produce stems with narrow, sharply toothed leaves. The buttonlike flowers—small, daisy-shaped with a muddy center—bloom in loose clusters by midsummer. Its common name reflects its use as snuff to induce sneezing (to cure headaches).

Yarrow is a common weed on the farm, growing at the edges of our pastures. I picked the wildflower for dried posies long before I thought of growing fancy cultivars in a wider range of colors. I have grown rose- and pink-colored variants from plants (*A. millefolium* 'Rosea') and from seeds ('Summer Pastels'), and I still think the wildflower is elegant in fresh bloom, its flowers a clear snow white (these gradually turn gray), blossoming all summer and well into the fall.

Cultivated yarrows, though, have great value as landscaping plants because of their bushy form—an attractive, low, green, ferny mound even when out of bloom—and wider range of flower colors, including not only the roses and pinks, but also salmon, lilac, and amber, some of them with prominent yellow centers (the stamens). These, however, are hybrids and do not grow as easily as the older cultivars of *A. millefolium* ('Cerise Queen' or 'Red Beauty'). In my experience, the seed-grown strain 'Summer Pastels' tends to produce mostly washed-out pinks, probably because they are closer to the wild and more vigorous, germinating more freely than the rest and crowding out other seedlings. This is the danger of growing seed strains as opposed to growing cultivars; the latter are grown from roots and always produce plants identical to the parent.

The classic sneezewort cultivar 'The Pearl', introduced in the late 19th century, is a well-known example of what happens when such a plant is grown repeatedly from seed, then offered to the public; the result is a deterioration in the original, improved form. I experienced this phenomenon when I purchased seeds advertised as 'The Pearl', a less rangy, more tractable garden plant than sneezewort with very tight, double white, pompon flowers. What I actually grew from this seed was a plant close to the wildflower, semidouble daisies with muddy centers. Once you have seen 'The Pearl' you can never mistake it for sneezewort (the wildflower). 'The Pearl' is common here on the island, growing as a garden escapee near old farmhouse sites. That is where I finally found a reliable source for my own garden, growing it from a few stem cuttings. Sneezewort joined my "wort garden," a naturalized planting of lungwort, bistort, and white mugwort in damp ground by the bridge that leads to one of our guest cabins. It's happy there, and I'm happy, too, since it's not tame enough to be planted within the confines of a garden.

The very desirable fernleaf yarrow, 'Coronation Gold' (*A. filipendulina*), with its 4- to 6-inch-wide mustard yellow heads (indispensable for wreaths and bouquets), can be grown from seed. A tall, striking plant that grows to 8 feet under favorable conditions (well-drained soil), it has come and gone in my garden, but it and the hybrid 'Moonshine', to 2 feet with silver-gray foliage and lemon yellow flowers, will be invited back again. I do admire the simple beauty of the pure white and light pink wildflower, but, like all gardening enthusiasts, I'm always interested in expanding my repertoire to include different forms and variations on pleasing themes.

Growing: Sow seeds (except of hybrids) outdoors in a coldframe during the summer, where seeds will germinate over the winter; or sow seeds indoors 12 weeks before the last frost at 70 degrees, just pressing them into the soil. Space plants outside 12 to 18 inches apart; yarrows do best if not crowded. Cut flowering stalks all summer to produce more blooms. In hot, dry weather, yarrows sag, sometimes losing their fresh colors (darker ones become lighter). Propagate the yarrows by division as often as they need it, at least every two or three years. Sneezewort will form large clumps in a naturalized setting; it will take care of itself (which is why you naturalized it). 'The Pearl' should be grown only from purchased plants; this is not, unfortunately, a guarantee that you'll get the right plant. 'The Pearl' can also be increased by stem cuttings taken during the summer and wintered-over in a coldframe.

Using: The yarrows, sneezewort, and 'The Pearl' make fine cut flowers ('The Pearl' is exceptional); all of them can also be dried for bouquets—yarrows are lacy fillers—or other crafts. Mark and Terry Silber, in their *Complete Book of Everlastings* (Alfred A. Knopf, 1988), give precise directions for picking yarrows to retain their color and form as much as possible (they will fade and shrivel, but will still be attractive): The little individual flowers that make up a flower head should all be completely open; close inspection is necessary. This is even more crucial when picking the wildflower since it grows in dry soil, causing its blooms to fade quickly. Pick sneezewort and 'The Pearl' when the flowers are fresh, in their early bloom.

ZA'ATAR (Bible Hyssop, Syrian Hyssop, Syrian Oregano)

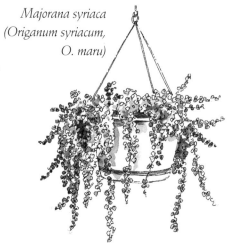

Majorana syriaca (Origanum syriacum, O. maru)

Majorana syriaca (Origanum syriacum, O. maru)

Labiatae (Mint Family)

Type: Tender perennial

Height: 2½ feet

Site: Sun

Soil: Well drained

Growing Zones: 8–10

Za'atar (an Arabic word pronounced Zah-tar) or hyssop (translation of the Hebrew word *ezov*) is a Middle Eastern herb closely related to the oreganos, as its several botanical names imply. Close to the ground and shrubby, it is able to grow, even thrive, in a dry, stony, desert landscape, a phenomenon that gained it an ancient reputation as a symbol of modesty or humility. Its many stems are covered with small, nearly heart-shaped, downy leaves that give the whole plant a grayish appearance (the hairs help it withstand drought conditions). White flowers appear in dense terminal clusters in midsummer.

Za'atar has a long history as a medicinal and flavoring herb. Its thymol concentration is probably responsible for its effective applications in treating tooth decay, gum infections, and coughs; hyssop tea is drunk after meals to aid digestion. Za'atar is also the Arabic name for a spice mixture (in which the herb is the main flavoring ingredient) baked into the crust of pita and other breads. The herb's flavor is sharp, a blend of thyme, marjoram, and oregano. Where it is unavailable, other herbs—notably spiked thyme, *Thymbra spicata*—are substituted in the spice blend.

My interest in herbs has greatly influenced my life, sometimes carrying me far from our backlands farm. One cold winter morning in 1988, Jigs hitched up the team to the bobsled, and took me over the ice-covered road to the railroad tracks a mile from the farm, where we hailed the train for the first leg of my trip to Israel to see the herbs and flowers I had been studying. Once there, my knowledgeable plant friends made sure I saw, felt, and tasted almost every one.

From one end of the tiny country to the other (altogether no larger than Cape Breton Island), I saw the herb whose identity had been in question for centuries, the hyssop of the Bible: "Purge me with hyssop," David begs after his affair with Bathsheba, "and I shall be clean; wash me, and I shall be whiter than snow" (Psalms 51:7). Its brushy stems were dipped in blood to mark the doorposts of the Children of Israel in the story of the first Passover as told in the Book of Exodus; the very same plant was used to hold a sponge full of vinegar to revive the dying Jesus (John 19:28–30). From the deserts of the Negev to the hill country in the Galilee, I saw this ancient symbol of the Jewish people, "lowly like the hyssop," growing "from the [sides of] rocks," as described in the Book of Kings. In the desert, people were gathering its plentiful winter leaves for tea, and at Neot Kedumim, the large Biblical Landscape Reserve between Jerusalem and Tel Aviv, I saw it in a planting of hyssops—the real and the false ones—all aromatic members of the mint family, among them blue hyssop (*Lavandula stoechas*).

I met Nogah Hareuveni, a slim, humble, intense man, then in his 60s, who, I felt, had grown from the soil like the hyssop, finding nourishment in difficult places. After years of struggle, his revelation that nature is an integral part of Judaism (a continuation of his parents' pioneering work) was becoming accepted. It was the self-evident truth of his vision that had drawn me thousands of miles to see for myself the landscape in which this point of view was born. It seemed as if my whole life, much of it a struggle with nature in one way or another, had been a preparation for understanding how herbs were used by the ancient sages to teach lessons on humility, as with the hyssop, to mark the distinction between sweet and bitter with a handful of weeds.

But, to tell the truth, I was also overcome by the sheer beauty of the herbs I saw everywhere growing as roadside weeds: the pebbly leaved salvias with their fragrant candelabras (perhaps ancient models for the menorah); the wooly-leaved horehound (a species of *Ballota*); the oreganos and thymes, so wonderfully fragrant; the larger-than-life rue and fennel growing on mountaintops. My herb world would never be the same.

Back home, I discovered that most of these herbs are available from specialty nurseries (Well-Sweep Herb Farm in New Jersey and Richters in Canada), and soon I was growing the hyssop of the Bible as a greenhouse plant in a hanging basket, where it does not reach the proportions of plants growing in the ground in frost-free areas, like Southern California. But it is the real thing, and when I pick the downy leaves to flavor my morning eggs, I can almost smell the desert again. And I found a source for the spice blend, za'atar, that I had eaten on pita bread fresh from the fire at a bedouin village.

Growing: Look for seeds or plants of *Majorana syriaca* under *Origanum* or Oregano in specialty seed and plant listings. It is usually offered as *Origanum syriacum* and may be called Syrian oregano; this is za'atar or Bible hyssop, same thing. Sow seeds as you would marjoram or oregano, 12 weeks before the last frost date, just pressing them into the soil; germination should occur in 8 to 14 days at 70 degrees. In cold climates, grow plants indoors under lights or in a greenhouse until temperatures are steadily warm. If you grow plants in containers that can be moved indoors at the end of the growing season, you can winter over za'atar in a cool, sunny window. In Zones 9 and 10, it grows as a small shrub, nice for landscaping in exposed sites, as in a rockery at the base of stones, where heat and moisture are easily captured. Soil should be somewhat alkaline and very well drained; the addition of sharp sand helps. Za'atar's gray-green foliage is a striking foil for tubs of bright yellow and orange signet marigolds *(Tagetes tenuifolia)*.

Using: Pick leaves anytime to use like oregano. I use za'atar leaves in salads, egg dishes, and herb butters. Dry leaves in a just-warm oven set no higher than 150 degrees F, then strip them from the stems and store them in a labeled jar away from light.

The spice blend, za'atar, is available at groceries specializing in Middle Eastern foods. It usually consists of about 3 parts crushed or powdered dried leaves of the herb za'atar (or a species of thyme), 1 part crushed roasted sesame seeds, 1 part ground sumac fruits (the nonpoisonous *Rhus coriaria,* similar in its tart flavor to our common staghorn sumac, *Rhus typhina*), and salt and pepper to taste. Use it to make my pita bread, now a feature of summer herb workshops, baked on the spot.

Jo Ann's Favorite Pita Bread

MAKES 1 DOZEN 5- TO 7-INCH ROUNDS

The best pita I ever experienced in the Middle East was baked in an outdoor oven called
a taboun, a rectangular tin box open at the front except for a narrow firebox at one end.
Inside the taboun is a manually operated revolving wheel on which the pita is baked,
each pita passing through the flames in turn until it is lightly browned and the za'atar-
and-olive-oil coating is sizzling. To experience the ultimate pita-with-za'atar, you would
either have to rig up a taboun (the results can't be duplicated in a conventional oven) or
visit Kaldia the baker in the bedouin village of Shibli at the foot of Mount Tabor in Israel.
Failing these solutions, however, follow the directions below.

2 heaping tablespoons za'atar spice blend, thinned with olive oil to
　　spreading consistency
1 tablespoon (1 packet) baking yeast
1 scant tablespoon salt
2 tablespoons sugar
3 cups water
6 to 7 cups unbleached white flour

Mix the za'atar with olive oil and set aside. Mix the yeast, salt, and sugar with
½ cup warm water, cover, and let stand for 10 minutes; stir the mixture to
make sure the yeast is all dissolved (it should be foaming). Add the rest of the
water and 4 cups of flour, then mix the dough vigorously, adding more flour as
needed to make it stiff. Knead 5 minutes, then cover the bowl and let the
dough rise in a warm place until doubled in bulk (about 45 minutes). Preheat
oven to 450 degrees F. Punch down the dough, cut it into 12 pieces (or 6 if you
want larger rounds), and roll out each piece about ¼ inch thick (or thicker, if
you want). Place them one at a time on an ungreased cookie sheet, patting each
into a roughly round shape. When the cookie sheet is full, gently press your fingertips into the top of the dough to make little indentations, then brush each
round with the za'atar–olive oil mixture. Bake immediately for about 8 minutes. The crust should be golden brown and the oil sizzling.

　　For stuffing, cut the bread in triangles and gently pull apart the dough
until you have a pouch. We always eat it hot, dipped into leftover za'atar–olive
oil. You can freeze uncooked dough immediately, but use it up within a few
weeks. Eat up the baked pita bread; it becomes stiff after a day or so.

A departing tussie-mussie for the reader

May your borage give you courage,
Your basil, love,
Your marjoram, happiness,
Your calendula, joy,
Your mint, wisdom and virtue,
And your sage, good health
To enjoy all the blessings of herbs.

Bibliography

Bremness, Lesley. **The Complete Book of Herbs.** Montreal: Reader's Digest Association (Canada) Ltd., 1989.
Comprehensive, good identifying photos.

Brownlow, Margaret E. **Herbs and the Fragrant Garden.** Kent, England: The Herb Farm Ltd., 1957.
A charming, pioneering classic.

Clarkson, Rosetta. **Herbs: Their Culture and Uses.** New York: The Macmillan Company, 1942.
Indispensable for herb uses; another pioneering classic.

Crockett, James Underwood, and editors. **Herbs.** (The Time-Life Encyclopedia of Gardening.) New York: Time-Life Books, 1977.
Thorough and reliable, like all the Crockett series.

DeBaggio, Thomas. **Growing Herbs: From Seed, Cutting, and Root.** Loveland, CO: Interweave Press, Inc., 1994.
Very practical, from an experienced grower.

Deno, Norman C. **Seed Germination, Theory and Practice.** Published by the author: 139 Lenor Drive, State College, PA 16801, 1993.
A different and persuasive way to understand the subject.

Facciola, Stephen. **Cornucopia: A Source Book of Edible Plants.** Vista, CA: Kampong Publications, 1990.
An incredible feat of research; very thorough and comprehensive.

Foster, Gertrude B., and Philip Foster, with Cathleen Maxwell. "Herbs for a Nosegay" (booklet). Falls Village, CT: The Herb Grower Press, 1966.

Foster, Gertrude B., and Rosemary F. Louden. **Park's Success with Herbs.** Greenwood, SC: Geo. W. Park Seed Co., Inc., 1980.
An invaluable reference by one of America's most knowledgeable herb writers.

Gardner, Jo Ann. **The Old-Fashioned Fruit Garden.** Halifax, Nova Scotia: Nimbus, 1989.
Growing and using directions for hardy fruits.

————. **The Heirloom Garden.** Pownal, VT: Storey Communications, Inc., 1992.
Growing old-fashioned flowers and herbs.

Hill, Madalene, and Gwen Barclay. **Southern Herb Growing.** Fredricksburg, TX: Shearer Publishing, 1987.
Excellent reference for the South and beyond.

Hopkinson, Patricia, Diane Miske, Jerry Parsons, and Holly Shimizu. **Herb Gardening.** New York: Pantheon Books, 1994.
Covers every growing region; a wide variety of herbs.

Hortus Third. Compiled and edited by the Staff of the Liberty Hyde Bailey Hortorium, Cornell University. New York: Macmillan, 1976.
Considered obsolete, but still invaluable for detailed descriptions of many species.

Kowalchik, Claire, and William H. Hylton, editors. **Rodale's Illustrated Encyclopedia of Herbs.** Emmaus, PA: Rodale Press, 1987.
Easy-to-use general reference.

Lust, John. **The Herb Book.** New York: Bantam Books, 1974.
Comprehensive reference on medicinal herbs.

Mazza, Irma Goodrich. **Herbs for the Kitchen.** Boston: Little, Brown and Company, 1947 (first published 1939).
Pioneering classic, never outdated.

Peterson, Roger Tory. **A Field Guide to Wildflowers.** Boston: Houghton Mifflin Co., 1968.
An indispensable guide.

Phillips, Rodger, and Nicki Foy. **The Random House Book of Herbs.** New York: Random House, 1990.
British book; reliable reference for herb uses; good identifying photos.

Shaudys, Phyllis. **The Pleasure of Herbs.** Pownal, VT: Storey Communications, Inc., 1986.
Useful information from the author, based on experience; many herb projects from herb enthusiasts.

————. **Herbal Treasures.** Pownal, VT: Storey Communications, Inc., 1990.

Silber, Mark, and Terry Silber. **The Complete Book of Everlastings.** New York: Knopf, 1988.
One of the best on the subject.

Simmons, Adelma Grenier. **Herb Gardening in Five Seasons.** New York: Plume, 1990 (first published by Hawthorne Dutton, 1964).
An endearing and pioneering work.

Source Appendix

United States

Companion Plants
>PO Box 88, Athens, OH 47501
>*A wide selection of plants and seeds.*

The Crownsville Nursery
>PO Box 797, Crownsville, MD 21032
>*Plants; choice herbs, such as bistort, are listed under Perennials.*

J.L. Hudson, Seedsman
>Star Route 2, Box 337, La Honda, CA 94020
>*Seeds; rare and unusual.*

Nichols Garden Nursery
>1190 North Pacific Highway, Albany, OR 97321
>*Plants and seeds; miscellaneous products including herbes de Provence.*

Sandy Mush Herb Nursery
>316 Surrett Cover Road, Leicester, NC 28758
>*Plants and seeds; extensive listing.*

Stokes Seeds, Inc.
>Box 548, Buffalo, NY 14240
>*Seeds; general selection; excellent growing information throughout catalog; extensive flower listings, some herby types, e.g., signet marigold.*

Sunnybrook Herb Farm
>Box 6, Chesterland, OH 44026
>*Plants; nice selection.*

Thompson & Morgan
>PO Box 1306, Jackson, NY 08527
>*Seeds; choice types often not listed under herbs, e.g., 'Zebrina Mallow' is under general listings.*

Well-Sweep Herb Farm
>317 Mt. Bethel Road, Port Murray, NJ 07865
>*Plants and seeds; wonderful selection of cultivars; miscellaneous products, including fragrance and essential oils.*

Wrenwood of Berkeley Springs
>Route 4, Box 361, Berkeley Springs, WV 25411
>*Plants; choice offerings, including tangerine southernwood.*

Canada

Country Green, Inc.
> Box 356, Campbellville, ON N0B 2J0
> *Plants, including a Windowsill Collection.*

William Dam Seeds
> Box 8400, Dundas, ON L9H 6M1
> *Seeds; Dutch company with a European flavor.*

The Herb Farm
> RR 4, Norton, NB E0G 2N0
> *Plants and seeds; craft supplies.*

Mulligan Seeds
> Box 700, Osgoode, ON K0A 2W0
> *Wildflower seeds, including bouncing bet and dame's rocket.*

Richters
> 357 Highway 47, Goodwood, ON L0C 1A0
> *Plants and seeds; enormous selection; ships to US.*

River View Herbs
> Box 92, Highway 215, Maitland, Hants Co., NS B0N 1T0
> *Plants; wide selection.*

Salt Spring Island Nursery
> 355A Blackburn Road, Salt Spring Island, BC V8K 288
> *Plants; good selection, including hardy types.*

Stokes Seeds Ltd.
> Box 10, St. Catharines, ON L2R 6R6
> *See Stokes Seeds, Inc., United States listing.*

Crafts Products Suppliers

Lavender Lane
> 5321 Elkhorn Boulevard, Sacramento, CA 95842
> *Tea bags, fixatives (including corn cellulose) fragrance and essential oils, bottles.*

San Francisco Herb Co.
> 250 14th Street, San Francisco, CA 94103
> *Fixatives (including corn cellulose), fragrance oils, herbs.*

Index

Accent plantings, 91-92
Achillea
  millefolium, 76, 269-271
  ptarmica, 20, 269-271
Aegopodium podagraria, 90, 206, 253
Air circulation, 40, 45, 89, 222
Air-drying, 50, 56-58
Ajuga spp., 90, 253
Alcea
  officinalis, 189
  rosea, 58, 76, 165-167
  rosea nigra, 165-167
Alchemilla vulgaris, 52, 58, 76, 174-175
Alecost. *See* Costmary
Allium
  schoenoprasum, 45, 52, 58, 66, 76, 134-137
  tuberosum, 138-139
Aloysia triphylla, 182
American
  cress. *See* Cress, Upland
  elder. *See* Elderberry
Anaphalis margaritacea, 52, 217-219
Anethum graveolens, 45, 58, 66, 76, 156-158
Angelica (*Angelica archangelica*), 76, 99-101
Angelica archangelica, 76, 99-101
Angelica candy, 100-101
Annual chamomile. *See* Chamomile
Annual herbs, full sun, 89
Anthriscus cerefolium, 45, 59, 131-132
Armoracia rusticana, 171-173
Aromatherapy, 61-62, 227, 239, 246, 262
Aromatherapy, 62
Aromatherapy Book, The, 63
Aromatherapy for Everyone, 62
Artemisia
  abrotanum, 53, 58, 76, 243-245
  absinthium, 53, 76, 265-268
  annua, 265-268
  lactiflora, 41, 52, 207-209
  pontica, 265-268
  vulgaris, 52, 76, 205-207
Art of Simpling, The, 128
Arugula (*Eruca vesicaria* var. *sativa*), 66, 101-102
Astringents, 90, 114

Band-aid plant, 177
Barbarea verna, 150-151
Basil (*Ocimum basilicum*), 35-36, 45, 58, 66, 76, 103-106
  Purple (*Ocimum basilicum*), 106-108
Basil Revolution, 104, 107
Bath salts, 62-63
Bee balm (*Monarda didyma*), 52, 58, 66, 109-111
Beer making, 168, 206
Bees, 114, 119, 188, 198, 249
  plants to attract, 92
Bergamot. *See* Bee balm
  lemon (*Monarda citriodora*), 111-113
  wild (*Monarda fistulosa*), 110, 113-114
Berry, Susan, 74
Bethlehem-sage. *See* Lungwort
Bible hyssop. *See* Za'atar
Bible-leaf. *See* Costmary
Biblical flora, 14-15, 173-174
Biblical Landscape Reserve, 273
Biennials, 140
Bistort (*Polygonum bistorta*), 114-116
Bitter herbs, 14, 133, 171-172
Black Currant Juice, 118-119
Black currant (*Ribes nigrum*), 116-119
Blue
  comfrey. *See* Comfrey
  mallow. *See* Mallow, common
Boneset. *See* Comfrey
Borage (*Borago officinalis*), 76, 119-121
Borago officinalis, 76, 119-121
Bouncing bet. *See* Soapwort
Bouquet garni, 258
Bouquets, dried, 65-66
Bremness, Lesley, 175
Bride's bouquet. *See* Sneezewort
Brownlow, Margaret, 266
Brush hook, long-handled, 53-54, 185
Buchanan, Rita, 240
Bugleweed (*Ajuga* spp.), 90, 253
Bunching method, traditional, 52-53
Burnet (*Poterium sanguisorba*), 45, 76, 121-122
Butterflies, 85, 114, 264
  plants to attract, 92
Butters, herb, 63

Calamint (*Calamintha grandiflora*), 123-124
Calamintha grandiflora, 123-124
Calendula (*Calendula officinalis*), 58, 66, 124-127
Calendula officinalis, 58, 66, 124-127
Candied Calendula Flowers, 127
Candied flowers, 64, 121, 127, 167, 191, 194, 265
Cape Breton, 19, 30, 50, 100, 135, 195, 215
Catmint. *See* Catnip
Catnip (*Nepeta cataria*), 52, 62, 127-129
Chamaemelum nobile, 129-130
Chamomile (*Matricaria recutita*), 49, 58, 76, 129-131
Chamomile, Roman (*Chamaemelum nobile*), 129-130
Cheese
    mallow. *See* Mallow, common
    spreads, 64-65
Chervil (*Anthriscus cerefolium*), 45, 59, 131-132
Chicory (*Cichorium intybus*), 132-134
Chinese
    chives. *See* Chives, garlic
    parsley. *See* Coriander
Chive Blossom Vinegar, 137-138
Chives (*Allium schoenoprasum*), 45, 52, 58, 66, 76, 134-137
    garlic (*Allium tuberosum*), 138-139
Chrysanthemum
    balsamita, 58, 76, 147-150
    parthenium, 52, 163-164
Cichorium intybus, 132-134
Cilantro. *See* Coriander
Clary (*Salvia sclarea*), 140-141
    annual (*Salvia viridis*), 141-143
Clary sage. *See* Clary
Coffee substitute, 133-134
Cold Beet Salad, 203-204
Coldframes, 27-29
Coles, William, 128
Comfrey (*Symphytum caucasicum*), 143-145
Common
    basil. *See* Basil
    marjoram. *See* Marjoram, wild
    oregano. *See* Marjoram, wild
    rose. *See* Roses, Virginia
    sage. *See* Sage
    thyme. *See* Thyme, cooking
Companion planting, 89, 255
Complete Book of Everlastings, The, 66, 78, 271
Complete Book of Herbs, The, 175
Complete Medicinal Herbal, The, 70

Composting, 31-32, 145
Containers, growing in, 35-39, 91-92
Cooking. *See* Culinary herbs
Cooking sage. *See* Sage
Coriander (*Coriandrum sativum*), 45, 76, 145-147
Coriandrum sativum, 45, 76, 145-147
Corn cellulose, 72
Cosmetic herbs, 77-78, 175
Costmary (*Chrysanthemum balsamita*), 58, 76, 147-150
Cottage Garden Flowers, 177
Cough drops, 170
Creeping Jenny (*Lysimachia nummularia*), 90, 253, 258
Creeping speedwell (*Veronica* spp.), 253
Cress, 45, 66, 76
    Garden (*Lepidium sativum*), 150-151
    Upland (*Barbarea verna*), 150-151
Culinary herbs, 11-12, 65, 77, 122, 132, 181
    basil, 103-108
    chives, 137, 139
    coriander, 147
    dill, 157
    growing indoors, 44-46
    marjoram, 196
    mints, 124, 183, 202-205
    nasturtium, 211-212
    parsley, 217
    rosemary, 227
    sage, 229-232
    savory, 237-238
    thyme, 260
    za'atar, 274-275
Curled cress. *See* Cress, Garden
Curly parsley. *See* Parsley

Dame's rocket. *See* Sweet rocket
Damping-off, 25
Dandelion (*Taraxacum officinale*), 76, 152-155
"Dandelion Times", 153
Dawson, Adele, 143-144
Dead nettle (*Lamium* spp.), 90, 253
DeBaggio, Tom, 44
Decoctions, 65, 68
Design elements, 90-91
Dill (*Anethum graveolens*), 45, 58, 66, 76, 156-158
Diseases, 25, 41-42, 89, 104, 222
Dried Black Currants, 118
Dried Flowers for All Seasons, 74

Drying
  alternative methods of, 53-59
  racks, 55-58
  traditional methods, 50-53
Duff, Gail, 148

Early American Gardens, 168
Edging, 83-85, 90, 176, 195, 236
  plants for, 92
Edible flowers, 66-67
Elderberry (*Sambucus canadensis*), 66, 76, 158-161
Elderflower-Mint Tea, 160
Elderflower Pancakes, 160-161
Elecampane (*Inula helenium*), 161-162
Eruca vesicaria var. *sativa,* 66, 101-102
Evelyn, John, 246

Fannie Farmer Boston Cooking-School Cook Book, 214
Fences, 87-89
Fertilizing, 37, 45
Feverfew (*Chrysanthemum parthenium*), 52, 163-164
Fines herbes, 67, 131, 132, 217
Fish, Margery, 177
Fixatives, 67-68, 250
Floral vinegars, 77-78
Flowering plants, 92
Flowers
  candied, 64, 121, 127, 167, 191, 194, 265
  cut, 112, 116, 191, 193, 248, 271
  dried, 65-66
  edible, 66-67
  language of, 76-77, 207, 276
  See also Nosegays; Tussie-mussies
Foot soaks, 73, 145, 206
Foster, Gertrude, 70, 77, 141, 152, 186, 195, 208, 267
Foster, Philip, 152
Fox, Helen, 170, 208, 225
Freezing, 59
French rose. *See* Roses, Apothecary
Fruits for the Home Garden, 116
Fuller, Samuel, 16
Full sun, 33, 89, 91
Fungus disease, 25, 42, 89, 104, 222

Galium odoratum (Asperula odorata), 67, 252-254
Garden
  heliotrope. *See* Valerian

  sorrel. *See* Sorrel
Gardner, Jigs
  construction by, 28-29, 32, 56
  harvesting, 53-54
  unusual herbs and, 11-12, 241
Gardner, Jo Ann
  in Cape Breton, 12-14
  in Vermont, 11-12
German chamomile. *See* Chamomile
Germination, 22-25, 27, 31
Ghost plant. *See* Mugwort, white
Gibbons, Euell, 153, 170
Goutweed, variegated (*Aegopodium podagraria*), 90, 206, 253
Gow choy, 138
Graywater, 40, 41
Great-flowered betony (*Stachys grandiflora*), 177
Greenhouses, seedlings in, 26-27
Grieve, Mrs., 244
Ground covers, 90, 188, 206, 252-253, 257
  plants for, 92
Growing Herbs: From Seed, Cutting & Root, 44

Habitats, wild, 86-87
  See also Naturalizing
Hamburg parsley. *See* Parsley
Hand-weeding, 35
Hard coats, treatment of, 23
Hardening-off, 27
Hardy lavender. *See* Lavender, English
Hareuveni, Nogah, 171-172, 273
Harrowsmith, 178-179
Harvest bed, 34-35, 87-89
Harvesting, 41, 49-50
  alternative methods of, 53-58
  traditional methods of, 50-53
Hassam, Childe, 166
Hay-chopper, hand-powered, 55
Heartsease. *See* Viola
Hedges, plants for, 92
Hedrick, U.P., 116
Herbal Skin Freshener, 149
Herb Companion, The, 179
Herbed
  Cottage Cheese Spread, 232
  Lamb Chops, 196
  Tea, 183
Herb Gardening in Five Seasons, 206, 267
Herb Grower, The, 141, 152-153
Herb Grower Press, The, 75
Herb-of-grace. *See* Rue

Herb
  Rolls, 260
  Renaissance, 267
Herbs
  flaking, 57-58
  flowering, 85-86
  growing indoors, 44-46
  relaxing, 62
  self-seeding, 43
  soothing, 62
  starting from seed, 20-24
  starting indoors, 24-27
  starting outdoors, 27-29
  stimulating, 62
Herb Salt, 126, 135, 157, 215
  origins of, 13-14
  recipe, 186-187
Herbs and the Fragrant Garden, 266
Herb teas. *See* Tea herbs
Hesperis matronalis, 247-248
High mallow. *See* Mallow, common
Hollyhock (*Alcea rosea*), 58, 76, 165-167
  black (*Alcea rosea nigra*), 165-167
Home Herbal, 70
Hop vine (*Humulus lupulus*), 52, 58, 76, 167-168
Horehound (*Marrubium vulgare*), 76, 169-170
  candy, 169-170
  silver (*Marrubium incanu*), 169-170
Horseheal. *See* Elecampane
Horseradish (*Armoracia rusticana*), 171-173
Hotbeds, 27-29
Hummingbirds, 83, 109, 110, 188, 209, 233
  plants to attract, 92
Humulus lupulus, 52, 58, 76, 167-168
Hundreds-and-thousands, 188
Hyssop (*Hyssopus officinalis*), 76, 173-174
Hyssop, Bible. *See* Za'atar
Hyssopus officinalis, 76, 173-174

Iced Herb Tea, 203
Iced Tea Deluxe, 203
Infusions, 68, 138, 168, 175
Insects, 41-42, 45, 149
Inula helenium, 161-162
Island bed, 83-86
Israel, trip to, 14-15, 142, 225-226, 228, 272-273
Italian parsley. *See* Parsley

Jackson, Bernard S., 136, 163

Japanese rose. *See* Roses, Rugosa
Jefferson, Thomas, 142, 189
Jekyll, Gertrude, 239
Jellies, 68-69, 108-109, 118, 160, 223, 254, 260
  mint, 204-205
Jew, returning, 14-15, 171-172
Jigs's
  Barbecued Chicken, 231-232
  Dill Crock, 157-158
  Horehound Candy, 170
  Mother's Sauce, 172-173
Jo Ann's
  Breakfast Mocha, 134
  Favorite Pita Bread, 275
  Quick Pesto, 106
Jo Ann's Kitchen & Garden, 11, 50, 55, 125, 158-159, 200, 215
  Herbal Foot Soak, 145
  Herb Guard, 244-245
  Herb Salt, 186-187
  Mint Blend Tea, 202-203
Johnny-Jump-Up. *See* Viola

Knitbone. *See* Comfrey
Knotted marjoram. *See* Marjoram

Ladies' tobacco. *See* Pearly everlasting
Lad's love. *See* Southernwood
Lady's mantle (*Alchemilla vulgaris*), 52, 58, 76, 174-175
Lamb's-ears (*Stachys byzantina*), 52, 76, 176-178
Lamium spp., 90, 253
Landscaping
  calendula, 125
  design elements, 90-91
  harvest bed, 87-89
  herbs for, 91-92
  hollyhocks, 166
  hyssop, 174
  integrated, 81-83
  island bed, 83-86
  lovage, 184
  marjoram, 195
  mugworts, 206
  roses, 220
  southernwood, 243-244
  yarrows, 270
Lavandula
  angustifolia, 49, 52, 58, 66, 178-181
  stoechas, 14, 180, 273

Lavender, English (*Lavandula angustifolia*), 49, 52, 58, 66, 178-181
Leaf shredder, 55
Leighton, Ann, 168, 254
Lemon
  balm (*Melissa officinalis*), 45, 52, 76, 181-183
  mint. *See* Bergamot, lemon
  verbena (*Aloysia triphylla*), 182
Lepidium sativum, 150-151
Levisticum officinale, 13, 45, 54-55, 57, 58, 183-187
Licorice-flavored herbs, 131, 245
Light requirements, 23
  full sun, 33, 89, 91
  partial sun, 33
  shade, 33, 91
Living With Herbs, origins of, 15-16
Lovage (*Levisticum officinale*), 13, 45, 54-55, 57, 58, 183-187
Love-in-a-mist. *See* Nigella
Lungwort (*Pulmonaria officinalis*), 83-85, 187-188
Lysimachia nummularia, 90, 253, 258

Macomber, Wendy, 253
Maintenance, general, 40-41
Majorana syriaca (*Origanum syriacum, O. maru*), 15, 173, 272-275
Mallow
  common (*Malva sylvestris*), 67, 189-191
  marsh (*Alcea officinalis*), 189
  musk (*Malva moschata*), 191-193
  tree (*Malva sylvestris mauritiana*), 190
Mallow-wort (*Malope trifida grandiflora*), 190-191
Malope trifida grandiflora, 190-191
Malva
  moschata, 191-193
  sylvestris, 67, 189-191
  sylvestris mauritiana, 190
Marigold, signet (*Tagetes tenuifolia*), 58, 76, 193-194
Marjoram (*Origanum majorana*), 45, 52, 76, 195-196
  wild (*Origanum vulgare* subsp. *vulgare*), 197-199
Marrubium
  incanu, 169-170
  vulgare, 169-170
Matricaria recutita, 129-131
Mealycup sage (*Salvia farinacea*), 39, 232-235

Medicinal herbs, 65, 69-70, 161, 181, 184, 269
  feverfew, 164
  lady's mantle, 175
  lungwort, 187
  musk mallow, 193
  pearly everlasting, 218
  rose, 219-220
  thyme, 258
  valerian, 261
  wormwood, 265-266
  za'atar, 272
Melilotus alba, 53, 58, 249-252
Melissa officinalis, 45, 52, 76, 181-183
Mentha pulegium, 76, 201
Mentha spp., 199-205
Mesclun, 132
Microhabitats, 13, 36
  fences, 87-89
Microwave, use of, 59
Milfoil. *See* Yarrow
Mint Jelly, 204-205
Mints (*Mentha* spp.), 20, 45, 52, 58, 67, 76, 199-205
Modern Herbal, A, 244
Monarda
  citriodora, 111-113
  didyma, 52, 58, 66, 109-111
  fistulosa, 110, 113-114
Moth repellent, 73, 256, 268
  recipes, 244-245
Mugwort, common (*Artemisia vulgaris*), 52, 76, 205-207
  white (*Artemisia lactiflora*), 41, 52, 207-209
Mulching, 39, 117-118, 145
Myrrhis odorata, 67, 245-247

Nasturtium officinale, 151
Nasturtium Sauce, 211
Nasturtium (*Tropaeolum majus, T. minor*), 67, 76, 209-212
Natural Fragrances, 148
Naturalizing, 86-87, 144, 255, 264, 269
  plants for, 92
Neot Kedumim, 273
Nepeta cataria, 52, 62, 127-129
Nichols Garden Nursery, 163, 181
Nigella damascena, 212-214
Nigella (*Nigella damascena*), 212-214
Nosegays, 74-77, 137, 177-178, 194

Ocimum basilicum, 35-36, 45, 58, 66, 76, 103-108

Ody, Penelope, 70
Officinalis, 119
Oils
  cooking, 70
  essential, 61-62, 67, 258
Old-Fashioned Fruit Garden, The, 117
Old
  warrior. *See* Wormwood, Roman
  woman. *See* Wormwood
Orange Blossom Potpourri, 149-150
Oregano, Greek (*Origanum vulgare* subsp. *hirtum*), 46, 198
Organic gardening movement, 30
Oriental garlic. *See* Chives, garlic
Origanum
  heracleoticum, 46, 198
  majorana, 45, 52, 76, 195-196
  vulgare subsp. *hirtum,* 46, 198
  vulgare subsp. *vulgare,* 197-199
Ornamental sages. *See* Sages, tender
Orrisroot, 67, 72
Oswego Tea. *See* Bee Balm
Overwatering, 44

Painted sage. *See* Clary, annual
Park's Success with Herbs, 70, 141, 186, 195, 267
Parsleys (*Petroselinum crispum*), 46, 58, 214-217
Partial sun, 33
Passover, 14, 133, 171-172
Paths, 85
Pearly everlasting (*Anaphalis margaritacea*), 52, 217-219
Pennyroyal, English (*Mentha pulegium*), 76, 201
Peppergrass. *See* Cress, Garden
Perennial herbs, 41, 43, 89
Perovskia atriplicifolia, 91
Petroselinum crispum, 46, 58, 214-217
Plants for Beekeeping in Canada, 193
Plant care, 45, 42
Pleasure of Herbs, The, 68
Polygonum bistorta, 114-116
Poterium sanguisorba, 45, 76, 121-122
Pot-marigold. *See* Calendula
Potpourri, 70-72, 149-150, 224
Potting mix, 24, 26, 44
Prechilling, 22-23
Preservation, 50-59
Propagation, 43-44
Protector plant, 227-228
Pulmonaria officinalis, 83-85, 187-188

Purple Basil
  Jelly, 108-109
  Vinegar, 108
Purple-top. *See* Clary, annual

Rabbit tobacco. *See* Pearly everlasting
Raised beds, 30-31
Ramsay, Jane, 193
Raworth, Jenny, 74
Recipes
  angelica, 100-101
  basil, 106, 108-109
  bath salts, 62
  black currants, 118-119
  candied flowers, 64, 127
  cheese spreads, 64-65
  chives, 137-138
  comfrey, 145
  costmary, 149-150
  dandelions, 155
  dill, 157-158
  elderberry, 160-161
  herb butters, 63
  horehound, 170
  horseradish, 172-173
  jellies, 68-69, 108-109, 204-205, 223, 254
  lemon balm, 183
  lovage, 186-187
  marjoram, 196
  mints, 202-205
  mocha, 134
  nasturtium, 211-212
  potpourri, 71-72, 149-150, 224
  rose, 223-224
  sage, 231-232
  savory, 238
  southernwood, 244-245
  sweet white clover, 251-252
  sweet woodruff, 254
  teas, 74, 160, 183, 202-203
  thyme, 260
  wine infusion, 253
  za'atar, 275
Red Bergamot. *See* Bee Balm
Red rose of Lancaster. *See* Roses, Apothecary
Ribes nigrum, 116-119
Richters, 193, 273
Riddle, use of, 57-58, 185-186
Rocket. *See* Arugula
Room fresheners, 73, 251-252
Root division, 43

Root system, development of, 29, 31
Rooting hormone powder, 43
Roquette. *See* Arugula
Rosa
  gallica, 219-224
  rugosa, 219-224
  virginiana, 219-224
Rose, Jeanne, 63
Roses, 58, 67, 76, 89-90
  Apothecary (*Rosa gallica*), 219-224
  Rugosa (*Rosa rugosa*), 219-224
  Virginia (*Rosa virginiana*), 219-224
Rosemary (*Rosmarinus officinalis*), 35-36, 46, 76,
  225-227
Rose Petal
  Jelly, 223
  Potpourri, 224
  Sandwiches, 223
  Vinegar, 224
Rosmarinus officinalis, 35-36, 46, 76, 225-227
Rue (*Ruta graveolens*), 76, 227-229
  fringed (*Ruta chalapensis*), 15, 228
Rumex acetosa, 240-243
Russian sage (*Perovskia atriplicifolia*), 91
Ruta
  chalapensis, 15, 228
  graveolens, 76, 227-229

Sachets, 72-73, 227
Sages, tender, 232-235
Sage (*Salvia officinalis*), 25, 46, 52, 58, 76, 229-
  232
Salad
  burnet. *See* Burnet
  rocket. *See* Arugula
Salads, 155, 203-204, 211-212
Salt substitute, 184
  See also Herb Salt; Seasonings
Salvia
  coccinea, 232-235
  farinacea, 39, 232-235
  officinalis, 25, 46, 52, 58, 76, 229-232
  sclarea, 140-141
  viridis, 141-143
Sambucus canadensis, 66, 76, 158-161
Saponaria officinalis, 238-240
Satureja
  hortensis, 46, 52, 235-238
  montana, 46, 235-238
Savory
  summer (*Satureja hortensis*), 46, 52, 235-238

winter (*Satureja montana*), 46, 235-238
Scarlet Bee Balm. *See* Bee Balm
Scented plants, 92
Screens, air-drying, 56-58
Scurvy grass. *See* Cress, Upland
Scythe, 53-54
Seasonings, 126, 181, 186, 217, 237-238, 272
Seedlings, 40, 182
  care of, 25-27
  planting out, 33-34
Seeds, starting, 20-24
  indoors, 24-27
  outdoors, 27-29
Self-seeding herbs, 43
Shade, 33, 91
Shattering, prevention of, 66
Shaudys, Phyllis, 68
Shining rose. *See* Roses, Virginia
Showy
  calamint. *See* Calamint
  savory. *See* Calamint
Silber, Mark and Terry, 66, 78, 271
Simmering Sweet White Clover Room
  Freshener, 251-252
Simmons, Adelma, 206, 267
Site, 29-30, 32-33
Skin fresheners, 77-78, 148-149, 175, 222
Sleep pillows, 167, 218
Snakeweed. *See* Bistort
Sneezewort (*Achillea ptarmica*), 20, 269-271
Soap solution, herbal, 240
Soap spray, 42, 45, 149
Soapwort (*Saponaria officinalis*), 238-240
Soil, 29-32, 40, 222
Sorrel (*Rumex acetosa*), 52, 240-243
Soup Seasoning, 238
Southernwood (*Artemisia abrotanum*), 53, 58,
  76, 243-245
Sowing, 20-25
Spanish lavender (*Lavandula stoechas*), 14, 180,
  273
Spiritual awakening, 14-15
"Spring Salad", 152-153, 155
Spring salads, 153-155, 186, 241-242
Stachys
  byzantina, 52, 76, 176-178
  grandiflora, 177
  officinalis, 177
Staking, 41
Stalking the Wild Asparagus, 153, 170
Stem cuttings, 43-44, 226

Stratification, 22-23
Summer Salad Extravaganza, 211-212
Sun requirements
full, 33, 89, 91
partial, 33
shade, 33, 91
Swags, 74
Sweet
Annie. *See* Wormwood, sweet
basil. *See* Basil
cicely (*Myrrhis odorata*), 67, 245-247
marjoram. *See* Marjoram
mugwort. *See* Mugwort, white;
Wormwood, sweet
rocket (*Hesperis matronalis*), 247-248
violet (*Viola odorata*), 262-265
white clover (*Melilotus alba*), 53, 58, 249-252
woodruff *(Galium odoratum (Asperula odorata))*, 67, 252-254
Symphytum caucasicum, 143-145
Syrian
hyssop. *See* Za'atar
oregano. *See* Za'atar

Tagetes tenuifolia, 58, 76, 193-194
Tanacetum
balsamita, 147-150
parthenium, 163-164
vulgare, 53, 76, 254-256
Tansy (*Tanacetum vulgare*), 53, 76, 254-256
Taraxacum officinale, 76, 152-155
Tea herbs, 58, 74, 111, 112, 124, 129, 131, 149, 167, 183
recipes, 160, 183, 202-203
Temple, Dottie, 40
Texas sage (*Salvia coccinea*), 232-235
Thaxter, Celia, 166
Thyme
cooking (*Thymus vulgaris*), 58, 257-260
creeping *(Thymus praecox* subsp. *arcticus (T. serpyllum)),* 257-260
Thymus
praecox subsp. *arcticus (T. serpyllum),* 257-260
vulgaris, 58, 257-260
Tincture, 193
Tires, as containers, 37-39
Tisanes, 74
Tisserand, Robert, 62
Tobacco substitute, 218
Treatment, 22-23
Tropaeolum majus, T. minor, 67, 76, 209-212

True lavender. *See* Lavender, English
True leaves, 25
Tussie-mussies, 74-77, 177-178, 206-207, 231, 276

Upright thyme. *See* Thyme, cooking
Urns, from tires, 37-38

Valeriana officinalis, 261-262
Valerian (*Valeriana officinalis*), 261-262
Vermifuge, 265
Veronica spp., 253
Vinegars, 77-78
Viola (*Viola tricolor*), 67, 76, 262-265
Viola
odorata, 262-265
tricolor, 67, 76, 262-265

Washing-machine water, reuse of, 40
Watercress (*Nasturtium officinale*), 151
Watering, 39-40
houseplants, 44-45
Weaver's Garden, A, 240
Weeds, discouraging, 34-35, 90, 176
Well-Sweep Herb Farm, 163, 228, 273
Wendy's May Jelly, 254
Wet conditions, plants for, 91
White
horehound. *See* Horehound
wormwood. *See* Mugwort, white
Wildflowers, 87, 249-251
Wild
mallow. *See* Mallow, common
pansy. *See* Viola
William-and-Mary. *See* Lungwort
Wilson, Ernest, 207
Wilted Dandelion Salad, 155
Wine, infusion of, 253
Winter cover, 41
Woolly betony. *See* Lamb's-ears
Wormwood
common (*Artemisia absinthium*), 53, 76, 265-268
Roman (*Artemisia pontica*), 265-268
sweet (*Artemisia annua*), 53, 265-268
Woundworts, 177
Wreath-making, 78, 199, 206, 219, 267, 268

Yarrow (*Achillea millefolium*), 76, 269-271
Years in My Herb Garden, The, 208

Za'atar *(Majorana syriaca (Origanum syriacum, O. maru)),* 15, 173, 272-275